Third Edition

Technology for Inclusion

Meeting the Special Needs of All Students

Mary Male
San Jose State University

Allyn and Bacon
Boston • London • Toronto • Sydney • Tokyo • Singapore

Executive Vice President, Education: Nancy Forsyth
Editor: Raymond Short
Editorial Assistant: Christine Svitila
Marketing Manager: Kris Farnsworth
Editorial-Production Service: Chestnut Hill Enterprises, Inc.
Manufacturing Buyer: Suzanne Lareau
Cover Administrator: Suzanne Harbison

Copyright © 1997, 1994, 1988 by Allyn & Bacon
A Viacom Company
160 Gould Street
Needham Heights, Massachusetts 02194

Internet: www.abacon.com
American Online keyword: College Online

A previous edition of this book was published under the title *Special Magic: Computers, Classroom Strategies, and Exceptional Students.*

Many of the designations used by manufacturers and sellers to distinguish their products are claimed as trademarks. Where those designations appear in this book and Allyn and Bacon was aware of a trademark claim, the designations have been printed in caps or initial caps.

Library of Congress Cataloging-in-Publication Data

Male, Mary.
    Technology for inclusion : meeting the special needs of all
students / Mary Male. — 3rd ed.
        p.   cm.
    Includes bibliographical references and index.
    ISBN 0-205-19654-3 (pb)
    1. Special education—United States—Computer-assisted
instruction. 2. Special education—United States—Data processing.
3. Educational technology—United States. 4. Mainstreaming in
education—United States.   I. Title.
LC3969.5.M37   1997
371.9′0285—dc20   96-41904
                                                        CIP

Printed in the United States of America

10 9 8 7 6 5 4 3 2   01 00 99 98 97

Contents

Preface

Each revision of this book has brought opportunities to reflect on both the magnitude of change in the field of special education and on the stability of the most powerful ideas. Students and their parents continue to press for access to technology that can expand opportunities for expression, communication, academic success, social participation and inclusion, and preparation for an independent life. Educators and service providers are energized by the experiences of their students and clients with technology and frustrated more than ever by funding shortages and bureaucratic barriers that delay meeting needs.

As with the earlier versions, ideas and examples for this book came from hundreds of hours of talking to students, parents, teachers, administrators, service providers, software and hardware designers, and professors who prepare special education personnel preparation. Classroom observations, reviews of research, and pilot tests of lessons, software, and hardware with a wide range of students provided first-hand knowledge of what works, what doesn't, and why.

Goals of This Book

By the time you finish this book, you will have done the following:

1. reflected on your vision of what technology offers your students and families;
2. reconsidered the importance of collaboration to maximize the impact of the use of technology on students and families;
3. reviewed a variety of applications of computers to determine ways computers can make your students powerful and your classrooms more effective in meeting student needs;
4. renewed your dedication to provide appropriate access to technology in spite of the challenges of dealing with change and an uncertain future.

How to Use This Book

The sequence of the book is designed to make sure that crucial steps and experiences in technology implementation are not overlooked; however, experienced computer users will feel comfortable skipping around in this book. Because of their origins in actual teacher practice, the examples, worksheets, and resource lists are likely to stimulate additional ideas for implementing technology programs.

The first section of the book focuses on identifying a vision (Chapter 1) and building collaborative relationships to support that vision. Chapter 2 is designed to help students learn to work together through cooperative learning at the computer. Chapter 3 provides ideas for working with parents to build a program that extends from school to home. In Chapter 4, the concept of a "Technology Team" for coordinating professionals so that skills and activities make sense and fit together is introduced. Chapter 5 shows how all the pieces can be tied together through the Individualized Education Program.

In the second section of the book, seven chapters focus on building teacher and student productivity from a number of perspectives. Chapter 6 addresses basic skills, and the ways a computer can be used to promote fluency where appropriate. In Chapter 7, functional and life skills beyond school are featured, from infancy through transition to adulthood. Chapters 8 through 12 focus on different kinds of applications and academic goals, including word processing, desktop publishing, data-base management, spreadsheets, telecommunications and the Internet, and multimedia.

The last section of the book provides information and resources for gaining access to technology. Chapter 13 addresses legislation, funding, and suggestions for assessing special access needs. Chapter 14 provides specific hardware and software recommendations and looks at the pros and cons of how schools provide access to computers. Chapter 15 concludes with suggestions for schools to consider as they are faced with continuous change and the need to question long-standing policies and practices.

Acknowledgments

Many people contributed to this book. I would particularly like to thank Chauncy Rucker and the extraordinary group of people he gathers at the ConnSense conference each summer, who are generous with ideas, insights, and experiences represented in this book—Amy Dell, Tom Holloway, Eileen Pracek, Deb Richards, Judi Sweeney, Jamie Wilkinson. Arjan Khalsa, Melinda Harrington, Suzanne Feit, and Cyndy Hoberman from IntelliTools provided countless hours of support and encouragement and innumerable ideas and the chance to explore them. Donna Dutton and the staff at a number of Alliance for Technology Access sites (particularly Mary Ann Glicksman in Los Angeles, Lois Symington and Alice Wershing in Knoxville, Tennessee, Lisa Wahl and Helen Miller in Berkeley, California, and Judy Timms in Charlotte, North Carolina) have gone above and beyond for me in gathering examples and data for the book. Jamie Judd-Wall has been a long-time colleague and unselfish with ideas and suggestions. Mary Anderson, a resource teacher in Arlington, Virginia, and close friend, colleague, and co-author, is conscientious and thoughtful in designing technology applications that have benefited numbers of students in her school and across the country. Richard Wanderman has always been a wonderful source of encouragement and inspiration.

I would also like to acknowledge the support and encouragement of the faculty at San Jose State University, who have supported our technology emphasis from the beginning Apple II+ days: Dr. Gil Guerin and Dr. Theodore Montemurro, the Division Head of Special Education. I appreciate the support and encouragement of Ray Short, my editor at Allyn and Bacon.

I am especially grateful to my family and friends for their patience and unflagging enthusiasm for my work. My son, Jonathan, now 8, has been a steady computer user ever since he could sit up and a fearless and discriminating tester of software, hardware, and lessons; he has helped me maintain a healthy perspective on what is important in life.

Last, but certainly not least, I acknowledge David Brick for being my own "Technology 911," with skill, patience, and humor, and for the joy and happiness he contributes to each day of my life.

Chapter *1*

Creating a Vision

Alan Kay, one of the pioneers in the development of the personal computer, has noted that until technology becomes as accessible as pencil and paper, we cannot expect technology to revolutionize the way students learn. Can you imagine telling students that their turn to use the pencil and paper will be a 30-minute period next Thursday? As Skip Via says,

> *We can no longer be content to operate one-computer classrooms and think that we are participants in the Information Revolution. That's like having one glove for a baseball team or one textbook for a classroom. If we want students to learn the kinds of skills that the business world already requires of them, then we had better be able to provide them with the necessary tools. How much technology is enough? When we think of computers as pencils rather than as subjects, we will have begun to reach that point. (1991, p. 1)*

This chapter will present snapshots of classrooms that have been successful in using technology (along with the best of everything else we know about effective instruction) to enable all students to succeed. In a number of schools, technology is an avenue for achieving large-scale change and reform in a number of areas. One large study found that "case study sites that were most successful in infusing technology throughout their entire programs were schools and projects that also devoted a good deal of effort to creating a schoolwide instructional vision—a consensus around instructional goals and a shared philosophy concerning the kinds of activities that would support those goals. In some cases preparing technology-savvy students was part of the school's original mission; in others, technology emerged over time as a means to achieve other goals, such as the acquisition of higher-order thinking skills. What appears to be important is not the point at which technology becomes a part of the vision but the coherence of the vision and the extent to which it is a unifying force among teachers" (Means, Olson, & Singh, 1995).

Objectives

By the end of this chapter, you will have:

1. Reflected on your own vision of your students' special needs and how technology might be used to increase the quality of their educational experience
2. Created a vision of your classroom, school, and community, reflecting on:

   • making diversity a strength

   • emphasizing learning strategies and processes, not just right answers

   • putting students in charge of the learning outcome, the means to achieve the outcome, or both (Russell, Corwin, Mokros, & Kapisovsky, 1989)

   • creating opportunities for maximum social and cognitive development within supportive environments

   • valuing the role of teacher and learner for all participants (teachers, students, and families)

3. Shared your vision with colleagues to determine the level of support for student-centered, curriculum rich learning at your school and in your community

A Vision in Focus

Creating a vision does not mean waiting until all the elements are in place before the work begins. Regardless of the degree of inclusiveness of the setting in which you and your students now work and regardless of the amount of technological resources currently available, the first step in the process of creating an exceptional classroom is to have a clear vision that can be achieved in incremental steps.

Even in the Apple Classroom of Tomorrow (ACOT) program, for example, where teachers worked in classrooms where there was one computer for every student, and every student was given a computer for home use, classroom instructional procedures did not change overnight. One teacher describes the impact of the ACOT program at the beginning of her third year:

> *Being on hall duty this year, I have a chance to hear how, in class after class the teachers' voices drone on and on and on. This allows little chance for the student to become an active participant. In today's schools there is little chance for the individual to actually change the curriculum, but we can make the way we deliver the curriculum very different. And that's where the technology comes into play: to make it more interactive, to encourage collaborative learning, to encourage exploration.* (Dwyer, Ringstaff, & Sandholtz, 1991, p. 50)

Via describes the success he has experienced in incorporating extensive use of technology into his inclusive classroom:

> *Students and teachers are using technology to work directly with source materials and to explore areas of interest within the regular curriculum. They are learning*

to research and gather information from a variety of sources, synthesize it, and create original reports and presentations. They control the technology for their own purposes, rather than being controlled by it for purposes established by software houses. Can you imagine a better way to integrate special students into "regular" settings? When students can work at their own pace, there is no "norm". Each individual can work to his or her potential and contribute to others' learning. And there can be expanded flexibility to include specialists or therapists in small groups. A classroom can be a resource room for everyone. (1991, pp. 6–7)

Six regular education teachers in two Charlotte, North Carolina, schools have been participating in a federally funded grant called "CompuCID" where the goal is to use technology effectively to promote inclusion of students with disabilities. A "technology team" is made up of a parent of a child with a disability and two special education teachers. The team is assigned to work in the schools with the staff, students, and parents. These team members disseminate information about innovative software to promote group learning, do problem solving with the teachers, and demonstrate how to use cooperative learning methods with computers. During the second year of the project, the enthusiasm for these techniques by both teachers and parents spread throughout the schools involved. Other teachers are now anxious to join the project. The "teachers teaching teachers" model has been encouraged, and the demonstration teachers are expanding their knowledge, some taking on specialty areas such as multimedia applications and acting as mentors for new CompuCID teachers (Carolina Computer Access Center, 1991).

Elements of a Vision: Focusing on the Results—What Is Success?

What, exactly, is a vision, and how does having a vision affect a teacher's day-to-day life with students? A vision is a consciously created fantasy of what we would ideally like to happen. A vision is not handed down from school administration; a vision must come from within each person. To develop a schoolwide vision, all participants must spend time together in a process of imagining what outcomes they want for parents and students. A vision is an expression of the spiritual and idealistic sides of our nature and comes from the heart, not the head. It should represent a substantial change from what exists currently, a quantum leap to making greater contributions to the lives of others. In the words of Thoreau, "If a man advances confidently in the direction of his dreams to live the life he has imagined, he will meet with a success unexpected in the common hours."

For teachers in special education, the emphasis on measurable goals and objectives, focusing on short-term outcomes, limits our opportunity for vision. In this book, you are encouraged to think big—how the world would be if we created opportunities for inclusion and educational success for all, with technology as a support.

Here are some questions to think about:

- What would be happening for your students if you had appropriate technology to support their participation in a variety of in- and out-of-school learning opportunities?
- Who would be a part of these learning opportunities?
- What kinds of structures would be needed for learning to be optimized?

- How would you plan for the rapid changes of technology over time?
- How would the learning opportunities change over time?

The vision of one elementary school in San Jose, California, illustrates the power of technology as a tool for change:

> *Students experience complex, challenging real-world problem solving requiring multiple abilities of thinking, discussing, writing, and analyzing. Students learn in mixed-age and non-graded classrooms, heterogeneous groupings, peer and cross age tutoring programs, cooperative learning situations; retention is not needed as a means to address low achievement. Teachers seek continuous professional growth, are recognized as leaders, mentors, and educational entrepreneurs; they earn professional advancement through career ladders. Collegial support, team teaching, and opportunities for collaborating with peers on projects are built into the school structure, schedule, and calendar. Students are supported by partnerships among parents, community, education, and business to enhance career-focused learning opportunities for all students. Students use state of the art equipment under the guidance of thoroughly trained teachers to support their learning outcomes with such tools as computers, scanners, CD-ROM, laserdisc players, video production equipment, telecommunications and multimedia. Student performance is measured by authentic, performance-based assessment practices that are complex and challenging.*
> (San Jose Unified School District, 1992, pp. 185–186)

A parent's vision may be expressed differently, but the "dreams" must be considered as a part of educational planning and building effective teams. "For many professionals, it is scary to hear a family's dreams because they seem 'unrealistic.' Professionals feel inadequate to deal with these dreams because they are not sure that they can make the family's dreams come true. However, even if the dreams seem 'unrealistic,' it is important for professionals to respect and validate the family's dreams" (Sloand-Armstrong & Jones, 1995). Four-year-old Lindsay's parents, for example, have the following dreams for their daughter:

1. We want Lindsay to talk.
2. We want Lindsay to have friends.
3. We want Lindsay to go to regular kindergarten.
4. We want Lindsay to contribute to society.

By listening to these dreams and incorporating them into a vision of inclusion supported by technology, the planning team can select from a range of assistive devices and instructional strategies to design goals and objectives that respect and aim for the vision.

Roles of Technology

More and more frequently, descriptions of classroom learning projects involving real-life, complex problem solving and use of technological tools are becoming widespread in the press and in professional journals. These descriptions express an evolving consensus about what teaching and learning will look like in the 21st century (Brandt, 1994). Brandt cites The Monarch Project as an example in which students map and chart the insects' progress and share their data over the Internet with students all over the world. This project gives students a chance to learn how to work together to gather and organize information and also achieve a social purpose of helping conservationists save a species in danger of extinction. Technological tools, according to Peck and Dorricott (1994), "allow educators to fulfill age-old dreams" about what learning can and should be. Dramatic shifts in the ways we think of teaching and learning will also transform what is possible for including students with special needs in a wider range of settings, because of the increasing accommodative, student-centered power of classrooms such as those described above.

Lewis (1993) describes the ABC model of what technology can do for learners with special needs:

Augment abilities

Students without speech, for example, can express their thoughts using a speech synthesizer; students with low vision can use magnification devices to have access to print.

Bypass disabilities

Students can use switches or voice commands to bypass the lack of motor control over hands and arms. Using e-mail can facilitate communication for students who have difficulty with transportation.

Compensate for disabilities

Students can use talking word processors to have their written work read aloud, or spelling and grammar checkers to assist with problems with composition. Students who have difficulty organizing their ideas can benefit from using mindmapping or outlining programs.

Teachers and parents alike describe with enthusiasm the benefits and roles technology can play:

- Improvements in academic performance and classroom behavior as well as increased motivation and more positive self-concept
- Changes in the ways students with disabilities are perceived by their peers; since they are able to accomplish more on their own, they are perceived as more capable (Lewis, 1993).

Process of Developing and Sharing a Vision for Technology and Inclusion

Begin with yourself. Take the time to reflect about yourself, your students, their families, the school culture, and the community. Write down your dreams.

Find a colleague with whom to share your reflections, who is also willing to go through similar reflecting/thinking processes. Bring up your ideas with your school faculty, school site council, and your administrators. Your school or district may already be involved in strategic planning efforts. Link what you are trying to do with ongoing school restructuring, reform, and strategic planning.

Involve parents of your students in the process. The idea is to check out your visions with those of key stakeholders (other teachers, service providers, parents, community leaders) to gather support for what you want to happen.

One model of strategic planning involves the following steps (Council for Exceptional Children, 1991):

- Develop a common vision (what should be)
- Scan the environment (what is currently happening)
- Assess the problems (the difference between what is and what should be, the barriers to and opportunities for change)
- Select outcomes
- Choose strategies and activities
- Build support
- Establish accountability/metrics to measure success

Whatever model of planning you choose, beginning with a compelling vision is the most important step. Figures 1-1 and 1-2 provide tools for brainstorming elements of your vision.

WHAT SHOULD BE	WHAT IS

FIGURE 1-1 Brainstorming Elements of a Vision

BARRIERS	OPPORTUNITIES

FIGURE 1-2 Problem/Opportunity Brainstorming

Activities

1. Write a one- or two-page paper that describes your vision of technology and inclusion for your students. How are effective learning situations structured? In what ways are learning opportunities inclusive? In what ways is technology utilized? What adaptations are required for students to have access to technology?
2. Visit an inclusive classroom in which technology is integrated. Interview the teacher and anyone who is involved in supporting the teacher's success. In what ways is technology being used? What adaptations are required? To what degree are differences in abilities, language, culture, and so on accommodated in this situation?

References

Brandt, R. (1994). Helping professional dreams come true. *Educational Leadership, 51*(7), 3.

Carolina Computer Access Center. (1991). How can computers help support the fuller integration of students with disabilities in regular education classrooms? Unpublished paper. Charlotte, NC: Carolina Computer Access Center.

Council for Exceptional Children (1991). National Institute on Comprehensive System of Personnel Development Collaboration—Strategic Planning. Reston, VA.

Dwyer, D., Ringstaff, C., & Sandholtz, J. (1991). Changes in teachers' beliefs and practices in technology-rich classrooms. *Educational Leadership, 48*(8), 45–52.

Lewis, R. (1993). *Special education technology: Classroom applications.* Pacific Grove, CA: Brooks/Cole Publishing Co.

Means, B., Olson, K., and Singh, R. (1995). Beyond the classroom: Restructuring schools with technology. *Phi Delta Kappan, 77*(1), 69–72.

Peck, K., and Dorricott, D. (1994). Why use technology? *Educational Leadership. 51*(7), 11–14.

Russell, S., Corwin, R., Mokros, J., & Kapisovsky, P. (1989). *Beyond drill and practice: Expanding the computer mainstream.* Reston, VA: Council for Exceptional Children.

San Jose Unified School District (1992). Midtown Elementary Academy: A magnet technology school of tomorrow. San Jose, CA.

Sloand-Armstrong, J., and Jones, K. (1995). Using family dreams to develop meaningful goals involving assistive technology. *Closing the Gap, 14*(2), 2, 6.

Via, S. (1991). How much technology is enough? *The Catalyst, 8*(3), 6–8.

$Chapter$ 2

Cooperative Learning and Social Development

Many educators fear that the use of computers will result in students becoming isolated from each other or the teacher. Other teachers are more concerned with the shortage of equipment and the logistical challenges of having students work together and share time at the computer. Still others are concerned with scheduling enough time at the computer to make any difference or are involved in creating opportunities for students of diverse learning needs to work together on computers in a mainstream setting.

In this chapter, cooperative learning is discussed as a means of providing access to computers for situations in which there are more students than computers. We stress not only academic and cognitive development but also social development, regardless of the number of computers available for students. Some of the important questions to consider include:

- How can computer activities be structured for group work stressing interdependence and individual accountability to enhance academic and cognitive development and communication skills?
- How can teachers use the computer to create positive interactions among students with diverse learning needs, abilities, and backgrounds?
- How can teachers ensure that computer experiences enhance the self-esteem of students?
- How should classroom use of computers be organized so that students develop independence, good work habits, and a sense of their own competence?

Objectives

By the end of this chapter, you will be able to do the following:

1. Use principles of cooperative learning to structure lessons using the computer as a tool.
2. Develop ideas for computer celebrations, clubs, or other events to provide visibility for the achievements of your students with computers.

3. Design your classroom so that students know when and how they can expect to use the computer.
4. Create opportunities for student recognition and rewards for achievements in using the computer.
5. Explore options for social development through community-focused activities.

Cooperative Learning at the Computer

Although the scarcity of computers has dictated that students must often work together at the computers in groups, cooperative learning refers to more than simply placing students in group activities. *Cooperative learning* can be defined as a way of structuring student interaction so that:

- Students know they can be successful only if their group is successful.
- They are accountable for their individual understanding and mastery of whatever is being taught.
- They are given specific instruction in the social skills necessary for the group to be successful.
- They are given the opportunity to discuss how well their group is working and receive feedback to improve future performance (Johnson & Johnson, 1994).

A summary of the differences between cooperative and traditional learning groups is provided in Table 2-1. A clear understanding of these differences will help you understand how to structure cooperative learning in your computer experiences (Male, Johnson, Johnson, & Anderson, 1986).

TABLE 2-1 A Comparison of Cooperative and Group Learning

Cooperative Learning	Traditional Learning
Positive interdependence	No interdependence
Individual accountability	No individual accountability
Heterogeneous	Homogeneous
Shared leadership	One appointed leader
Shared responsibility for each other	Responsibility for self
Task and maintenance emphasized	Only task emphasized
Social skills directly taught	Social skills assumed
Teacher observes and intervenes	Teacher ignores group functioning
Groups process their effectiveness	No group processing

Source: From *Cooperative Learning and Computers: An Activity Guide for Teachers* by M. Male, R. Johnson, D. Johnson, and M. Anderson, 1986, Educational Apple-cations (125 Sylvar Street, Santa Cruz, CA 95060). Reprinted by permission of Mary Male.

Cooperative learning groups are based on positive interdependence among group members; goals are structured so that students need to be concerned about the performance of all group members as well as their own. In order for the situation to be cooperative, students must perceive that they are positively interdependent with other members of their learning group. This may be achieved by having mutual goals (goal interdependence); by dividing the work task (task interdependence); by dividing materials, resources, or information among group members (resource interdependence); by assigning students differing roles (role interdependence); and by giving joint rewards (reward interdependence).

The students' mastery of the assigned material is assessed to ensure individual accountability. Each student is given feedback on his or her progress, and the group is given feedback on how each member is progressing so that the other group members know whom to assist and encourage. All group members are accountable for mastering the assigned material. In traditional learning groups, individual students are often not held accountable for providing their share of the group's work, and occasionally students will "hitchhike" on the work of others.

Cooperative learning groups are typically heterogeneous in ability levels and personal characteristics, whereas traditional learning groups are often homogeneous in membership. All members in cooperative learning groups share responsibility for performing leadership functions in the group, whereas traditional learning groups frequently have a leader assigned to be in charge.

In addition to the shared responsibility for leadership, students are held responsible for each others' learning. Students are expected to provide help and encouragement to each other in order to ensure that all members do the assigned work. In traditional learning groups, members are seldom held accountable for each other's learning. The goals of cooperative learning groups focus on bringing each member's learning to the maximum while maintaining good working relationships among members. Traditional learning groups focus primarily on completing the assignment.

Cooperative learning groups present an opportunity for the teacher to observe the groups and give feedback to students on how effectively they are working. Students are also given the time and procedures to process how effectively they are working together. Students need to have a chance to analyze how well their learning groups are functioning and the extent to which they are using their collaborative skills to promote the learning of all group members and to maintain effective working relationships within the group. Students may then plan how to work with each other more effectively the next day and in the future (Johnson, Johnson, & Holubec, 1993).

Synergy of Cooperative Learning and Computers

When cooperative learning and the computer are combined for instruction, the computer, depending on the software, does one or more of the following:

- Presents the learning task
- Provides strategy instructions
- Controls the flow of activity (e.g., signals when a new task should be initiated)
- Monitors learning activities in an objective and efficient manner

- Provides reinforcing messages for good performance on all aspects of the task
- Keeps track of students' responses for future analysis
- Tailors learning activities to the students based on responses to tasks within the learning sequence
- Provides tests on the training materials and, based on students' responses, branches to further strategy instructions
- Performs computations to free the cooperative group from lengthy calculations, thus members can spend more energy on problem solving and conceptual learning
- Provides expert content

Cooperative learning groups allow students to serve as models for each other. Students assist each other in analyzing and diagnosing the problems being addressed, explain to each other the material being learned, teach relevant concepts and procedures to each other, keep each other on task, and share their satisfaction and sense of accomplishment with each other.

Two studies have compared computer use in cooperative, competitive, and individualistic learning (Johnson, Johnson, & Stanne, 1986a, 1986b). Results of these studies indicate that computers and cooperative learning promoted greater quantity and quality of daily achievement, more successful problem solving, and higher performance on factual recognition, application, and problem-solving test items than did computers and competitive and individualistic learning. The combination of cooperative learning and computers had an especially positive impact on female students' attitudes toward computers. The combination of competition and computers had an especially negative impact on female students' achievement, achievement motivation, confidence in their ability to work with computers, attitudes toward computers, and attitudes toward the subject being studied.

Essential Components of Cooperative Computer Lessons

Although there may be differences in the ways in which researchers have identified the essentials of cooperative learning, there seem to be some basic principles that are common among most of the formal cooperative learning strategies being used by teachers. The following description of the essentials is designed to assist you in structuring your own version of cooperative learning.

Assignment to Teams and Team Preparation

The purpose of team assignment is to assure a good heterogeneous mix of students, taking into account gender, race, cultural and language differences, problematic behaviors, and past performance (achievement and communication skills). In the past, schools have made every effort to group students homogeneously by age, ability, and the like, with limited success. Cooperative learning offers teachers an opportunity to capitalize on the benefits of heterogeneity and to abandon the nearly impossible task of finding homogeneous groups. These strategies work particularly well in mainstreaming and inclusive classroom situations.

Some teachers prefer to randomly assign students to teams in order to keep team assignment simple and to demonstrate to students that they are expected to work together in groups, no matter where they are assigned. Assignment to teams can be as simple as having students count off to a certain number or dealing a deck of cards and having students gather in groups of four.

Team preparation activities build a sense of team identity and spirit as well as trust among team members. Teachers may ask students to select a name for their team and display it on a class bulletin board. Getting-acquainted activities or values-clarification activities that are tied into computer use may be conducted as team members are developing working relationships (Anderson, 1989).

Creating Positive Interdependence among Students

Positive interdependence is the feeling among team members that no one is successful unless everyone is successful. Following are examples of the types of interdependence:

- *Goal Interdependence:* "You're not finished until everyone in the group can explain the pattern for sorting" (*Sammy's Science House, Thinkin' Things*).
- *Task Interdependence:* "Each of you will be an expert on a different aspect of the story—one on the setting, one on the characters, one on the plot. You must agree on how to put your story together."
- *Resource Interdependence:* "I will give only one worksheet to the group. You must record your group's prediction of what the product will look like on the worksheet."
- *Role Interdependence:* "Each of you will have a job. One of you, for example, will be the Checker. The Checker's job is to make sure that everyone can explain the way they arrived at their answer. I will be giving your group credit for how well each of you does your job."
- *Reward Interdependence:* "Your grade will be made up of the sum of the individual grades on the test."

Most students have had much practice in competitive classroom goal structures (and many have failed in such settings) and some have had experience in individualized special education classrooms; few have had practice in positive interdependence. Therefore, positive interdependence will need to be concretely and clearly communicated, especially when first presented. Otherwise, students may use their usual ways of working to get the job done, and the group will experience problems. For example, before you start your groups, establish why it is important to work in the groups. Make sure students understand the benefits of working together, using statements such as, "You will want to work closely with each other so that your group grade will go up," "You will receive bonus points for your grade for every student who makes 100 percent in the group," and "If your group does all of its work correctly, you can earn the opportunity to be a computer tutor in the kindergarten class."

Individual Accountability

Most teachers who have experienced learning in traditional groups or who have tried using traditional learning groups in their classrooms find that the addition of individual accountability ensures that each student contributes to the group. It helps the teacher in monitoring exactly how much each student has contributed or the level of mastery of each student of the target skills. For example, in a cooperative computer activity each student must be able to explain the activity, produce a printout, or score at a certain level on a quiz. All students must know in advance that they will be responsible individually for demonstrating mastery.

Direct Teaching of Social Skills

Teachers who use cooperative learning successfully place as much importance on the mastery of key social skills as they do on the mastery of the use of the computer for instructional tasks. Most teachers begin with a single social skill, such as praising; they provide examples of praising, solicit examples from students, and frequently list behaviors and words that characterize praising. In addition to providing systematic instruction in these targeted social skills, teachers monitor the groups, using an observation sheet, so that groups receive bonus points or a portion of their grade based on their use of social skills. A sample list of social skills is included in Table 2-2.

Processing

The teacher not only observes the collaborative skills within the groups but also provides structured opportunities for students to discuss and process what happened within their group. The best way to ensure that the effectiveness of the groups continues to improve is to provide time for students to share what they contributed to the group, how the group helped each student learn, problems that the group was able to solve, and problems with which the group would like help. In this way, the teacher creates a feeling that everyone is in this together, sink or swim.

Learning Together: A Cooperative Learning Strategy

Learning Together is a cooperative strategy that illustrates the use of the essential components of cooperative learning (Johnson & Johnson, 1994). In a Learning Together lesson with computers, the teacher would do the following:

1. Assign students to heterogeneous teams and do team building as necessary to establish trust and friendship.
2. Present the group goal (the payoff for working together).
3. Review the group skill to be emphasized (checking, praising, summarizing, etc.).
4. Make sure at least one student in each group can operate the software program.
5. Explain how each student's understanding or contribution to the team effort will be evaluated.
6. Observe the group working both at the computer and at a table as the members plan their strategies and complete their assignment at the computer.
7. Keep records on (or observe) who should receive special recognition points of social skill mastery or on problems that should be discussed during the processing phase.
8. Review the group product.
9. Check for individual participation, understanding, and contribution.
10. Recognize outstanding group performance.
11. Lead the processing discussion.

Two sample lessons incorporating the Learning Together strategy are included in Figures 2-1 and 2-2.

TABLE 2-2   Social Skills at Various Grade Levels

Grade Level	Task Skills	Maintenance Skills
Lower Elementary	Check others' understanding of the work	Encourage
	Give ideas	Use names
	Talk about work	Invite others to talk
	Get group back to work	Respond to ideas
	Repeat what has been said	Look at others
	Ask questions	Say "thank you"
	Follow directions	Share feelings
	Stay in seat	Disagree in a friendly way
		Keep things calm
Upper Elementary/ Middle School	Check others' understanding of the work	Encourage
	Contribute ideas	Use names
	Stay on task	Encourage others to talk
	Get group back to work	Respond to ideas
	Paraphrase	Use eye contact
	Follow directions	Show appreciation
	Stay in own space	Disagree in a friendly way
		Keep things calm
Senior High/Adult	Check others' understanding of the work	Encourage
	Give information and opinions	Use names
	Stay on task	Encourage others to talk
	Get group back to work	Acknowledge contributions
	Paraphrase	Use eye contact
	Seek information and opinions	Express appreciation
	Follow directions	Share feelings
		Disagree in a friendly way
		Reduce tension
		Practice active listening

Source: From *A Guidebook for Cooperative Learning* (p. 57) by D. Dishon and P. Wilson O'Leary, 1984, Learning Publications (PO Box 1326, Holmes Beach, FL 33509). Reprinted by permission of Pat Wilson O'Leary.

Celebrating and Sharing Computer Skills with Others

Recognition, celebration, and sharing of computer achievements can have a powerful impact on student motivation and skill development. The recognition and support received from peers result in enhancement of self-esteem, self-confidence, and motivation, all of which transfer to other situations. Miriam Furst, teacher of students ranging from those

FIGURE 2-1   HyperCard Vacation Lesson Plan

Grade Level: 8–12

Subject: Geography

Length: five 40-minute class periods

Step 1: Select a Lesson

In this lesson student groups make a software program that plans a trip and gives information about a place they would like to visit.

Step 2: Make Decisions

Group Size: 2–3

Group Assignment: Students select groups according to places they would like to visit.

Materials Needed: HyperCard, HyperStudio, or LinkWay; encyclopedias/references.

Assigning Tasks: Keyboarder (rotates) who listens to group ideas and responds to suggestions as he or she uses the keyboard and mouse. Decision-making to be shared by all team members.

Step 3: Set the Lesson

Task: The teacher introduces the topic of places in the world by asking students the place they have visited that is farthest away from where they live now. The teacher explains that students will be working in teams who will visit, by way of computer, some place in the world.

Students think about the continent in the world they would like to visit. They are directed to parts of the room according to the continent they have selected. When they find 1–2 other people with similar interest, they sit in a group and agree on a specific destination for their simulated visit. The entire class brainstorms some of the things that are done when planning a trip: buy tickets; find out about the country—its weather, historical sites, national heroes, monuments, animals, parks; set an itinerary.

The teacher directs the class as they create a stack about their destination. Cards, buttons, and fields are created for the stack.

Positive Interdependence: Each group member contributes ideas and helps plan and make the program. Each group member helps the group make decisions.

Individual Accountability: Each group member creates at least one card of the stack and does special research focusing on one topic of the group's destination.

Criteria for Success: a completed stack.

Specific Behaviors Expected: contributing ideas, listening to others' ideas, sharing the keyboarding work, helping the group come to consensus.

Step 4: Monitor and Process

Evidence of Expected Behaviors: students reading about the destinations, discussing and sharing ideas, planning and creating the stack.

Plans for Processing: All groups will have a chance to use other groups' stacks. There will be a session to reflect on what was learned about their destination and about the group process of listening to each others' ideas and making decisions.

Step 5: Evaluate Outcomes

Task Achievement:

Group Functioning:

Notes on Individuals:

Suggestions for Next Time:

FIGURE 2-2   Learning Together Lesson Plan (Where in the World Is Carmen Sandiego?)

Students are detectives using clues to catch a thief who is hiding in one of thirty cities. The *World Almanac and Book of Facts* helps in exploring cities and countries.

Subject Areas: Problem solving and logical thinking; geography

Grade Level: 5 and up

  I. *Objectives*:

    A. Students will be able to use problem solving and logical thinking skills while working with clues to solve a mystery.

    B. Students will be able to use the dictionary and *World Almanac* as reference tools.

    C. Students will gain information to enlarge their understanding of geography.

    D. Students will be able to ask team members why they are advocating an action and will be able to listen for the response.

  II. *Materials Needed:* Where in the World Is Carmen Sandiego? program manual, *World Almanac,* dictionary, police dossiers in software booklet, paper and pencil, marbles, jar, job cards, evaluation forms

  III. *Time Required:* One class period per activity

  IV. *Procedures*

    A. Preparation

      1. Assemble needed materials.

      2. Practice program of Where in the World Is Carmen Sandiego?, solve several cases.

    B. Set

      1. Ask students what mystery programs they have seen on TV. Ask what the role of the detective is.

      2. James Bond always started with an assignment. Today you have an assignment to catch a thief. You will use clues about Carmen Sandiego's gang, and clues about cities and countries to solve the mystery. Your team will work together in the investigation.

    C. Input

      1. As a total class, use the program Where in the World Is Carmen Sandiego? to solve a case. Ask three random questions to decide on a menu option. Then use another three students for the next option.

      2. Ask three students what to do next; ask each for their reason for this decision, and listen to the response. Get agreement on their next action for the case. Repeat with additional decisions and additional ideas from three students.

      3. Assign students to heterogeneous teams.

      4. Set the group goal. "Your team will work together on a case assignment today to catch a thief. You may use the Almanac, the dictionary, the police dossiers in the manual, and the hints that you get as you run the program. As you decide what

Continued

FIGURE 2-2 *Continued*

to do next, you are to ask each member for his/her idea and then listen carefully to the response. Then you are to agree on your course of action."

5. To help you accomplish your task there are job cards at each computer. Please distribute these among team members. You may make suggestions to the reference people and the recorder. All of you are to use the social skill of asking for a reason and listening to the response.

6. Every group that catches a thief will be permitted to put a marble in the jar. When the jar is filled we will have a class party. In the meantime, every group that puts a marble in will have a day when they are first in the lunch line.

D. Guided Practice

1. Students will work in their teams to catch a thief.

2. Teacher observes and records instances of team members asking others for the reason behind their ideas. Teacher also records students listening for the responses of others.

E. Closure

1. Each individual fills out an evaluation form.

2. With the total class together, the teacher calls on students to give comments on work in their group. Afterwards the teacher gives comments with examples of what asking for a reason sounded like and what the behavior of listening to a response sounded like.

F. Independent Practice

1. Teams work on additional cases in succeeding days adding marbles to the class jar as they are solved.

2. Teams can get together their members and work on cases before or after school or during unscheduled times.

Note-Taking Guide for
Where in World Is Carmen Sandiego?

Country	Capital	Population	Geography	Flag	Money	Products

Source: From *Cooperative Learning and Computers: An Activity Guide for Teachers* by M. Male, R. Johnson, D. Johnson, and M. Anderson, 1986, Educational Apple-cations (125 Sylvar Street, Santa Cruz, CA 95060). Reprinted by permission of Mary Male.

with severe learning problems to gifted students who may have difficulties in making and keeping friends, describes her experiment with "Computer Celebrations." She describes one class:

Annie is playing a spelling game. The computer will show her one of this week's spelling words. In a second or so the word will disappear, and Annie will try to spell it. Annie has not failed a spelling test this year. Annie is learning to focus her attention! She's finding that if she pays less attention to peripheral distractions— the sound of traffic outside, children's voices in the hall, her own inner dialogue— she can attend to the words flashed on the screen and increase her score.

Ray, Carol, and Jeannie are giggling and laughing as they tell me what to type into the computer. They have almost finished writing a question-and-answer program about animals, and now they're thinking of possible responses the computer can give to wrong answers. They already have a number of classmates lined up who are anxious to see the final product. These students are learning that even though they can't read very well, their thoughts and ideas are of value and interest to others!

Debbie is using a computer to practice multiplication. Standardized tests show that her skills have risen by one year in the past three months. She knows that she has to repeat a piece of information many times before she can remember it. But now she's also finding out that she can and will achieve a breakthrough if she is willing to stick to a task long enough. (1983, p. 11)

Suzanne Feit reports on a student in her class:

Heather is a girl who is mainstreamed in my second-grade class with an aide. She is nonverbal with very limited fine and gross motor control. Utilizing a switch and scanning alphabet, she is now able to write, spell, and do all of her assignments on the computer. Prior to this, Heather was transported 1½ hours by bus each way to a class where her communication was limited to a "yes" or "no" pasted on her tray. The costs for the current program with an aide are less than the transportation costs for the other program. And she has learned so much! She uses a talking word processor and is working independently on reading programs to develop language patterns and syntax. I encourage the other students to work with Heather, and she has shown them how to make personal number lines using Print Shop and printing at 5% size. (1991)

Ann Grady and Judy Timms observed the following classroom situation:

Rick, a student who had been labeled as "autistic" because of his social isolation from other students, is mainstreamed in my sixth grade class. He began demonstrating dramatic improvements in his social interaction after working in a computer group. I had been told that he should just remain sitting in his chair during homeroom, the class for which he was being mainstreamed. Using the computer, we introduced him to software programs that he could easily master and then assigned him to instruct a few other students. By the end of the school year, he was actively involved in all classroom activities and, to the great delight of everyone involved, was socializing daily with peers and adults, both in and outside of class. (Timms, 1991)

Furst's class collected samples of their finest work and designed an invitation (see Figure 2-3). Parents, family members, school board members and classmates received invitations. Similar to a recital, the program featured a description of the event and listed the name of the designer (see Figure 2-4). The pride of these students in showing their pro-

FIGURE 2-3   Invitation to a Computer Celebration

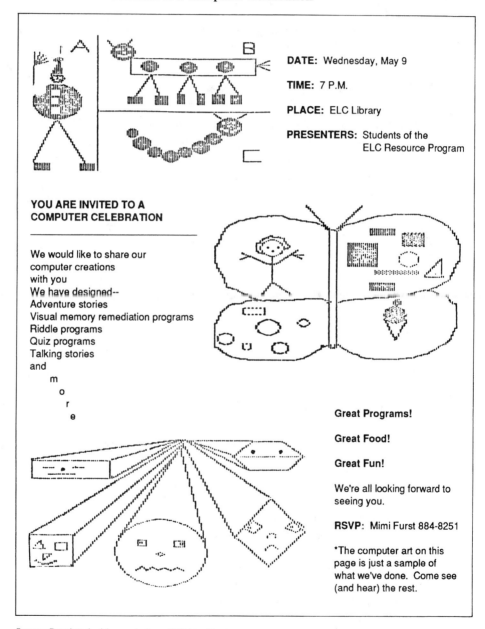

Source: Reprinted with permission of Miriam Furst.

FIGURE 2-4   **Program for a Computer Celebration**

COMPUTER CELEBRATION
Schedule of Events

Program Name	Program Designer
1. CHRIS	Chris Wallace

Chris designed the first in our series of visual memory remediation programs. This game really makes you read and observe carefully.

| 2. BLOODY MURDER | Mara Howell
Lucia Nowlin |

A branched adventure program—watch out!

| 3. SPORTS | Chris McFarland |

As well as designing this program, Chris also programmed a great deal of it. Better brush up on your sports before trying this one!

| 4. IFY'S MULTIPLICATION | Ify Semanas |

Ify has designed a program to motivate children to practice multiplication. Notice the special feature at the end.

| 5. GRADUATE | Shawn Kiley |

A clever way to help children improve visual discrimination.

| 6. ANGLES | Nathan Clark
Dana Freeman |

A pre-geometry program that also helps visualization skills. Dana and Nathan discovered some interesting properties of triangles, squares and parallelograms. They share them with you in this program.

| 7. CHARLIE'S STORY | Charlie Marquez |

Charlie gets attacked by a giant shark. Hear him tell the story himself. Find out if he survives!

| 8. HOUSE | Diana Nowlin
Erin Wells |

A Halloween adventure through a haunted house. If I were you, I'd bring a friend along for protection!!

INTERMISSION—REFRESHMENTS

Source: Reprinted with permission of Miriam Furst.

grams and the pride of their families and friends for these students who were not accustomed to academic and social recognition illustrate the importance and impact that a computer environment can have on social development.

In San Francisco's Community School, the special education resource room is the only room with computers. The students in the resource room were the first to learn how to use them, and they became responsible for helping other students (and teachers) learn how to operate the computers.

Sande Tatum, special education resource teacher, became the sponsor of the school's computer club, and time was provided once a week for the club to meet during school hours in the resource room. During the club meeting, specific computer activities were featured, and students could share with each other what they had learned in an informal way. The computer club provided opportunities for "mainstreaming in reverse," with students discovering that exciting and important things happened in the resource room.

In a school in Nashville, students are recruited for the Apple Corps. These students have a chance to become experts with certain software and then teach students and teachers how to use it. These students also help produce instructional material for lower class grades or for their own class (Symington, 1991). Mary Anderson's students are also active instructional materials designers. They use programs such as HyperStudio to make learning activities for younger children (Anderson, 1995).

In another Nashville school, students in a Higher Order Thinking Skills (HOTS) class can invite a friend to one class each month. This gives the students an opportunity to demonstrate the skills they have learned with computers and problem solving. Often their friends have difficulty with programs that have been mastered by the HOTS students. The result is that the HOTS students have to simplify programs for their friends; consequently, their own self-esteem increases. They also get realistic feedback on their own skills in comparison to their peers (Symington, 1991). Using the HOTS Word Problem Processor (Figure 2-5), heterogeneous groups create word problems, take four problems to another group and challenge that group to solve their problems and vice versa.

FIGURE 2-5   HOTS Math Word Problem Processor

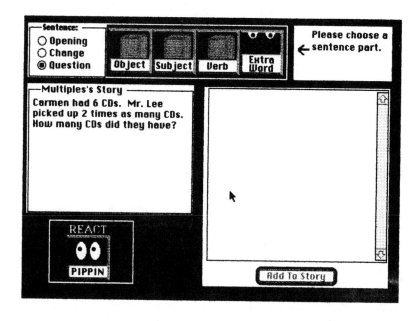

Classroom Designs to Promote Social Development

The Center for Special Education Technology (1991) describes three illustrative scenarios of classrooms where computer use promotes social as well as academic development:

Scenario 1

Students are clustered around a computer using word processing. They are in the prewriting stage and are making a vocabulary list about a topic. Each student gives an idea which is added to the list on the screen. If someone doesn't know what to say, others give suggestions. When the list is complete, it may be printed out and students can go to their desks to write their story, or the group may continue working together to create a group story.

Scenario 2

A group around the computer is using problem-solving simulation software. Each group member is performing a different role. One member is designated as the keyboarder, one as the manager to identify group consensus, one as the reference person to consult additional materials which are available, and one as the recorder to keep notes on information the group gets from the computer. They work together talking over the information on the computer screen and the options available to solve the problem. When it is finally solved, they share their success. For the next episode, they change roles until everyone has a chance to do each of them. At the end of the lesson, they discuss successful strategies with the class and reflect on how the group process worked in their group.

Scenario 3

Students read different reference books as they focus on one aspect of the topic being studied. Then they gather at the computer to use a database. Together they have the information to complete each of the fields for the database entries. Later they may merge this information with what the whole class has collected and analyze all of the information.

A list of software appropriate for these scenarios is included in Table 2-3. Research evidence documents the effectiveness of classroom activities such as those described above. In one study (Mevarech, Stern, & Levita, 1987), students were given an achievement test and then assigned at random to an individualistic setting or a paired learning setting, with each pair being approximately equivalent in scores on the achievement test. After two months, students were asked to complete questionnaires on their attitudes toward classmates, computer learning, and cooperative learning. The results showed that students became more altruistic toward their partners in the cooperative setting and preferred cooperative to individualistic learning. Their achievement was also slightly higher than that of the students in the individualistic setting, although not statistically significant.

An additional list of ideas for promoting social development with the computer is featured in Figure 2-6. These ideas have been tested by the CompuCID project in Charlotte, North Carolina, with promising results (Timms, 1991).

TABLE 2-3 Social Development Software and Publishers

Software	Publisher
Yukon Trail	MECC
Oregon Trail II	MECC
Maya Quest	Sunburst
Pilgrim Quest	Sunburst
Africa Trail	Sunburst
Colony Quest	Sunburst
Amazon Trail	Sunburst
Decisions, Decisions	Tom Snyder
Nigel's World	Lawrence Productions
Where in the . . . series	Broderbund
Sim City	Maxis
Dig It: Egyptians	Terrapin
ClarisWorks	Claris
Microsoft Works	Microsoft

Recognition and Rewards

With the emphasis on teamwork in computer activities, the teacher may want to develop strategies and materials to help students understand their roles at the computer and in their groups. Role cards can be developed that describe behaviors and expectations for students to fulfill (see Figure 2-7). Roles should be rotated regularly so that all students have the opportunity to master all the computer and social skills necessary to be a good team member. Students can also apply for particular computer jobs or roles (see Figure 2-8).

Recognizing positive behaviors is a powerful tool for maintaining discipline, and some students are highly motivated by special stickers or certificates of recognition that can be taken home. The certificates can be designed with a general format by the teacher, who fills in the specific noteworthy action. Certificates can also be done by students, who are encouraged to notice and acknowledge each other. Three samples are included in Figure 2-9 (Broad, 1991).

Community-Focused Activities to Promote Social Development

Alliance for Technology Access (ATA) centers across the country (see Figure 3-1) have been promoting community involvement in activities that offer rich social development opportunities. The Kids Linking Kids project in Santa Monica, California, offers students in the middle school an opportunity to work with students at a nearby elementary school in an after-school computer exploration situation (Dutton, 1991).

FIGURE 2-6   Great Ideas to Promote Social Development with the Computer

- Combine text and graphics to make book reports.
- Make book jackets for a story or book or for a World Wide Web page.
- Make a poster to "sell" a book.
- Make a travel brochure to advertise a story setting for a vacation.
- Publish a classroom newsletter.
- Use a word-processing program with graphics to write pen pals.
- Develop story starters to send to pen pals via the Internet.
- E-mail interesting questions/information to other schools.
- Use a crossword puzzle program to study vocabulary words.
- Use a crossword puzzle program to practice using descriptors.
- Use TimeLiner to plot important school events in chronological order.
- Use TimeLiner to plot important personal events.
- Make banners or illustrations to decorate class bulletin boards.
- Scan students' pictures and have others use positive words to describe the students.
- Print invitations to parents/school staff to classroom events.
- Write poems and include graphics and voice of student reading the poem.
- Use a graphics program to make wordless picture books.
- Create a class book (one page per student).
- Create flyers to illustrate ways to recycle goods.
- Allow student experts to tutor fellow classmates or schoolmates on computer or software use.
- Use a graphing program such as The Cruncher or Graph Club to graph science project results.
- Make a videotape of students using computers and allow parents to borrow the tape for viewing.

Source: Reprinted with permission from Carolina Computer Access Center, Charlotte, NC.

FIGURE 2-7   Role Cards

The Negotiator helps to resolve disagreements by looking for compromises, identifying partial agreement, or coming up with a new alternative idea.

The Summarizer checks to make sure everyone's ideas have been considered before the next part of the design is entered.

The Checker makes sure all of the words are spelled correctly before the card is printed.

The Praiser lets people on the team know when they are doing a good job.

Source: From *Cooperative Learning and Computers: An Activity Guide for Teachers* by M. Male, R. Johnson, D. Johnson, and M. Anderson, 1986, Educational Apple-cations (125 Sylvar Street, Santa Cruz, CA 95060). Copyright © 1986 by Mary Male. Reprinted by permission.

FIGURE 2-8   Computer Job Application

Chip-In
Job Application

Name _____

Date _____

Address _____

City _____ State _____ Zip _____

Phone _____ Sex: M _____ F_____ Age _____ Grade _____

Day(s) Available _____

Time/Class Period(s) Available _____

Chip-In Job Desired:

  1st Choice _____

  2nd Choice _____

List special Chip-In job qualifications _____

_____

_____

_____

_____

_____

Personal Statement:

_____ Yes   _____ No   _____ Written   _____ Taped

_____ Included   _____ Will arrive by _____

  References: (teachers, computer pals, others who know you and your work habits)

  1. _____

  2. _____

Chip-In job applicant signature _____

I, _____, hereby give permission for _____

to obtain my work records.

SIGNATURE _____ DATE _____

Source: From *CHIPS: Computer Humanization in Positive Steps* by P. Kaplan et al., 1984, Denver, CO: Love Publishing. Reprinted with permission of the publisher.

FIGURE 2-9   Recognition Certificates

_____ has been a part of a Cooperative Learning Computer Team that has earned the most points on word processing lessons in the computer laboratory. The winning team gets lunch at McDonald's on Friday, June 7, compliments of Ms. Diaz. The students will be traveling by automobile during the regular lunch period with Ms. Diaz.

_____ has my permission to go with Ms. Diaz by automobile on Friday, June 7, to McDonald's for lunch.

_____
Parent Signature

Computer Whiz Kid Award

Student's Name _____

Has earned _____

For Creative Cooperative Computing Competence!

Computer Operator's License

_____
Student's Name

is certified to operate the computer and help others.

_____
Teacher's Signature

Source: From _The Writing Team with the Writing Machine_ by C. A. Broad, 1991, Educational Apple-cations (125 Sylvar Street, Santa Cruz, CA 95060). Reprinted by permission of the author.

Hello, Neighbor is a project developed at Beekman Hill School (New York), located in a densely populated, heavily trafficked urban area, where students commute to school and are unfamiliar with the neighborhood. In fact, many people in the neighborhood are unaware of the school. The program integrates social studies, communication skills, math, art, and computer use. Students interview community members, photograph people and places of interest, and make files and reports describing their experiences. Reports include name and address of the facility, name of the person in charge, services offered, and other relevant data. Students use map skills, dioramas, puppet theater, and role-playing to enrich their experience. Using computers, they record their reports with word processing and data bases. Using desktop publishing, students publish a quarterly newsletter for distribution in area shops and homes.

Neighborhood excursions are included in the projects, as are visits from merchants and other community members to the school. A Neighborhood Resource Booklet is produced at the end of the project (and is easily updated by using computers). A culminating activity is an assembly program to which all participants (students, their families, community members) are invited to view a display of students' work and receive a copy of the Neighborhood Resource Booklet (van de Vender, 1991).

Summer computer camps at the CompuCID sites in Charlotte, North Carolina, have offered a way to educate parents about computer technology as well as involve them as active participants in the project (Timms, 1991). These special camps have included a variety of students of various ages, ability levels, and physical challenges—all using computers to write stories, create original drawings, and make comic books. Children and parents have had the opportunity to contact other students and parents across the country by way of the Internet.

Activities

1. Design a cooperative computer lesson using a piece of software in which you are interested. Try it out. Write a short paper that describes your experience. Include your lesson plan.
2. Begin preparing your students for a computer celebration. What work on the computer are they most proud of? Begin brainstorming ideas with your class for the software and demonstrations to be featured in the computer celebration.
3. Survey your school for current ways in which students are (or can be) computer tutors or instructional materials developers for other students or teachers. Make a list of what is currently in place and what ideas you have for expanding these activities.
4. Survey your community for projects such as Kids Linking Kids, Hello, Neighbor, or a computer summer camp. If no such projects exist, design an action plan to begin one. Share your plan with your school administrator or service club.
5. Contact the Alliance for Technology Access center nearest you or other community or school resource and request information/updates on the programs they offer to promote social development, such as the ones described in the chapter. How did these programs begin? What made them successful? What challenges did they present? What have the results been so far?

References

Anderson, M. (1989). *Partnerships: Teambuilding at the computer.* Arlington, VA: Ma-jo Press.

Anderson, M. (1995). Using HyperStudio in a Resource Room. Presentation at San José State University.

Broad, C. (1991). *The writing team with the writing machine.* Santa Cruz, CA: Educational Apple-cations.

Center for Special Education Technology (1991). *Computers and cooperative learning.* Reston, VA: Council for Exceptional Children.

Feit, S. (1991). Personal communication.

Furst, M. (1983). Building self-esteem. *Academic Therapy,* 10(1), 11–15.

Johnson, D., and Johnson, R. (1994). *Learning together and alone: Cooperative, competitive, and individualistic learning.* Englewood Cliffs, NJ: Prentice-Hall.

Johnson, D., Johnson, R., and Holubec, E. (1993). *Circles of learning.* Edina, MN: Interaction Book Company.

Johnson, R., Johnson, D., and Stanne, M. (1986a). The effects of cooperative, competitive, and individual-istic goal structures on computer-assisted instruction. *Journal of Educational Psychology,* 77(6), 668–677.

Johnson, R., Johnson, D., and Stanne, M. (1986b). Computer-assisted instruction: A comparison of cooperative, competitive, and individualistic goal structures. *American Educational Research Journal,* 23(3), 382–391.

Male, M., Johnson, D., Johnson, R., and Anderson, M. (1986). *Cooperative learning and computers: An activity guide for teachers.* Santa Cruz, CA: Educational Apple-cations.

Mevarech, Z., Stern, D., & Levita, I. (1987). To cooperate or not to cooperate in CAI: That is the question. *Journal of Educational Research,* 60(2), 68–72.

Symington, L. (1991). Presentation at the 1991 Special Magic Symposium, Minneapolis, MN.

Timms, J. (1991, October). Presentation at the Special Magic Symposium, Minneapolis, MN.

van de Vender, D. (1991). Hello, neighbor! *Computers & Cooperative Learning Newsletter* 1(1), 2.

C h a p t e r 3

Building Partnerships between Parents and Professionals

The entire history of special education is intertwined with issues of parent participation in creating appropriate programs for their children. The initial passage of the Education of All Handicapped Children's Act in 1975 was largely in response to parents' organized lobbying efforts (Weintraub, 1975); the passage of the Individuals with Disabilities Education Act (IDEA) and the Americans with Disabilities Act (ADA) in 1990 was also based on significant parents' support.

"Many families of children with disabilities have a vision of what they want for their children's lives, and they are working to actualize that vision. The vision begins by having all children learn side-by-side in an integrated classroom to ensure that they all have the skills and experiences necessary to live together in the community" (Buswell & Schaffner, 1990, p. 219). Many families are well aware of the possibilities that technology offers to enhance inclusion and are actively promoting integration through technology in the following ways:

- The parents of a high school student with Down syndrome and a visual impairment use a scanner so that regular classroom materials call be enlarged and printed out for her use in class and in homework.
- Parents across the country joined forces with Apple Computer, Inc., to form the National Special Education Alliance. Now an independent organization with a new name, the Alliance for Technology Access (ATA) got its initial start from a group of parents and professionals who saw ways of meeting the learning needs of their children through technology.

- Parents in the CompuPlay project take the opportunity to check out software for their children and use it with support from professionals who can show them how the software works and various ways of using it to promote learning and social goals.

The benefits of establishing solid partnerships in program planning with parents have been extensively documented in the literature of special education (Calvert, 1971; Kelly, 1973; Kingsley, 1971; Turnbull & Turnbull, 1978; Stainback & Stainback, 1990). In the area of computer technology, parent involvement is particularly important (Hagen, 1984; Dutton & Dutton, 1990). Through their own professional contacts, parents may create links to the computer industry so that hardware and software are accessible for students with a wide range of learning needs (Brightman, 1985). Some parents are computer experts with invaluable technical expertise. Parent-involvement efforts also can provide networks of assistance and support to other parents who are often groping for information on how technology can assist their child (Brand, 1985). Teachers cite the importance of students having access to computers at home as well as at school, so that benefits can be maximized. Parents can also assist professionals by raising money for computer hardware, software, and training, as well as by providing classroom assistance where appropriate (Rotenberg, 1983).

The purpose of this chapter is to increase your interest in involving parents in your computer programs and to make you aware of successful programs started by parents.

Objectives

By the end of this chapter, you will be able to do the following:

1. Identify benefits of coordinating computer efforts with parents.
2. Discuss important features of a parent-involvement program.
3. Plan strategies to involve the parents of your students in your computer program.

The Benefits of Parent/Professional Partnerships

Although most educators express support for the concept of parent involvement in all aspects of education programming, many have not reached out to parents in the exploration of computer technology for exceptional learners. Some educators are self-conscious about their lack of technical expertise in this evolving area; some are not even aware of the variety of ways parent involvement could enhance their efforts to provide technology for their students. Educators are discovering that parents have a number of assets, among them the following:

- Community contacts that may be helpful in supporting efforts to provide access to computer resources
- Technical expertise in the field of computers
- A fascination with the development of computer technology and a willingness to assist in a variety of capacities to assure access for their child
- The desire to achieve maximum results for their child's program and an interest in having a computer at home

- The ability to help other parents become involved in computer technology so that rapid dissemination of information can occur
- The ability to put pressure on school systems and legislative bodies to provide access to equipment and software in ways that professionals cannot

Assuring Parent Involvement

Educators must take care in examining their assumptions about parent-involvement activities, whether they involve the computer or not. Statements such as, "They never show up for the IEP meeting" or "We planned a parent meeting, but only a few parents attended" reflect the need for greater sensitivity to the broad range of responsibilities parents face, particularly those with a child who has a disability. Delores Hagen (1984), longtime activist in providing access to computer technology for persons with disabilities, describes the situation in this way:

The future education for the handicapped is the responsibility of public education. The implementation of the technology to improve the quality of that education is also their responsibility. If that responsibility is lived up to, the future for the handicapped will certainly be brighter than it is today.

The public education system, by definition, must include parents as well as educators. There must be interest and involvement from the home front. We cannot send the children off to school in the morning and assume that the responsibility ends there.

The size and structure of today's educational system has presented problems for many parents. The buildings as well as the curriculum are foreign when compared to the smaller, intimate educational environments of just a few years ago. Some parents are intimidated by the bureaucracy that has somehow insulated them from day-to-day education of their children. Some call it parent apathy—parents too busy to care. More likely, it is parent intimidation. As a result, the system has become less responsive to the needs of society.

Communication between parents and the system seems to have broken down. By implication this means communication between society and education has diminished.

The advent of the microcomputer age may serve to solve this communication problem. As the dialogue between microcomputers presents itself on the home computer screen, the parent involvement in the educational process will return. (p. 95)

Following are some factors that may enhance parent involvement in all types of activities, including computer-related events (Dutton, 1991):

1. Involve parents in the planning of events.
2. Invite adult role models of people (with and without disabilities) who are successful in using technology.

3. Schedule activities at times when parents are available—in the evening or on weekends—and be realistic. In single-parent families or families where both parents work, taking care of a child with disabilities, other siblings, and work responsibilities may leave little time for anything else.

4. Set up a telephone tree so that parents are contacted personally by other parents; this will help overcome such barriers as transportation, language, fear, and so on.

5. Review the formality of the structure for getting parents together. Is it clear that parents are equal partners, or are status differences reinforced?

6. Provide child care so that baby-sitting costs do not become an issue and so that both parents can attend.

7. Set up a calendar of opportunities for participation rather than a series of one time events. In this way, plans can be made in advance and, over time, parents can get acquainted with each other and with professionals in informal ways.

8. Try a variety of ways of getting the word out to parents, not just written notices sent home with students or mailed out. Stories in newspapers about events, personal contacts by both professionals and other parents, and displays on bulletin boards of upcoming events and past activities can be motivational.

9. Don't give up.

Model Programs for Involving Parents

Successful efforts to involve parents in technology are taking a variety of forms and producing exciting results. The descriptions of the following programs are merely illustrative examples. They are designed to serve as a catalyst for the creation of new programs and services to link parents and professionals.

Closing the Gap

Delores and Budd Hagen, parents of a child with profound hearing loss, founded Closing the Gap out of their need to learn how computers could help their child. Closing the Gap began in 1981 as a newspaper for sharing technology information among professionals in rehabilitation and special education, as well as among persons with disabilities, their families, and friends. So many requests for training were received by the Hagens as a result of their newspaper that they began traveling all over the country to provide consultation and training services.

In 1984, the Hagens opened their Closing the Gap Training Center in Henderson, Minnesota, where people could receive intensive, personalized training. The center features state-of-the-art computer labs, adaptive devices, and a large software library.

Services provided by Closing the Gap include the following:

- The newsletter, published six times a year, reviews (and explains in easy-to-understand terms) software and hardware that have had the most successful applications of computer technology for the disabled. It also includes a yearly comprehensive catalog of products and services that feature computer technology for persons with disabilities.

- A bookstore offers materials to aid in the planning, selection, and implementation of microcomputer technology for persons with disabilities.
- A training and resource center provides workshops, seminars, and consultations that offer individuals the opportunity to determine which specific assistive devices and software programs are applicable to their particular situation.
- Tailor-made in-service, and on-site training is provided to meet the needs of the host organization.
- A yearly international conference is held in Minneapolis, where consumers, professionals, and parents can share the best applications of computer technology for persons with disabilities.

Alliance for Technology Access

The Alliance for Technology Access (ATA) is composed of a network of computer resource centers working in partnership with technology vendors, parents, professionals, and persons with disabilities with the vision of "redefining human potential through the powerful and imaginative use of technology" (ATA, 1990, p. 1). More than 40 ATA centers nationwide (see Figure 3-1) provide the following services:

- Collaborative consultations take place between staff and families or individual users. These consultations provide opportunities for one-on-one investigation of computers, adaptive equipment, and software, as well as information and resource sharing.
- Telephone support is available for the hundreds of people calling monthly for technical assistance and referrals.
- Open houses and other awareness events are open to all visitors. Software tryouts, library browsing, state-of-the-art equipment, and software demonstrations are featured during these open houses. An example of a calendar of events for the Center for Accessible Technology in Berkeley is presented in Figure 3-2.
- Speakers share information, demonstrate new products, and provide opportunities for hands-on exploration.
- Presentations are made to consumer, parent, professional, and community groups about the untapped potential of technology for people with disabilities.

The Alliance is also actively involved in school systems through its CompuCID project, described in earlier chapters. This project seeks to answer the question: How can computers help support the integration of students with disabilities who are being mainstreamed into regular public school classrooms? With demonstration sites in Seattle, Washington; Santa Monica, California; Knoxville, Tennessee; Charlotte, North Carolina; and Denver, Colorado, this project utilizes a technology team composed of an educator, a person with disabilities or a parent, and one or more interested persons, such as an occupational or speech/language therapist. Schools and centers are linked by a telecommunications system so that lessons and experiences can be shared quickly and easily, thus enabling students to learn from each other.

FIGURE 3-1 ATA Resource Centers

ALLIANCE FOR TECHNOLOGY ACCESS

Offices: 2175 East Francisco Blvd, Suite L • San Rafael, CA 94901
Voice (415) 455-4575 • Fax (415) 455-0654 • E-mail: atafta@aol.com

RESOURCE CENTERS

Alabama

Birmingham Alliance for
  Technology Access Center
Birmingham Independent
  Living Center
206 13th Street South
Birmingham AL 35233-1317
205/251-2223 (V/TTY)
dkessle1@ix.netcom.com

Technology Assistance for
  Special Consumers
P.O. Box 443
Huntsville AL 35804
205/532-5996 (V/TTY)
tascal@aol.com

Alaska

Alaska Services for
  Enabling Technology
P.O. Box 6485
Sitka AK 99835-7615
907/747-3019
asetseak@aol.com

Arizona

Technology Access Center of Tuscon
4710 East 29th Street
P.O. Box 13178
Tuscon AZ 85732-3178
520/745-5588, ext 412
tactaz@aol.com

Arkansas

Technology Resource Center
c/o Arkansas Easter Seal Society
3920 Woodland Heights Road
Little Rock AR 72212-2495
501/227-3600
atrce@aol.com

California

Center for Accessible Technology
2547 8th St., 12-A
Berkeley CA 94710-2572
510/841-3224; 841-5621 (BBS)
cforat@aol.com

Computer Access Center
5901 Green Valley Circle, Suite 320
Culver City CA 90230
310/338-1597
cacofsmca@aol.com

Sacramento Center for
  Assistive Technology
4370 Mather School Rd.
Mather CA 95655-0301
916-361-0553
scatca@aol.com

Special Awareness
  Computer Center
Rehab Unit North
2975 North Sycamore Drive
Simi Valley CA 93065
805/582-1881
saccca@aol.com

Special Technology Center
590 Castro Street
Mountain View CA 94041
415/961-6789
stcca@aol.com

Team of Advocates for
  Special Kids
100 W. Cerritos Ave.
Anaheim CA 90802
714/533-8275
taskca@aol.com

Florida

CITE/Center for Independence,
  Technology & Education
215 E. New Hampshire St.
Orlando FL 32804
407/898-2483
comcite@aol.com

Georgia

Tech-Able
1140 Ellington Dr.
Conyers GA 30207
770/922-6768
tekablegal@aol.com

Hawaii

Aloha Special Technology
  Access Center
710 Green Street
Honolulu HI 96813
808/523-5547
stachi@aol.com

Illinois

Northern Illinois Center
  for Adaptive Technology
3615 Louisiana Road
Rockford IL 61108-6195
815/229-2163
ilcat@aol.com

Technical Aids & Assistance
  for the Disabled Center
1950 West Roosevelt Road
Chicago IL 60608
312/421-3373 (V/TTY)
taad@interaccess.com

Indiana

Assistive Technology Training and
  Information Center
P.O. Box 2441
Vincennes IN 47591
812-886-0575 (V/TTY)
inattic1@aol.com

Kansas

Technology Resource Solutions
  for People
1710 West Schilling Road
Salina KS 67401
913/827-9383 (V/TTY)
trspks@aol.com

Kentucky

Bluegrass Technology Center
169 N. Limestone Street
Lexington KY 40507
606/255-9951 (V/TTY)
bluegrassc@aol.com

EnTech: Enabling Technologies
  of Kentuckiana
Louisville Free Public Library
301 York Street
Louisville KY 40203-2205
502/574-1637
entecky@aol.com

Special Link
36 W. 5th Street
Covington KY 41011
606/491-2464 (V/TTY)
spclinkky@aol.com

Continued

FIGURE 3-1 *Continued*

Maryland

Learning Independence Through
  Computers, Inc.
28 E. Ostend St. Suite 140
Baltimore MD 21230
410/659-5462
lincmd@aol.com

Massachusetts

Massachusetts Special Technology
  Access Center
12 Mudge Way 1–6
Bedford MA 01730-2138
617/275-2446
mastacma@aol.com

Michigan

Living & Learning Resource Centre
Physically Impaired Association
  of Mich.
600 West Maple Street
Lansing MI 48906-5038
517/487-0883;800/833-1996(MI)
llrcmi@aol.com

Minnesota

PACER Computer Resource Center
4826 Chicago Avenue South
Minneapolis MN 55417-1098
612/827-2966 (V/TTY)
pacercrc@aol.com

Missouri

Technology Access Center
12110 Clayton Road
St. Louis MO 63131-2599
314/569-8404
mostltac@aol.com

Montana

Parents, Let's Unite for Kids
MSU-B/SPED Bldg., Room 267
1500 N. 30th Street
Billings MT 59101-0298
406/657-2055 (V/TTY)
plukmt@aol.com

New Jersey

Computer Center for People
  With Disabilities
c/o Family Resource Associates, Inc.
35 Haddon Avenue
Shrewsbury NJ 07702-4007
908/747-5310
ccdanj@aol.com

The Center for Enabling
  Technology
622 Route 10 West, Ste 22B
Whippany, NJ 07981-0272
201/428-1455
cetnj@aol.com

New York

Techspress
Resource Center for
  Independent Living
401-409 Columbia Street
P.O. Box 210
Utica NY 13503-0210
315/797-4642
txprsny@aol.com

North Carolina

Carolina Computer Access Center
Metro School
700 East Second Street
Charlotte NC 28202-2826
704/342-3004
ccacnc@aol.com

Ohio

Technology Resource Center
301 Valley St.
Dayton OH 45404-1840
513/222-5222
trcdoh@aol.com

Rhode Island

TechACCE33 Center of
  Rhode Island
300 Richmond St.
Providence RI 02903-4222
401/273-1990 (V/TTY)
accessri@aol.com

Tennessee

East Tennessee Technology
  Access Center, Inc.
3525 Emory Road, NW
Powell TN 37849
423/947-2191 (V/TTY)
etstactn@aol.com

Technology Access Center of
  Middle Tennessee
Fountain Square, Suite 126
2222 Metrocenter Blvd.
Nashville TN 37228
615/248-6733 (V/TTY)
tactn@aol.com

West Tenn. Special Tech.
  Access Resource Center
60 Lynoak Cove
P.O. Box 3683
Jackson TN 38305
901/668-3888
startn@aol.com

Utah

The Computer Center for Citizens
  with Disabilities
c/o Utah Center for Assistive
  Technology
2056 South 1100 East
Salt Lake City UT 84106
801/485-9152 (V/TTY)
cccdut@aol.com

Virgin Islands

Virgin Islands Resource Center
  for the Disabled, Inc.
P.O. Box 308427
St. Thomas, US VI 00803-8427
809/777-2253

Virginia

Tidewater Center for
  Technology Access
Special Education Annex
960 Windsor Oaks Blvd.
Virginia Beach VA 23462
804/474-8650 (V/TTY)
tcta@aol.com

West Virginia

Assistive Technology
  Learning Center
P.O. Box 8962
South Charleston WV 25303
304/744-4370
glueata@aol.com

Eastern Panhandle Technology
Access Center, Inc.
P.O. Box 987
Charles Town WV 25414
304/725-6473
eptac@aol.com

FIGURE 3-2 Center for Accessible Technology Calendar

October 1995

Sunday	Monday	Tuesday	Wednesday	Thursday	Friday	Saturday
1	2	3	Yom Kippur 4	5	6	7
8	Columbus Day 9	10	OPEN RESOURCE 4-6 11	12	13	Beginning Mac 10 am (Pre-register) 14
15	16	17	OPEN RESOURCE 4-6 18	19	20	Playgroups (Pre-register) Ages 4-7 & 7-9 21
22	23	24	OPEN RESOURCE 4-6 25	26	27	28
29	30	31				

November 1995

Sunday	Monday	Tuesday	Wednesday	Thursday	Friday	Saturday
			1	2	3	Beginning IBM 10 am (Pre-register) 4
5	6	7	OPEN RESOURCE 4-6 8	9	Ke:nx Workshop 6:45 am (pre-reg) 10	Bay Bridge Run Software & L D 10-noon 11
12	13	14	OPEN RESOURCE 4-6 15	16	17	18
19	20	21	CLOSED 22	CLOSED 23	24	25
26	27	28	OPEN RESOURCE 4-6 29	30		

December 1995

Sunday	Monday	Tuesday	Wednesday	Thursday	Friday	Saturday
					1	2
3	4	5	OPEN RESOURCE 4-6 6	7	8	9
PICKLE CIRCUS BENEFIT 2 pm 10	11	12	OPEN RESOURCE 4-6 13	14	15	16
17	Hanukkah 18	19	20	21	22	23
24	Closed til Jan 2nd 25	26	27	28	29	30

Center for Accessible Technology
(510) 841-3224
Site Address:
2525 8th Street, Berkeley
Mail: 2547 8th St. 12-A
Berkeley CA 94710

Call, fax or e-mail!
Our internet address is:
CforAT@aol.com
The DCCG BBS can be
called at 510-841-5621.
The fax is
510-841-7956.

Open Resource:
Open to all for software preview, demonstrations, questions & answers.

Playgroups:
Open to members, please call to pre-register. There will be two groups on October 21, children ages 3-5 from 10 am-10:45 am, and those ages 6-8 from 11:15 am to noon.

Beginning Mac:
Free 2 hr. class on the Mac operating system and basic access features.

Beginning IBM:
Free 2 hr. class on the DOS & Windows 3.x operating system and basic access features.

Software & LD:
Talking word processing and word prediction software for the Macintosh from Don Johnston Inc.

Ke:nx Workshop:
Powerful switch access for the Macintosh, Ke:nx allows you to create custom scanning for any software. Call for details before October 20, if interested.

FIGURE 3-2 *Continued*

Thank You!

Gifts Since July 18, 1995
Rogers, Judith
Levi Strauss Inc.

United Way & Campaign Donors
Barrera, Ginny LaVine
Betleyoun, Fred
Darnell, Jack
Emerson, Lawrence
Faulkner, Martin
Findlay, Jolene
Frederickson, D.
Gee, Julia
Geliebter, Mark
Ho, Ching Yee
Iantuono, Alexander
Isola, Frank
Kahn, Eric
Kaur, Manjeet
Kendall, Bruce
Liu, Helen
Loughrey, Micheal
Ma, Mary L
Medina, Marlene
Miranda, Jr., Rufino
Muller, Richard
Parra, Marilyn
Patrizi, Debra
Peralta, Irene
Politan, Robin
Sack, Tyler
Schatz, B.E.
Sysum, Scott
Toms, Maureen
Trujillo, Tamara
Walker, Jean
Whitaker, Carl

In-Kind Gifts since July 18, 1995
Bennett, Barbara
Don Johnston Inc.
Haberberger, Carol
IntelliTools
Key Curriclum Press
Kraber, Richard
Laureate Learning Systems, Inc.
Niebuhr, Deanna
Wanderman, Richard
Woodward, Chuck

Recent Grants
Children's Support League
City of Berkeley
McKesson Employee Gifts
  Committee

Benefits

Our mission is ....
- to provide technology support for parents, teachers, and children and adults with disabilities.

- to demonstrate that computers and adaptive technology are powerful tools of ability, offering independence and integration into the mainstream.

- to redefine human potential by making technology a regular part of the lives of people with disabilities.

Membership provides:
- support to keep the doors open.

- staffing to help answer your calls and questions.

- a free consultation scheduled with a Center staff member to guide your exploration of adaptive technology. The appointment can be for an individual or family.

- drop-in times held almost weekly for on-going exploration, support, trouble-shooting, and loan.

- loan of Apple II software and selected hardware items.

- the Real Times newsletter, published five time per year, with reviews of products, previews of new technology, and related information.

- Saturday morning playgroups for young children and parents, held five or more times per year.

- discounts on selected Center classes, such as keyboarding.

- discounts on refurbished Macintosh computer and selected software through the User Group Connection.

MEMBERSHIP FORM
(Please Print)

Name_____

Name of Person w/ Disability (if different)

_____

Birth date (if a child)_____

Address_____

City_____

County_____State_____

Zip _____

Title/Position_____
Agency/Business
Affiliation_____

School District (if applicable)

_____

For funders information, are you:
❏ Asian   ❏ African-American
❏ Hispanic ❏ Caucasian
❏ Native American ❏ Other

Please check the areas of interest:
❏ Orthopedic   ❏ Visual
  ❏ Hearing/Deaf   ❏ Speech
❏ Emotion/Behavior ❏ Learning
❏ Developmental
❏ Multiply Impaired
❏ Other:_____
Date of Birth (if under the age of 18):_____

+++++++++++++++++++++++++++++++++++

Membership Options:
❏ $30 for a one-year membership
❏ $55 for two years
❏ $75 for three years
❏ $5 for an out-of-town, or newsletter-only membership
❏ I am enclosing a larger gift to help the Center do even more.

Sliding Scale (for families & individuals with disabilities)
❏ I can't pay $30, but can pay $_____
❏ This is a renewal.

Center for Accessible Technology
2547 8th ST. 12-A, Berkeley CA 94710

Western Center for Microcomputers in Special Education

Western Center's purpose is to interpret and clarify for educators and parents the latest microcomputer research, development, products, and applications. Modified equipment is developed and sold, and a quarterly newsletter, called *The Catalyst,* has been published for 10 years. The Western Center was started by a team composed of Sue Swezey, parent of a son with autism whose favorite pastime is computer graphics; Dr. David Uslan, an educator whose background includes considerable computer expertise; and Dr. Howard Johnson, a scientist with extensive technical expertise. The advisory committee and editorial staff now include Skip Via, a special education teacher in Fairbanks, Alaska, and Dr. Richard Riedl, an Associate Professor of Computer Education at Appalachian State University in North Carolina. The Western Center provides helpful, easy-to-use information and a means of exchanging ideas (Swezey, 1991).

Services Needed by Parents and Professionals

In reviewing the programs that have had the greatest impact, the common thread among them is the cooperation and sharing between parents and professionals. Computer technology seems to foster this cooperative spirit. Because the technology changes so rapidly, ideas must come from all directions. A rule of thumb seems to be that if one designs a program to serve the needs of parents and individuals with disabilities first and foremost, one will end up serving professionals too. (The reverse is not necessarily true, however.)

The first area of need for most parents (and professionals) is awareness—how their child will access the computer—or, in the case of students with learning difficulties, identifying the broad categories of use that will be most appropriate given the student's learning needs. After the types of access and use are identified, parents may need assistance in selecting hardware, software, peripherals, and adaptive devices. The options are bewildering, as can be attested by the plethora of articles on how to select a computer.

The third area of need is hands-on assistance in how to use the equipment, including how to troubleshoot when things are not working properly. Technical computer expertise is helpful, though not essential; many of the problems nervous first-time users experience can be solved by someone who has had just a little more practice.

Parents may also need direction in finding sources of funds to provide needed computer technology. Students with physical disabilities may be eligible for computers to use at home through vocational rehabilitation, regional centers, special low-incidence funds, and the like. Grant programs may offer assistance to students with particular types of needs. When appropriate, computers should be written into the individual education plan (IEP).

Getting Started

Most of the successful programs reviewed here began with a strong personal commitment rather than a formal planning process with committees, recommendations, and policy decisions. The following suggestions were contributed by the founders of the programs described in this chapter, based on their own experiences.

1. Get a group together to talk informally about needs and ideas that people would like to bring to life. An agenda might include:

- Personal introductions (parents might talk about their interests in computers; adults with disabilities might share how technology has enhanced life on the job and at home; parents might share about their own child and what a computer does or might do)
- Demonstrations of a sample of software and adaptive devices
- Videotape of a child using a particular piece of software or a classroom where technology supports full inclusion (Carolina Computer Access Center, 1991)
- Brainstorming ideas for events or services that could be planned
- Action planning and dividing up tasks

2. Begin systematically collecting information about who is doing what—an expandable data base of names, addresses, jobs, specific interests and talents, current uses of computers, and so on. Collect relevant articles and share them (decide who will subscribe to which periodicals so that you can cover more ground).

3. Create a computer technology event for your school, district, or community. Apple Computer, Inc., distributes a kit of materials for a family computing event. The event doesn't have to be fancy—it is simply an opportunity for sharing, with a focus on children, adults, families, and computers. The cooperative effort needed to make such an event successful will provide a model for future projects.

4. Hold an informal open house. Let each student (or pairs) demonstrate for parents a particular application or piece of software. Have parents rotate from machine to machine.

5. Start a newsletter or a computer column in an existing newsletter.

6. Try an approach that no one has thought of yet, particularly if parent involvement has not been successful in the past. Be creative!

7. Establish an informal ongoing users' group that meets on a regular basis and provides a framework for parents and teachers to share with one another.

8. Expand your thinking to include grandparents (Symington, 1991).

9. Ask people what they want or need (a special group on a particular topic, a guest speaker, information about telecommunications, etc.) and then try to offer it.

Activities

1. Survey your local district for opportunities for parent involvement in education and computers. What sorts of activities have been tried? What were the results? What future activities are planned? Are parents recruited as leaders of these activities?
2. Review a copy of the *Classroom Connect, CUE Newsletter, Electronic Learning, Technology & Learning, Teaching and Computers, Closing the Gap,* or *The Catalyst* for articles related to the diverse needs of the learners in your classroom. Clip or photocopy articles and place them in files

for future reference or for future parent requests for information. Make sure your school or district subscribes to these publications.

3. Select one of the ideas suggested in this chapter and try it out with a parent and student (or a group of parents and students). What response did you get? What will you do next?

4. Organize a committee to promote parent involvement in special education and computer technology. Develop an action plan. Add some new ideas to those presented in this chapter.

5. Visit one of the programs discussed in this chapter for information on current activities. Write a description of what you saw, learned, or experienced.

References

Alliance for Technology Access (ATA) (1990). Portrait of the Alliance. *Perspectives. 1*(1), 1.

Brand, J. (1985, July). Presentation at Special Magic Symposium, San Jose, CA.

Brightman, A. (1985). Keynote address for Closing the Gap conference.

Buswell, B., & Schaffner, C. (1990). Families supporting inclusive schooling. In W. Stainback & S. Stainback (Eds.), *Support networks for inclusive schooling.* Baltimore: Paul H. Brookes.

Calvert, D. (1971). Dimensions of family involvement in early childhood education. *Exceptional Children, 37,* 655–659.

Carolina Computer Access Center (1991). *Demonstrating technology for special needs* (videotape). Charlotte, NC: Charlotte Mecklenburg Schools.

Dutton, D. (1991). Unpublished review of this book.

Dutton, D., & Dutton, D. (1990). Technology to support diverse needs in regular classes. In W. Stainback & S. Stainback (Eds.), *Support networks for inclusive schooling.* Baltimore: Paul H. Brookes.

Hagen, D. (1984). *Microcomputer resource book for special education.* Reston, VA: Reston Publishing.

Kelly, E. (1973). Parental roles in special educational programming—A brief for involvement. *Journal of Special Education, 1*(4), 357–364.

Kingsley, L. (1971). Parents can help with school difficulties. *Exceptional Parent, 1,*13–15.

Rotenberg, L. (1983). Put parents on your computing team. *Teaching and Computers, 1*(2), 18–20.

Stainback, W., & Stainback, S. (1990). *Support networks for inclusive schooling.* Baltimore: Paul H. Brookes.

Swezey, S. (1991). A privileged observer. *The Catalyst, 8*(2), 1.

Symington, L. (1991). Unpublished review of this book.

Turnbull, R., & Turnbull, A. (1978). *Parents speak out: The view from the other side of the mirror.* Columbus, OH: Merrill.

Weintraub, F. (1975). Recent influences of law regarding the identification and placement of children. In E. Meyen, G. Vergason, & R. Whelan (Eds.), *Alternatives for teaching exceptional children.* Denver: Love Publishing

$$Chapter \quad 4$$

The Technology Team

Collaboration and teamwork are recurring themes in this book. Given a scarcity of resources, effective collaboration will increase access to technology for all students. Chapter 3 concentrated specifically on building partnerships between parents and professionals; in this chapter, the focus is primarily on promoting access through partnerships between teachers and administrators, teachers and technology specialists, and general education and special education personnel.

Objectives

By the end of this chapter, you will be able to do the following:

1. Identify sources of support for you and your students in making sure technology needs are met
2. Establish a technology team and conduct a planning meeting to address the technology needs of your students
3. Set up an accountability system to track services and project needs for your students

Defining Roles and Responsibilities for Technology Support

The Individualized Education Planning (IEP) team, which includes an administrator, teacher, and parent, may be a natural starting place for beginning to assure that technology is considered as an integral part of a child's program. The IEP team, however, must have people with the necessary technology expertise, and technology must be considered in the development of each student's program. For this reason, some schools have specially-designated Technology Teams to make sure that teachers and students have the support needed for technology to have the maximum impact on the success of a child's program. Whether the IEP or a Technology Team approach is adopted, the role of the site administrator is critical.

To move from segregated or pull-out programs for students with special needs toward more mainstreaming and inclusion, the principal must be knowledgeable and actively involved. Technology provides a means but it is not the end in itself. An active principal can arrange time for teachers to learn to use the technology, plan together, and team teach; redirect physical location of classrooms; advocate and assist with fund-raising for needed equipment, services, and programs; and arrange training in specific skills and technologies. Table 4-1 illustrates the administrative support needed for the teachers in the technology-rich Apple Classroom of Tomorrow program to be successful. Notice how essential active participation of the principal is at every phase of this evolutionary process (Dwyer et al., 1991).

A school-site computer expert is essential to keep equipment in operating order and to reduce technical frustrations on the part of teachers who are attempting this major change. Many schools simply turn over the use of the computer to such an expert, who typically teaches programming, keyboarding, or computer skills in isolation from the curriculum (Lieber & Cosden, 1989). A team approach is more effective. This team is composed of members who combine computer expertise, curriculum expertise, and skills in linking with district and community resources and provide a strong foundation for beginning and maintaining a change effort around inclusive classrooms and technology.

Teamwork depends on each person having a clear understanding about roles and responsibilities. In a new situation, flexibility is required, and, in the spirit of experimentation, you may want to try things out for a while. Most important is that teamwork requires planning time, especially in the beginning. A successful classroom requires support to address adequately all the special needs and characteristics. Teachers must have immediate access to that support as technology is implemented, so that early efforts are successful and will lead to more risk-taking. Speech/language, occupational, and bilingual specialists, along with teachers and technology specialists, have important perspectives to share. Russell, Corwin, Mokros, and Kapisovsky (1989) describe the following key roles for the teacher (but these roles could also be filled by others on the technology team within a school or school district):

1. *Introducer:* The introducer helps get students started. Most students will need simplified help cards or posters and the basics for getting started with a piece of software. Some students who are reluctant to risk failure may need specific encouragement to just try something—anything—when they are not sure what to do next.

2. *Technical Advisor:* Deciding who needs what kind of help is essential. Not every student needs keyboarding instruction, but some will. Some pieces of software will work better with worksheets or other supports to help students organize information or keep track of their progress. Some students may get hung up if the program behaves in unexpected ways; the technology advisor helps students practice ways to make the software work.

3. *Arranger:* Setting up, monitoring, and intervening when necessary in cooperative learning groups become important skills in this role.

4. *Visitor:* In the beginning, the teacher will need to be available to circulate and help with problems until the students feel comfortable with the software, whether they are working in groups or working on their own. Although the teacher needs to be available, it is important not to dominate the situation and to know when to leave.

TABLE 4-1 Support for Instructional Evolution in Technology-Intensive Environments

Phase	Expectations	Support
Entry	• Identification of volunteer team • Installation of critical mass of technology to make it a constant feature of the classroom	• Provide advance planning time to develop shared vision • Provide daily team planning time as permanent feature of schedule • Excuse staff from as many district requirements as possible • Create opportunities for staff to share experiences with nonparticipant colleagues
Adoption	• Maintenance of established instructional patterns and course of study • Use of word processors for writing • Use of CAI software for drill and practice of basic skills	• Provide nuts-and-bolts technical support to develop teachers' confidence and ability to maintain hardware and facilitate children's use • Provide CAI and word-processor software training
Adaptation	• Smooth integration of word processing and CAI software into existing instructional program, resulting in increased teacher and student productivity • Modifications in course of study to take advantage of time opened by increase in productivity	• Develop flexible schedule to permit peer observation and team teaching • Introduce and discuss alternative pedagogies • Train staff in use of tool software: spreadsheets, databases, graphics, HyperCard, communications • Introduce videodisk and scanner technology
Appropriation	• Experimentation with interdisciplinary project-based instruction • Experimentation with team teaching • Experimentation with student grouping • Experimentation with scheduling	• Routinize peer observation and group discussions of events and consequences • Re-examine project mission and goals • Build awareness of alternative student assessment strategies, that is, performance-based assessment and portfolio assessment strategies • Encourage and support conference attendance and teacher presentations
Invention	• Implementation of integrated curriculum • Balanced and strategic use of direct teaching and project-based teaching • Integration of alternative modes of subject assessment	• Encourage collaboration between teachers and researchers • Encourage teachers to write about and publish their experience • Explore telecommunications as a way to keep teachers in contact with innovators outside of district • Create opportunities for teachers to mentor other teachers

Source: From "Changes in Teachers' Beliefs and Practices in Technology-Rich Classrooms" by D. Dwyer, C. Ringstaff, and J. Sandholtz, 1991, *Educational Leadership, 48*(8), p. 51. Reprinted with permission of the Association for Supervision and Curriculum Development. Copyright 1991 by the Association for Supervision and Curriculum Development. All rights reserved. Also reprinted with permission of D. Dwyer, Ph.D., Project Manager and Principal Scientist, Apple Classrooms of Tomorrow.

5. *Silent Partner:* Knowing when not to intervene is as important as intervening appropriately. The computer will promote student self-sufficiency—if teachers do not get in the way.

6. *Booster:* Some teachers have a ground rule to check with teammates before asking the teacher. This procedure will help students learn to deal with frustration without depending on the teacher too much. In this way, teachers can schedule individual time with each student to review progress, share successes, and empathize with frustrations.

7. *Mentor:* Teachers need to provide an opportunity for students to reflect on what they are learning and how they are learning it. Teachers should model that reflectivity themselves by offering students the opportunity to give feedback on what works and does not work and thinking about how to improve over time.

8. *Learner:* Perhaps the most important role is to model for students the willingness to take risks, to try something in which the outcome is uncertain, and to deal with the frustration of things that do not work out, as well as to celebrate the successes.

Successful Technology Team Models

In Lawrence, New York, a "Pathways Team" was formed at each school, composed of teachers from several consecutive grade levels, the administrator, and support personnel such as the resource teacher and social worker. The teams met to develop curriculum activities to support integration of students with disabilities using a variety of technologies. Periodically, the teams from all the school sites would meet to share progress with particular students, ideas for curriculum adaptations, and explore new technologies (Moeller, Jeffers, Zorfass, & Capel, 1995). The role of facilitator on the team was considered of such importance that two facilitators were used: one to train teachers and one to secure resources (funding, equipment, software) and arrange for professional development time, select consultants to help with implementation, schedule activities, and conduct ongoing evaluation of progress.

School districts with Alliance for Technology Access centers nearby have taken advantage of the centers' expertise and range of equipment and software to meet the needs of their students. The CITE center in Orlando, Florida, for example, offers a summer computer camp at which a wide array of communication devices and switches were available to try out. Parents could observe their child's success with a variety of equipment and software and had ideas to share with school personnel when the IEP team met to plan the next year's program. Based on the team's recommendations, appropriate equipment and software were purchased (Alliance for Technology Access, 1995).

Lauren Scrivo, eight years old, from Fairfield, New Jersey, had a similar success experience. She and her family worked with the Center for Enabling Technology in Whippany, New Jersey, where they discovered Ke:nx software and a trackball for easier movement of the cursor. An adaptive keyboard, the Magic Wand, provided a more appropriate input system, and using Co:Writer (word prediction), Lauren was able to work much more quickly. CET worked with her parents and school to purchase these new tools and a classroom computer. The school also made architectural changes to make the school more accessible. "Everyone at the school—from the principal on down—has embraced the concept of full inclusion and is committed to making Lauren's experience a success," reported her mother. "We have nothing but praise for their efforts" (Alliance for Technology Access, 1995, p. 31).

The Planning Meeting

The first step in setting up a technology team at a school site is to determine the composition of the team. The team membership will vary for each student, depending on the needs, but some members will be the same. Figure 4-1 provides a list of people who might be appropriate for a technology support team (Alliance for Technology Access, 1994).

Technology should be an integral part of program planning for all students with special needs; no IEP is complete without an assessment of a student's technology needs. If a student is served in more than one setting and by more than one teacher or specialist, a coordinated approach to how technology will support each aspect of the student's program should be explored. Selection and funding of hardware, software, assistive devices, training, and equipment maintenance are all considerations to be addressed during planned meetings.

During the initial technology team meeting, an action plan should be developed so that all team members have identified responsibilities and a timeline is clear to all team members. A sample action plan is included in Figure 4-2. The agenda for the meeting should include a chance for all team members (including the student, if appropriate) to brainstorm dreams and goals for what using technology might produce (Armstrong & Jones, 1995), goals, objectives, and activities that could be pursued, and resources. Following the brainstorming, team members could select the highest priority activities and outcomes and com-

FIGURE 4-1   Potential Technology Team Members

- Parents
- Partners
- Advocates
- Professional service providers
- Other people with disabilities or their parents
- Computer-using children
- Computer enthusiasts
- Rehabilitation counselors
- Job coaches
- Employers
- Teachers
- Funders
- People with a good knowledge of you, your environment, funding, legislation, community resources, assistive technology

FIGURE 4-2 Technology Team Action Plan

Activity	Date Due	Person(s) Responsible
Evaluate computer access	10-1	physical therapist
		ATA center staff
Try out software	10-15	teachers
		computer specialist
		ATA center staff
Seek funding for system/software	11-1	administrator, parents
Provide training for staff/parents	12-15	ATA center
		computer specialist

plete the action plan. A follow-up meeting should be scheduled to assure that team members are accountable for their outlined responsibilities.

Tracking Services and Projecting Needs

Students' needs and technology will change. If possible, leasing equipment instead of purchasing it may be a more cost-effective option. In addition, a school or district technology team should look at the changing needs of its students, so that as one student moves into a

FIGURE 4-3 Data Base to Track Student Technology Needs

Student Last Name:

Student First Name:

School:

DOB:

Type of Computer:

Date Purchased:

Assistive Devices:

Software:

Funding Source:

Technology Goals:

more sophisticated system, another student may benefit from the equipment as it becomes available. Portability is another issue for students whose needs are met in different settings. A laptop computer may be more cost-effective than a desktop system if a student needs it in several places during a school day.

Most schools and districts are not accustomed to planning for rapid changes that technology requires. Technology teams need to develop a data base (see Chapter 9) to keep track of equipment and software so that as student needs change, the team can reallocate more appropriate equipment to a particular student or situation. When decisions are made for this year's needs, what the student will need next is also an important consideration. A sample record for such a data base is provided in Figure 4-3.

Activities

1. For the students in your school or program, summarize the process used currently to assure that their technology needs are met. List three ways in which this process might be enhanced by the use of some of the ideas in this chapter.
2. Compare and contrast the expertise needed by an IEP team and a technology team. What are three advantages and three disadvantages of having a combined IEP/technology team versus separate teams?
3. Select one student in your program who would benefit most from having a technology team to review his/her technology needs. Assemble a team and follow the steps suggested in the chapter to conduct a planning meeting and generate an action plan.

References

Alliance for Technology Access (1994). *Computer resources for people with disabilities.* Alameda, CA: Hunter House.

Alliance for Technology Access (1995). Real people, real technology, real solutions. *Exceptional Parent,* 25(11), 30–31, 32, 34.

Armstrong, J., and Jones, K. (1995). Using family dreams to develop meaningful goals involving assistive technology. *Closing the Gap,* 14(2), 1, 6.

Dwyer, D., Ringstaff, C., & Sandhortz, J. (1991). Changes in teachers' beliefs and practices in technology-rich classrooms. *Educational Leadership,* 48(8), 45–52.

Lieber, J., & Cosden, M. (1989). A survey of computer lab specialists in elementary schools in southern California. *Journal of Research on Computing in Education,* 2(2), 3–13.

Moeller, B., Jeffers, L., Zorfass, J., and Capel, H. (1995). Forging special pathways. *Electronic Learning,* 15(3), 18–19.

Russell, S., Corwin, R., Mokros, J., and Kapisovsky, P. (1989). *Beyond drill and practice: Expanding the computer mainstream.* Reston, VA: Council for Exceptional Children.

Chapter 5

Integrating Technology with Individualized Education Programs (IEPs)

Most educators recognize the need to establish goals and objectives and to monitor progress for students. Every student with special needs (special education, bilingual education, Chapter I, etc.) is required by law to have an individualized plan. Developing the plan can be a difficult and time-consuming process; many educators are viewing technology as one means of relieving the mechanical aspects of this task, which will then allow more time for emphasizing the content of these plans.

Some of the difficulties encountered in writing high-quality individualized plans include the following:

- Many worthwhile goals are difficult to measure and quantify (e.g., John will improve his self-concept).
- Objectives that are easy to measure may lead to isolated skill development and a very narrow curriculum focus (e.g., Given 20 sight word flashcards from the reader, Susan will correctly read them aloud).
- Teachers wonder if they should write separate objectives for computer use, and parents wonder if computer use should be included in their child's individualized plan.
- Administrators would like to use technology to reduce the drudgery of handwritten individualized plans, yet most wonder what effect a computer and printer would have on the planning meeting with parents in which the plan is developed.
- Teachers question the validity of "computerized objective banks" for individualized planning; at the same time, writing goals and objectives can be tedious as well as re-

petitive, and may not result in a higher-quality result than objectives selected or modified from a data bank.

In this chapter, you will investigate the impact of technology on assessing special needs and student progress and the use of electronic portfolios. You will review issues and instructional objectives for individualized plans that incorporate computer activities. You will also explore alternatives for increasing your productivity by using technology to assist with assessment, report writing, and individualized planning.

Objectives

By the end of this chapter, you will be able to do the following:

1. Identify ways technology can enhance assessment procedures for determining special needs and pupil progress
2. Review computer activities and integrate them into classroom thematic units and students' individual plans
3. Write meaningful goals and objectives which incorporate computer use
4. Identify ways that technology can enhance productivity in assessment, report writing, and individualized planning

Assessing Special Needs

In order to make good decisions about how to use technology effectively in the assessment process, it is important to reexamine assessment practices for appropriateness. As schools undergo restructuring, assessment is the topic of much debate and scrutiny (Newman, 1991; Wolf, Bixby, Glenn, & Gardner, 1991). Teachers should give careful consideration to software in four areas: informal assessment, curriculum-based assessment, standardized assessment, and electronic portfolios.

Technology-based assessment offers one or more of the following features (McCain, 1995):

- Self-administration
- Software control of item presentation
- Response evaluation based on conceptual models or algorithms
- Decision making based on rules and criteria
- Prescription based on expert knowledge
- Direct links between assessment and recommendations for instruction

Some of the options in special education assessment currently available include several types of tests. Some tests can switch to the language preference of the student as appropriate. Others include video segments from which students must make choices and decisions about the appropriate course of action to take (moral dilemmas). Students make selections by touching the screen rather than having to read the responses.

Assessment tools are also available which include a variety of formats for direct observation, entry of anecdotal information, checklists, and comments from a variety of sources (student, teacher, parent). The Grady Profile, for example, is a multimedia software package utilizing HyperCard stacks (see Chapter 12 for more information on HyperCard). One screen allows students to record reading samples; another screen allows a scanned sample of a student's handwritten work. QuickTime movies of a student performing a task or behavior are also easy to include. Almost every screen has a checklist that can be customized by the user to record teacher, parent, and student assessment of each item. A variety of reports can also be created from the data and printed from a word processor (Barrett, 1994). Figure 5-1 provides an example of a Grady Profile Checklist screen for a sample student.

Another example of a technology-supported assessment system to record direct observation data is the Learner Profile. The program operates in three stages: planning, observing, and reporting. At the beginning of the observation period, the teacher prints out a page of bar codes, containing a seating chart (with a separate bar code for each student), a set of bar codes for the behaviors that the students were expected to exhibit that day, qualifiers for

FIGURE 5-1   Sample Grady Profile Checklist

Einstein's Academy for the Advancement of Science and Violin
Middle School Division

Demo-Student, Ann   **Reading**

Legend

– = Performance is less than expected	**Evaluation:** 4/4/94
✓ = Performance is at expected level	**Evaluator:** Miss A. Nelson
+ = Performance exceeded expected level	**Skill-Set:** Reading Comprehension
	Date: 10/14/95

Student	Parent	Teacher	
✓	✓	+	Displays independent behaviors
+	+	+	Reads a variety of materials
✓	+	✓	Returns to text to verify/clarify
+	✓	+	Makes reasonable predictions
+	+	+	Can sequence events in a story
✓	✓	+	Uses reading to improve writing
+	✓	+	Talks meaningfully about story
+	+	✓	Can summarize the contents of works of both fiction and nonfiction

Miscellaneous Remarks

This is the first semester report for all students at Einstein. We the faculty hope you like our new output format. It is part of our new student profile system.

Notes

---

those observations, and attendance codes. The teacher observes students working, strokes across a bar code for the student, and strokes across the behavior observed. The program uses a Videx credit-card-sized optical reader that can later be dropped into an interface box connected to a Macintosh. The data is organized by student, class, or observed behaviors by a relational data base for later editing and summarizing.

Informal Assessment

In the area of informal assessment, educators have at least three choices:

1. Software with built-in record-keeping features (e.g., Diascriptive Reading I, II, and III; Math Assistant I, II).

2. Mini-authoring or modifiable software in which teachers can enter the desired instructional content into the shell of a program, thereby allowing a way to design and monitor progress with software that has been tailored for individual needs (e.g., QuickFlash, Classroom Toolbox, M-ss-ng L-nks, The New Game Show, Tic Tac Show, TouchWindow LessonMaker, Ten Clues).

3. Multimedia accompanied by HyperCard, Linkway, Classroom Toolbox, or TutorTech offer educators options in designing whole-learning environments or microworlds. Using these approaches, educators can view student learning styles in ways other than traditional language-based, linear-sequential models.

Curriculum-Based Assessment

Curriculum-based assessment is characterized by frequent collection of student performance data that are typical of classroom curricula with frequent, specific feedback to students and parents. One program that subscribes to the curriculum-based philosophy is the DLM Math Fluency series, which includes subtraction, addition, multiplication, and division. It is designed to improve students' inefficient counting strategies by building mastery and fluency in basic math facts. Another program is Monitoring Basic Skills Progress, a series of three programs (Basic Math, Basic Spelling, and Basic Reading) that utilize parallel tests administered and scored by the computer to provide the teacher and parent with feedback, reports, and graphics on student progress.

Standardized Assessment

A wide range of programs are available that have one or more of the following capabilities in regard to a particular standardized test, such as the Woodcock-Johnson Achievement Test, the Wechsler Intelligence Scale for Children-Revised (WISC-R), and the Peabody Individual Achievement Test (PIAT), and so on:

1. Diagnostic programs
2. Interpretation of test results
3. Information management of test results and data
4. Report writing
5. Generation of instructional strategies, goals, and objectives

To locate programs for various assessments, consult the *Psychware Sourcebook* (Krug, 1989) for profiles of each product.

In addition to the possibilities of computerized assessment and computation of scores, the use of a word processor with copy and paste features can improve productivity immeasurably. Sample paragraphs saved under different descriptive titles can be edited and merged into an individualized report.

Electronic Portfolios

As schools move toward more performance-based and authentic assessment approaches and toward instruction based on multiple intelligences, both low-tech and electronic portfolios are becoming more prevalent. In fact, in some states (e.g., Kentucky and Vermont), portfolios are required for some grades statewide. Just what is an electronic portfolio, and what information does it add to our knowledge and understanding about what students can and cannot do? An electronic portfolio is a student folder that includes a selection of work over time and the student's evaluation of the contents (Johnson, 1994).

Gardner's vision of classrooms of the future (1991) features student-created multimedia exhibits to demonstrate their understanding of different curricular topics. Students create multimedia book reports, biographies, math story problems, and science projects. They store their "works" on audio tapes, videotapes, and computer disks. Each student gets the opportunity to show their work in a public exhibition on a rotating, periodic basis (D'Ignazio, 1994).

Integrated software tools with word processing, data base, and spreadsheets were commonly used in portfolios (such as Microsoft Works, ClarisWorks, and KidWorks) in which students express their ideas graphically and in pictures, tables, and charts. Students would include explanations of their thinking, in writing or in their own recorded voices or QuickTime movies.

At Van Cortlandt Middle School in New York, all eighth-grade students were required to create a multimedia portfolio including word processed documents, scanned images, video clips, and audio clips using HyperStudio (Milone, 1995). All students were expected to show competence in five areas: aesthetics, problem solving, research, and out-of-class activities, such as hobbies and volunteer work. At the end of the year, these areas serve as the basis by which a panel of parents, teachers, and peers evaluate the portfolios. The portfolios are also presented at an open house at the school and are transferred to video for parents to take home.

One teacher reported, "Many of the students who were doing average or below average work produced remarkable portfolios. We discovered that we could not predict who could create the best portfolios. The process of creating an opening screen, choosing work to be included, and actually creating the portfolio empowered students and made them feel more responsible for their work" (Milone, 1995, p. 29).

At Horizon Community Middle School in Aurora, Colorado, students also used HyperStudio for their electronic portfolios. A teacher there commented, "Many of the students who are put off by high-stakes tests are less anxious and more enthusiastic about portfolios. Some of the students who were underachieving academically found the portfolio project to be an incentive to push themselves. Students had the opportunity to present their portfolios to a large audience using either an LCD projection panel or multiple televison screens around the room. Students reviewed their work in collaboration with the teacher to determine if they met state-set standards in various subject areas" (Milone, 1995, p. 32).

Two schools in Florida, A.D. Henderson in Boca Raton, and Ahfachkee School on a nearby Seminole reservation, used a template for Linkway Live called Multimedia Assessment Tool. These portfolios contained not only student work but management information as well. The home page for each student contains a picture and buttons that can be clicked to show bus information, a historical picture of the student's school record, attendance, and academic objectives. Samples of what students put in their portfolio included:

- Spelling: a scanned image of a student's spelling test with the student doing a voice-over reading
- Writing: a handwritten letter with student voice-over
- Math: scanned samples of a student's work from the beginning to the end of the year (problems, as well as written and voice-over explanations of the process used to solve the problems)
- Science: a video of the student engaged in a seed experiment, explaining what she is doing

The portfolio also included video footage of a student-teacher conference (Milone, 1995, p. 36).

Writing Meaningful Goals and Objectives

Goals are broad, general statements of direction and categories of skills that can be used as guidelines for designing more specific instructional objectives and learning activities. Objectives may or may not include a specific piece of software. Some parents and teachers feel that specifying the software may be important; others worry that specifying software may work against the student's ability to transfer the needed skill to situations when technology is not available. One way of balancing these two opinions is to specify software when appropriate and to include specific objectives for transferring the skill to other, non-technology situations. The examples in Figure 5-2 illustrate different skill areas and types of objectives (Feit, 1991).

Teachers may also want to include problem-solving goals, objectives, and software into their instructional program. The goals listed in Figure 5-3 (Russell, Mokros, Corwin, & Kapisovsky, 1989, pp. 63–64) can be used with or without technology.

Because the use of computers in education is a relatively new phenomenon, there are no tests specifically designed that will reliably and validly measure the impact of computer use on learning, particularly for other than drill-and-practice software. For this reason, educators will need to use other means to document the kinds of learning being targeted in the individualized plan. For example, one teacher noticed a student who typically never completed a task without checking with the teacher at each step before proceeding to the next. Using the computer, the student began to demonstrate a new independence in completing a task and, in fact, began explaining to other students how to proceed.

FIGURE 5-2   Integrating Computer Use into Goals and Objectives

---

John—Written Language

Goal: John will use the computer to correct spelling errors in his compositions and to practice combining sentences to improve the quality of his writing.

Objective: John will work independently on the computer, editing his work after joint review with the teacher. His sentence length will increase from four words to six or seven words, with all words correctly spelled when the composition is resubmitted.

Mike—Written Language

Goal: Mike will use the computer to write his book reports each month.

Objective: Mike will write a book report using guided writing (prompts) with ClarisWorks. He will be able to distinguish fiction from nonfiction, opinion vs. fact, the main idea, and the main character. He will describe one incident from the book in his own words. He will select one character from a book and discuss at least one strength and one weakness.

Tom—Math

Goal: Tom will learn and be fluent with his addition facts to 10.

Objective: Tom will use the DLM Math Fluency program to practice his math facts for 10 minutes a day, four to five times per week, with follow-up worksheets for homework once a week.

Suzy—Written Language

Goal: Suzy will write short stories with correct grammar and spelling.

Objective: Suzy will use The Writing Center to write a story with beginning, middle, and ending paragraphs and select an illustration and share it with a partner. After editing with a partner, Suzy will print out a second draft and conference with the teacher. Following the conference, Suzy will do final editing and print out a final story, free from spelling and grammatical errors.

Bob—Social Studies

Goal: Bob will organize his thoughts, outline, and write a social studies report.

Objective: Bob will use an outlining or mapping program such as ACTA. He will research a specific topic and insert relevant topics into outline form for review. He will expand his outline into a report for sharing with a small group. After editing, he will conference with the teacher and do editing for the final report.

David—Keyboarding

Goal: David will learn to touch type.

Objective: Using Typing to Learn, David will complete four to five 15-minute sessions per week, with the keys covered with a cloth, hands typing underneath.

Source: From *Special Magic: Computers, Classroom Strategies, and Exceptional Students* by M. Male, 1988, Mountain View, CA: Mayfield Publishing. Reprinted with permission of the author.

Can such an outcome be measured with the Wide Range Achievement Test or the Woodcock-Johnson Test? Probably not, but it can be observed and documented. Systematic observation, anecdotal record keeping, and structured interviews are important alternatives to norm- or criterion-referenced achievement tests for measuring progress.

FIGURE 5-3 Problem-Solving Goals for Individual Plans

Organizational Skills

- Note-taking
- Gathering facts
- Categorizing
- Comparing and contrasting
- Creating and using organized lists
- Identifying patterns
- Sorting necessary and unnecessary information

Reasoning Skills

- Reasoning deductively
- Finding multiple solutions
- Constructing a sequence of events
- Modifying a sequence of events
- Reasoning backwards from a result to the sequence which led to it
- Using trial and error effectively
- Moving from sole use of trial and error to a range of other strategies
- Using a process of elimination to isolate the solution
- Solving problems with minimal clues
- Varying one aspect of a situation at a time to isolate critical attributes
- Evaluating partial solutions
- Testing solutions
- Making sense out of contradictory or ambiguous information
- Evaluating relative importance of different elements in a situation

Learning to Learn

- Working on a project not completed in one class period
- Responding to situations flexibly
- Learning to tolerate errors
- Concentrating on a task
- Controlling impulsive answers
- Using errors as information to guide next steps
- Sticking to a goal

Social Skills

- Cooperating with a peer or small group
- Communicating with peers about content and strategy
- Taking turns
- Becoming a "student expert" or "computer tutor"
- Taking a leadership role

Content Area Skills

- Working with maps
- Improving language development
- Recognizing shapes and colors

Source: From *Special Magic: Computers, Classroom Strategies, and Exceptional Students* by M. Male, 1988, Mountain View, CA: Mayfield Publishing. Reprinted with permission of the author.

The following suggestions will help teachers develop ways to document student progress:

1. Observe systematically what the students are doing and learning with the computer applications that are built into the program. Keep a journal for each student of what software the student is using, how the student is using it, for what length of time, and with what result. (Older students can keep their own journals.)

2. Review each student's individualized plan. Are the goals and objectives meaningful or do they tend to fragment learning into easily measurable but isolated bits? If they are fragmented, perhaps the entire plan needs revision to incorporate computer objectives into more comprehensive goals and objectives.

3. Reflect on the most important learning outcomes that the computer will promote (self-esteem and motivation alone are probably not enough).

4. Draft some sample annual goals and objectives for students who have demonstrated increased language, cognitive, or basic skills achievement from using a computer, and ask their parents to review them with you.

5. Brainstorm with other teachers for ways to document the achievement of these goals and objectives. Ask parents for their assistance in the documentation process. (How does the student describe a particular computer experience? Does talk of the computer activity come up spontaneously or by parent initiation?)

6. Try out the documentation system with a specific student; develop an observation form, an anecdotal record-keeping system, and a checklist or rating scale, and field test it with the student.

7. Review the results. Modify the data-gathering tools. Share ideas with one or more educators who are using computers with their students.

Here is another approach to develop specific objectives. Select a piece of software that has benefited a particular student or group of students and that addresses learning needs not dependent solely on that specific software. Brainstorm objectives that could be met with the software and correlate them with goal areas of the individualized plan. Table 5-1 illustrates a teacher's objectives for one student (or an entire class) using the Hot Dog Stand simulation from Survival Math software. Note that although the teacher plans to use a particular piece of software, these objectives are not limited to its use. Other simulations or paper-and-pencil tasks could be used instead.

Table 5-2 provides a second example of a goal and objective matrix, using The Factory software. Table 5-3 illustrates correlation of goals and objectives for a student with severe disabilities who is using the computer and the IntelliKeys. These examples illustrate the following:

- One piece of software can address objectives in every area (math concepts, psychomotor skills, language, social-emotional development, reading, self-help, and career and vocational guidance).
- Objectives may be, but do not need to be, software specific.
- Objectives can fit into lesson planning and direct instruction.

TABLE 5-1   Developing IEP Objectives from Software (Survival Math)

	Goals	
	Students will take intellectual risks.	**Students will communicate about intellectual content.**
Academic/Cognitive		
Math		
Concepts	Given a simulated business and a starting balance, student will make decisions and document results. Student will use feedback to make subsequent decisions.	
Operations	Student will calculate unit cost, total cost, expenses, income, and profit.	
Language		
Written		Student will prepare a written summary of results at the end of each round.
		Student will proofread written summary for capitalization, punctuation, and spelling.
Verbal	Student will develop a strategy and present a rationale.	
Reading		
Decoding	Student will read and define basic vocabulary: income and expenses, cost per unit, balance.	
Comprehension		Student will discuss meanings and relationships of the key terms.
Psychomotor		
Spatial		
Visual Sequencing/ Memory/Discrimination	Student will copy information from screen into appropriate columns on paper.	
Eye–hand	Student will organize results on paper.	
Social/Emotional		Student will work with a partner to make decisions satisfactory to both.
Self-Help	When a decision results in an unfavorable outcome, the student will use this information to adjust future decisions.	
Career	Student will experiment with impact of variables and economic goals/motivation on outcomes.	Given different variables and goals, different outcomes result. Student will discuss the relationship between outcomes and variables.

Source: From *Special Magic: Computers, Classroom Strategies, and Exceptional Students* by M. Male, 1988, Mountain View, CA: Mayfield Publishing. Reprinted with permission of the author.

TABLE 5-2 Developing IEP Objectives from Software (The Factory)

	Goals	
	Students will take intellectual risks.	**Students will communicate about intellectual content.**
Academic/Cognitive		
Math		
Concepts	Given an example, student will determine how many degrees of rotation are needed to reproduce the example.	
Operations		
Language		
Written		
Verbal	Student can describe the sequence of steps needed to reproduce a given design.	Student will pose a problem example for another student to duplicate. Student will discuss a strategy to duplicate a design.
Reading		
Decoding		
Comprehension		
Psychomotor		
Spatial	Student can create a design to be duplicated.	
Visual Sequencing/ Memory/Discrimination	Given a design, student can sequence the steps needed to duplicate the design.	
	Given a design, student can identify the component parts of the design.	
Eye—hand	Student can use a paper model or a computer to perform the steps needed to duplicate a design.	
Social/Emotional		Student will work with a partner and come to a consensus on a series of steps to duplicate a design.
Self-Help	Given a design and an incorrect effort to duplicate it, student will modify work and attempt a new solution, without teacher assistance.	

Source: From *Special Magic: Computers, Classroom Strategies, and Exceptional Students* by M. Male, 1988, Mountain View, CA: Mayfield Publishing. Reprinted with permission of the author.

TABLE 5-3　Developing IEP Objectives That Utilize Adaptive Devices

	Goals		
	Students will communicate basic needs/wants.	**Students will demonstrate understanding of cause and effect.**	**Students will instigate 2-way conversation.**
Academic/Cognitive			
Math			
Concepts			
Operations			
Language			
Written			
Verbal	Given an overlay, student will ask for a drink.	Given an overlay, student will choose the square to match an object.	Given an overlay, student will answer and ask questions in return.
Reading			
Decoding			
Comprehension			
Psychomotor			
Spatial			
Visual Sequencing/ Memory/Discrimination			
Eye—hand			Given a wobble switch, student will operate a program.
Social/Emotional		Given an overlay with song titles, student selects one for teacher to sing. Given an overlay with two choices, "go" and "stop," student chooses one. (If choice is "go," he is moved in a circle: "stop" results in cessation of movement.)	
Self-Help	When asked, "What do you want?", the student can select an option for the computer to say.		
Career	Given a set of two choices, student will make a selection.		

Source: From *Special Magic: Computers, Classroom Strategies, and Exceptional Students* by M. Male, 1988, Mountain View, CA: Mayfield Publishing. Reprinted with permission of the author.

Activities

1. Make a list of five ways you are currently using technology to assist with assessing special needs and pupil progress. List five ideas you have for enhancing your use of technology in the area of assessment after reviewing the examples in this chapter.
2. Obtain a copy of the Grady Profile or Learner Profile and try it out. Print out the results for a sample student.
3. For a case study student or one in your program, write three goals and three objectives which incorporate the use of technology.
4. Design a template of a required form, which you customarily complete by hand, using your favorite word processor. Complete the form on the computer and evaluate the amount of time you could save using technology.
5. Design a form letter using an integrated productivity tool such as Microsoft Works or ClarisWorks to use with a data base of student information. Practice using the Mail Merge option. Make a list of five situations in which this approach could be used to save time and improve communication with parents or other staff.

References

Barrett, H. (1994). Technology-supported assessment portfolios. *The Computing Teacher,* 21(6) 9–12.

D'Ignazio, F. (1994). The classroom as knowledge theme park. *The Computing Teacher,* 21(7), 35–37, 50.

Feit, S. (1991). Unpublished review of this book.

Gardner, H. (1991). *UnSchooled minds: How children think.* New York: Basic Books.

Johnson, J. (1994). Portfolio assessment in mathematics: Lessons from the field. *The Computing Teacher,* 21(6), 22–23.

Krug, J. (1989). *PsychWare sourcebook* (3rd Ed.). Austin, TX: Pro-Ed.

McCain, G. (1995). Technology-based assessment in special education. *T.H.E. Journal,* 23(1), 57–59.

Milone, M. (1995). Electronic portfolios: Who's doing them and how? *Technology & Learning,* 16(2), 28–36.

Newman, F. (1991). Linking restructuring to authentic student achievement. *Phi Delta Kappan,* 72, 458–463.

Russell, S., Mokros, J., Corwin, R., & Kapisovsky, P. (1989). *Beyond drill and practice: Expanding the computer mainstream.* Reston, VA: Council for Exceptional Children.

Wolf, D., Bixby, J., Glenn, J., and Gardner H. (1991). To use their minds well: Investigating new forms of student assessment. In G. Grant (Ed.), *Review of Research in Education,* 17, 31–74, Washington, DC: American Educational Research Association.

Chapter 6

Building Fluency in Basic Skills

The options for cognitive and academic development with the computer are virtually unlimited. For students with physical disabilities who may not have been able to express themselves verbally or in writing, the computer opens the door to their capabilities. For all students, the computer is an infinitely adaptable tool with unrestricted possibilities.

Hart describes his first experience at the computer with his young grandson, Andrew, who had oxygen deprivation at birth:

> *Andrew was thrilled to be able to sit down with Grandpa and play with the computer. The first program I tried with him was the Alphabet Circus. I was totally unprepared for what I was about to observe. I saw the boy's mind and attitude light up before me. All of this was reinforced by the song and the little dancing characters built into the program to reward him when he had chosen the right answer. It has now been eight months since I started to work with him, and it is still a thrill to see his face light up as he works with the computer. I truly feel that computer-assisted learning has tremendous possibilities for children with learning disabilities. (1990, p. 7)*

Gerow provides further examples with three of her students:

> *Tony is a skinny, frail boy of eighteen who sits in a wheelchair most of the day. He doesn't talk or seem to communicate much except when his face lights up with an electric smile, or darkens into a frown. His hands are contractured, and he doesn't use them skillfully to do much, but today they pressed the space bar on an Apple computer to make a program "go." It was a program with bright colored creatures that talk, and make funny noises, and move around a lot. The program is called "Creature Features." His look was one of intense concentration, his laugh delighted. Tony learned that he could make something happen.*

Linda walked up and spoke softly, "I want to use the computer now." She is a tall, pretty girl who has severe problems with coordination, especially eye-hand co-ordination. This has prevented her from learning to read or write. She is diagnosed as schizophrenic and takes medication to control her behavior. She comes into the lab every day and works at the computer for 10–15 minutes until her mistakes start to bother her. Then she quits for awhile. Today she laughs as she presses the space bar to "Make Breaker Jump." She seems excited to realize she is making him go. Her ability to concentrate and to look at what she's doing seem to be improving.

Nearby, Sandy is using "Stickybear Math" to teach himself subtraction. Sandy was diagnosed as autistic only a few years ago. One year earlier, his behavior was so severe that he required a locked time-out program for the safety of himself and others in the class. He didn't work any math problems and hardly spoke. Today he does two-digit addition and subtraction with carrying or borrowing, and talks in complete sentences five words long. He loves the computer and asks for his favorite program every day. He's also doing well at a cafeteria job serving lunches for the school. (1988, p. 7)

Objectives

By the end of this chapter, you will be able to do the following:

1. Set criteria for reviewing software in basic skill areas of reading, writing, math, social studies, and science.
2. Identify appropriate software for students who need to develop fluency.
3. Determine situations in which such software might be appropriate.

Selection of Software

For many students, their only experience with computers has been with drill and practice programs. One of the main goals of this book is to challenge educators to provide students opportunities to benefit from all the possibilities that computers have to offer—not just the ease and appeal of "electronic workbooks." Nevertheless, some students benefit substantially from intensive practice sessions on specific skills and concepts and make greater progress using computers than using workbooks, flashcards, and the like. Software is available to identify students' needs, present problems, diagnose error patterns, give immediate corrective feedback, and move the student to higher levels as soon as a mastery criterion is reached. Six types of software are available that may be appropriate in situations to increase a student's skills in a curriculum area (Lewis, 1993).

1. Tutorials (to present new information)
2. Drill and practice (practice in a skill that has already been introduced)
3. Educational game (graphics, sound, and animation in an arcade format which provides drill and practice)

4. Discovery (an environment with no right or wrong answers in which a student can explore, such as sound-symbol correspondence in alphabet programs or cause-and-effect programs)

5. Simulations (students make decisions and see the consequences of those decisions)

6. Problem solving (frequently includes more than one right answer and focuses on both the process of finding an answer as well as the answer itself)

Criteria suggested by Alliance for Technology Access (1994) include the following:

- Easy-to-read screens
- Consistency
- Intuitive characteristics
- Logical labels
- Instructional choices
- Friendly documentation
- On-screen instructions
- Auditory cues (prompts or hints given in digitized or synthesized speech; helpful for those who may struggle with reading directions)
- Visual cues (prompts or hints that assist the user to respond to the problem)
- Built-in access methods (aids that enable use of switches, alternate keyboards, etc.)
- Alternatives to a mouse (for those users who may prefer keyboard access)
- Optional cursors (options that allow the user to make the cursor more visible or easier to manipulate)
- Creation of custom programs (authoring capability to enter word lists, math problem sets, etc.)

Software Examples by Subject Area

Tables 6-1 through 6-4 provide teacher-tested software and sources for basic skill development in major school subject areas.

Keyboarding

Many teachers and parents are curious about when to offer or require keyboarding training to students. Some students struggle as much with locating the appropriate keys on the keyboard as they do with handwriting. Is keyboarding a developmental skill? Research is not conclusive. However, in order for word processing to be a really useful tool, students need to be able to type words faster at the keyboard than they can using handwriting. Many students at about the third-grade level begin asking for keyboarding software and training, because they are aware how much their lack of keyboarding skills slows them down.

In searching for appropriate keyboarding programs, two criteria are important:

1. The use of meaningful words for practice

2. The ability to control the rate of presentation and the rate of advancement to higher speeds and skill levels. In Mario Teaches Typing, for example, the user has little control at

TABLE 6-1   **Reading and Writing Software**

Software Title	Source
Imagination Express	EdMark
Arcademic Skill Builders in Language Arts	DLM
Bailey's Book House	Edmark
Capitalization Machine	SWEPS
Reader Rabbit	Learning Company
Reading Maze	Great Wave
Storybook Weaver	MECC
First Words	Laureate
First Categories	Laureate
First Verbs	Laureate
First Letter Fun	Laureate
Language Experience Recorder	Teacher Support
Supermunchers	Teacher Support
Phonics Workout	Bill and Richard's
Reading Machine	SWEPS
Write On!	Humanities
Spelling Machine	SWEPS
Vocabulary Machine	SWEPS
Word Munchers	MECC
Writing to Read	Edu-Quest
Writing to Write	Edu-Quest

TABLE 6-2   **Math Software**

Software Title	Source
Math Workshop	
Math Blaster Plus	Davidson
Math Blaster Mystery	Davidson
Graph Club	Sunburst
Balancing Bear	Sunburst
Arithmetic Critters	MECC
Countdown	Sunburst
Conquering Fractions	Sunburst
Treasure MathStorm	Learning Company
Number Maze	Great Wave
Millie's Math House	Edmark
Number Munchers	MECC
Survival Math	Sunburst

TABLE 6-3   Science Software

Software Title	Source
The Rain Forest	
Sammy's Science House	Edmark
Nature of Science	
Science Inquiry	
Lunar Greenhouse	MECC
Widget Workshop	Broderbund

the very beginning levels over speed and advancement. The familiar arcade game character is appealing, however, and students will continue to practice at the lowest levels until mastery is achieved.

Selecting Situations for Use of Basic Skills Software

Three variables affecting the teacher's use of basic skills software include technology expertise/comfort level of the teacher, skill level/technology expertise of the student, and curricular emphasis of the classroom. In general, these programs should be used in combination with other, more empowering applications of technology. As teachers move toward more thematic teaching, they can find ways to combine software programs to provide a combination of drill and practice, exploration, simulation, and other kinds of experiences.

TABLE 6-4   Social Studies Software

Software Title	Source
Timeliner	Tom Snyder
Decisions, Decisions	Tom Snyder
Choices, Choices	Tom Snyder
Nigel's World	Lawrence
Where in the World . . . Europe series	Broderbund
Amazon Trail	MECC
Oregon Trail	MECC
SimCity	Maxsis
SimEarth	Maxsis
American Discovery	Great Wave
Picture Atlas of the World	Edu-quest
USA GeoGraph	Edu-quest
World GeoGraph	Edu-quest
Safari Search	Sunburst

FIGURE 6-1

ENDANGERED SPECIES THEMATIC UNIT

SCIENCE

CONCEPT
• Different animals
  and characteristics
• Endangered animals

BOOKS
Animals Do the Strangest Things
by L. & A. Hornblow
The Zabajaba Jungle
by W.Steig

SOFTWARE
The Treehouse [Brøderbund]

SOCIAL STUDIES

CONCEPT
• Career options for working
  with endangered animals
• Reasons why animals are
  becoming extinct
• Problems and solutions
  for endangered animals

BOOK & MAGAZINE
I Can Be An Animal Doctor
by K. Lumley
Ranger Rick

SOFTWARE
The Whole Neighborhood
[Queue]

MATHEMATICS

CONCEPT
• Measurement
• Survey uses and processes
• Bar graph uses

BOOK
Fabulous Animal Facts
by R. G. Geiman

SOFTWARE
Muppet Math [Sunburst]

THEME — ENDANGERED SPECIES

ART

CONCEPT
• Effects of various materials
  and media for projects

MUSICAL RECORDING
The Bear's Mountain
by K. Tejima

SOFTWARE
Puppetmaker [Sunburst]

LANGUAGE ARTS

CONCEPT
• Characteristics of different
  genres

BOOKS
Gorilla by A. Brown
Fables by A. Lobel
*Sing a Song of Popcorn:
Every Child's Books
of Poems*
by B. S. de Regniers

SOFTWARE
Animal Rescue [Sunburst]
Puppet Plays [Sunburst]

MUSIC

CONCEPT
• Animal movements

MUSICAL RECORDING
Animal Antics
by H. Palmer

SOFTWARE
Kidstime [Great Wave]
The Treehouse [Brøderbund]

A unit on endangered species, for example, enables the teacher to choose different kinds of software for different subject areas and activities, but all related to the overall theme. Figure 6-1 shows a diagram of the kindergarten teacher's plan and choices for software (Wepner & Seminoff, 1995).

In determining when to use software a teacher should:

1. Try to think of as many creative ways as possible to use one flexible piece of software.

2. Think about ways of using different pieces of software that approach the same skills from different modes or styles of presentation. In this way, the teacher can gain diagnostic insights from the software that are most effective in achieving a particular curricular goal.

Activities

1. Interview three teachers about the types of software they use with students. What criteria do they use to select software? How are their criteria similar to or different from those in this chapter? What is the percentage of their use of drill and practice software compared to other applications presented in this book?

2. Select a piece of software that you have never used and try it out with a student. List the strengths and limitations of the software from your experience of working with the student. Interview the student to determine the student's perceptions of the software's benefits or limitations.

3. Design a thematic unit as outlined in Figure 6-1 and list the software you would select for each subject area.

References

Alliance for Technology Access (1994). *Computer resources for people with disabilities.* Alameda, CA: Hunter House.

Gerow, A. (1988). The computer adaptive technology project. *The Catalyst,* 6(3), 7–8.

Hart, J. (1990). Andrew and the computer. *The Catalyst,* 7(3), 7–8.

Lewis, R. (1993). *Special education technology: Classroom applications.* Belmont, CA: Wadsworth Publishing Co.

Wepner, S., and Seminoff, N. (1995). Saving endangered species: Using technology to teach thematically. *The Computing Teacher,* 22(1), 34–36.

Chapter 7

Functional and Life Skills

just sitting in a chair not talking
just sitting in a chair not walking
just sitting in a chair not using your board.
one day you would throw them away
or you ain't no friend of mine.
when i can walk and talk and sit.
just play the game and you can win.
i will fight until i am 50009008
and in my grave.
i can do some things
but i want to do more.
just sitting in a chair not having fun.
just sitting in a chair not playing.
just sitting in a chair not moving.
maybe one day it will come true.
just sitting in a chair watching your friends.
i hope it comes true.

Jason was 10 years old when he wrote that poem (Burcat, 1995); at 16, technology has changed his life substantially. He uses a Liberator for augmentative communication, a power wheelchair, finds information using an encyclopedia on his CD-ROM, and loves to play computer games with friends—Concentration and SimCity, in particular. He has a specially equipped SEGA system for NBA Life 95. All aspects of his life are enhanced by access to technology.

Academic development and productivity are significant areas in which technology can play a major role. However, technology can also play a major role in offering options for recreation and leisure, art and music, and social and career development. This chapter focuses on how technology can offer enriching options beyond school.

Objectives

By the end of this chapter, you will be able to do the following:

1. List ways in which technology can improve the quality of life for the students you serve in situations outside of school
2. Select technology options for developing functional and life skills specific for specific situations
3. Ensure that all aspects of a student's life are addressed by the educational program and supported by technology where appropriate

Infants, Toddlers, and the Early Childhood Years

What is the best way to select technology interventions for very young children? Regardless of any special needs, babies and very young children need a wide variety of opportunities to explore, control their environment, and communicate with caregivers.

Toys

Adapted toys, appropriate for any baby, can be made inexpensively at home using resources purchased from companies specializing in adapted toys, such as *From Toys to Computers: Access for the Physically Disabled Child* (Wright & Nomura, 1989), or checked out from a lending library established specifically for that purpose, such as CompuPlay projects across the country, set up by the National Lekotek Center. Battery-operated toys, for example, can be operated by manipulating a switch, so that the child has control of the activity. Infants as young as three months old have used a combination of toys and computers to discover relationships between what they do and their environment. These activities can also stimulate motor development when the toys and switches are positioned in certain ways. Because these toys and computer activities are appealing to babies with a wide variety of abilities, these tools are perfect for an inclusive environment—in the home, in a play group, or in an educational program. After getting used to operating switch-adapted toys, a child can make an easier transition to operating a computer.

Siegel and Freels describe a starting place with one child:

> *Krystle is a two and a half year old multiply handicapped child. Her communicative signals are extremely limited. "Ahhh" sounds are her primary way of interacting with the people around her. These sounds seem to say "pay attention to me." Her mother interprets her tongue clicking sounds as a sign of hunger. Krystle smiles and vocalizes to get Mom to repeat an action rhyme. When positioned upright, she will watch Mom move around the room. She looks for the family dog when his name is called. If asked to make a choice between eat and drink (i.e.,*

spoon and cup) she usually looks at the object at her right since it takes less effort to turn her head in that direction. She infrequently reaches out to hit at hanging toys. And she uses a switch which is wired to a door chime in order to get another drink of juice at snack time. (1989, p. 20)

Computers

At the very early ages, communication, language, cognition, and movement are all inter-twined in the learning process. The computer can assist with providing experiences to enhance and supplement strengths and skills, or to compensate and accommodate for limitations and disabilities. Designed to fit each child's meaning system and reality, the computer explodes physical limitations and perceived mental limitations. Meyers describes one situation:

Three computer peripherals, the Unicorn Board, the Adaptive Firmware Card, and the Echo speech synthesizer, made the computer accessible to Kevin, a severe-ly physically handicapped, totally blind toddler. He was 20 months old when he first used a computer. He had never explored an object with his hands, and he rare-ly vocalized. He had one reflex that brought his hands up when he tried to bring them down and another that caused his head to turn to one side when he reached for an object in front of him. Kevin's favorite time of the day was when his mother sang songs with him. The computer was programmed through the Adaptive Firm-ware card so that each time he touched the highly sensitive Unicorn membrane keyboard he could say the word "sing" in the speech output (using an Echo speech synthesizer). When Kevin hit the keyboard, making the computer say "sing" in speech output, his mother and uncle would immediately break into one of his fa-vorite songs. He learned to bring his hand down on the keyboard purposefully dur-ing the first session. His mother and uncle immediately responded to his request, saying, "Oh, you said sing! Okay, we'll sing 'Wheels on the Bus.'" This helped him understand a powerful function of language—to get something done. His suc-cessful communication motivated him to try to type then say his first word, "sing," in his own speech. For the next session, the keyboard was divided into two parts. He could tell his mother and uncle to sing his choice of his two favorite songs. With another activity developed for the same session, he could control what happened during his snack, asking for juice or cereal. Because the teaching methods were personally meaningful, and because they helped him interact with people who were familiar and important to him, he immediately learned how to use technology as a friendly tool. (1990, p. 9)

The following is another example:

Jonathan (age 3) has used a computer since he was six months old. He began with the Muppet Learning Keys, cackling with delight when pressing a key activated a Sesame Street character. At about eighteen months, he moved on to the Macintosh and developed very precise motor control of the mouse, pointing and selecting what he wanted from programs such as McGee or The Playroom with the greatest of care. Now he treats the computer as a tool and a companion, experimenting with speech output, telling stories to Mom, who types them in, and then selecting the "Read Aloud" button to hear his stories read over and over again—far more often than even patient Mom could bear to do it. When friends come to visit, he brings them straight up to the computer, where he proudly offers to show them his skills and to let them have a turn making a picture or putting a piece of a puzzle into PuzzleMaker. In this way, he participates as an equal with a wide age and ability range of people—just as he will have to be prepared for in real life!

Guidelines for successfully incorporating technology at very early ages include the following:

- Assume that there are no prerequisites for language acquisition and that every child has the capacity to learn.
- Use the child's own reality and meaning system to construct activities, not isolated tasks constructed in a hierarchy of prerequisites (cause and effect, switch use, picture recognition, toy recognition, visual scanning on the computer).
- Make sure the child's positioning needs are assessed and addressed so that the appropriate type of switch or keyboard can be used.
- Use the computer to promote social skills and increase interaction with peers or caregivers.

Some of the characteristics of software that have been the most popular with very young children include the following:

1. Ease of operation, with limited requirements for keyboarding and easy use of adaptive devices

2. Clear, concise documentation so that the program is up and running without the need for an adult to study a manual

3. Color, graphics, and sound

4. Adaptability so that the program can be modified to fit a different need or varied to keep it challenging

Adolescence

Pressures to prepare for making difficult choices begin to build in adolescent years. These may be personal choices involving sex, drugs, truancy, and the like, or they may be related to choosing a career or deciding whether to apply for college or continued training in a particular field.

The computer can be used in a number of ways to help students acquire information they need to make these decisions, look at the consequences of decisions in a simulated environment (S.M.A.R.T. Choices), and practice skills they will need once they are out of school and on their own. Table 7-1 provides a sample of software programs that teachers

TABLE 7-1   Social Skills and Commercial Software

Software Program	Social Skills
Blueprint for Decision Making	Decision making and problem solving in peer and authority figure relationships, dealing with group pressure
Choices, Choices	Decision making, problem solving, cause-effect, dealing with group pressure, expressing feelings, and listening skills in peer relationships
Taking Responsibility	Honesty, decision making, and responsibility in peer and authority figure relationships
On the Playground	Initiating and maintaining relationship skills, decision making in peer relationships
Following Directions: Life Skills Series Set 1	Following directions and listening
Interviewing: Life Skills Series Set 1	Receptive and expressive verbal and nonverbal communication skills, nonverbal communication skills, understanding the feelings of others
On the Job: Life Skills Series Set 1	Asking a question, asking for help, giving and following instructions
The Mirror Inside Us: Life Skills Series Set 1	Knowing and expressing feelings, dealing with anger and criticism, and rewarding oneself

From Walker & Williamson, CTG Aug/Sept, 95.

have used with success in working with adolescents to develop appropriate social skills (Walker & Williamson, 1995).

Multimedia authoring programs with QuickTime movies (the teacher can set up role plays and record them or record actual situations) can also be effective in presenting real or simulated social skill situations to which students must respond. Preparing students for job interviews or dealing with agencies is another important part of adolescent functional skill programs. Joanne Davis (1989) used Talking Flashcards to help students memorize biographical information. She also used authoring programs to help with customized lessons in money skills and telling time. Table 7-2 provides an overview of functional skills software that may be appropriate for your students.

TABLE 7-2   Functional Skills Software

Software Title	Producer
Edmark Functional Word Series: Signs Around You—1 and 2	Edmark
Touch Money	Edmark
A Day in the Life . . . Instruction	Curriculum Associates

Recreational Activities

What is recreation for some people may be livelihood and vocation to others, which makes this category somewhat subjective. For example, Jim plans to be a graphic artist for an entertainment company; he uses the computer to design graphics, do layout, and produce finished products. Johnnie Wilder, noted composer and rock group leader, uses the computer to compose his music, as did Frank Zappa and as do a number of other top musicians. Johnnie Wilder, however, is paralyzed from the neck down following an automobile accident. All three of these men love what they do and would do it even if they were not being paid; therefore, one could call their interests "recreational." The theme of recreation using the computer across all age groups is explored in depth in the next chapter. For those people who love music and art, or who are interested in games and simulations, the computer offers unending possibilities.

Music, art, and games on the computer can engender curiosity, excitement, and opportunities for social interaction in those students for whom these aspects of education are all too elusive. Who knows what might be the key to motivate certain students who have experienced failure for a long time? The answer might be found in generating a picture and printing it out in a professional-looking format. It might be experimenting with music software and producing an original tune to accompany a lesson, or it might be making a greeting card or comic strip. It might even be coloring a simple picture on the screen.

Music

Using a musical instrument digital interface (MIDI), a device that allows for transfer of data between a computer and a musical instrument, the user can create, record, edit, and play sounds that simulate an entire orchestra. At a simpler level, students can play premade songs, revise them and record the changes, or write songs using the speaker on the computer. Other examples of music activities with the computer include the following:

- The teacher may program familiar songs, perhaps with the help of the students' music teacher if necessary. The students then make selections and play back songs of their choice. Students may also print out scores of the musical compositions.
- Students may transcribe favorite songs from sheet music or song books to add to the library of tunes from the computer.
- Students may experiment with composition, first with melody only, and later with harmony. One student might try adding harmony to a melody written by another.
- Students may devise games of "Name That Tune" for each other by writing and playing back only a few notes, or by writing a rhythm without melody, or a melody without rhythm, for others to identify.
- Students may move to music or act out simple stories by using the music written or transcribed by students in the class (Melly, 1986). Sutin (1990) describes a discovery approach that allows students to learn about music by composing and playing. Programs that do not use standard notations immediately involve the student in making creative decisions about pitch, rhythm, and form in music.

In Brooklyn's Public School 36K, students work at five stations equipped with MIDI keyboards and two percussion pads. As students play, computer software translates their musical efforts into notation. Miriam Klein, principal, points out "They don't have to know how to read or write regular music, but in creating the music, they learn about musical notation." She finds that the music software helps students with fractions, with science (sound waves and principles of hearing), and other subjects as well, not to mention social skills, as students work together on their musical pieces and give feedback to each other. The learning takes many different directions.

Music Software

Music Construction Set-Electronic Arts
Jam Session
Instant Music
Kidstime
Stickybear Music
Music Mouse
Music Shapes

Art

Computer graphics are very easy to use. Many imaginative and inexpensive art packages on the market today provide easy access to art for children as well as adults. Graphics programs for all ages can provide hours of constructive recreation and leisure activity to students at all levels of ability and interest. The student with a physical impairment can participate by using assistive devices when pencil, pen, crayon, and paintbrush are impractical. Computer graphics can also be highly motivating. Even the most elementary attempt can be so satisfying that a student may experience a feeling of great accomplishment. Printouts can be taken home to share with parents and other family members.

Art Software

Print Shop
Kid Pix
Electric Crayon
SuperPaint (use with HeadMaster)
Big Book Maker
Creative Writer
IntelliPaint

Games

Games can be designed for review of academic content, for development of problem-solving and strategy skills, or purely for fun. The dice game in The Playroom offers young children a means for learning about taking turns, planning a strategy for getting the most out of each move, and number sequence.

For older students, games can stimulate curiosity about the world (Where in the World Is Carmen Sandiego?). They can also use authoring tools to make their own games and test them out with other students or to design games for younger students.

Games Software

Sim City
Where in the World Is Carmen Sandiego? series
Agent USA
Cross Country USA
The Voyage of the Mimi

Transition to Work/Adulthood

The computer skills students have built throughout their years in school can have major impacts on several areas in their adult lives, such as job/vocational options, personal/professional productivity, recreational activities, and access to information and resources.

Job/Vocational Options

Not everyone will want to become a computer scientist, engineer, or programmer, but almost everyone who has successful skills with computers will be able to find a job. Data entry, reservationist, cashier, clerical, graphic arts, mechanics—all these fields require computer skills. Students who have developed these skills, whose needs for access have been evaluated and updated as new and improved devices have been implemented, will have advantages over other job applicants. Table 7-3 provides an overview of software helpful in gathering information about or providing skills in career/vocational development.

TABLE 7-3 Career/Vocational Development Software

Software Title	Producer
Blueprint for Decision Making	Lawrence Productions
Career Surveys	Conover Company
Functional Skills Screening Inventory	Functional Assessment and Training Consultants
Job Readiness	Lawrence Productions
Job Attitudes	Lawrence Productions
Job Search and Local Job Bank	Conover Company
Job Success Series	Lawrence Productions
Jobs in Today's World	Lawrence Productions
On the Job Series: Career Interests, Communication Skills, Competency-Based Mathematics I & II, Problem-Solving	Conover Company

Environmental Control

Many people are becoming accustomed to various remote control or computerized devices in their homes, such as those used for televisions and videocassette recorders, microwave ovens, clocks, thermostats, and the like. Whether these devices offer merely convenience or a means of providing environmental control, these options present people with the opportunity for normalized, independent living with reduced dependence on others for comfort and even survival. With current technology, the computer can be used to control a security system, turn lights on and off, operate kitchen appliances, and even have a robot deliver dinner.

Access to Information and Resources

Access to the Internet (see Chapter 11) provides a means for getting and sending needed information instantly, without having to leave one's home. Electronic mail enables those with a variety of needs and abilities to communicate without the interference or stigma of wheelchairs, sign language, and so forth—electronic equality for all!

Long-Range Planning for Technology across the Life Cycle

One purpose of this chapter was to illustrate several principles about incorporating appropriate technology into one's life.

1. There is no minimum age.
2. There is no maximum age.
3. Computer skills are not developmental, and prerequisites should not apply.
4. Computer skills are infinitely expandable to new situations, software, and hardware.
5. Computer skills benefit people of varying levels of abilities, interests, and ages and can be adapted to virtually any situation.

In making decisions about the types of technology, software, and so on to be used, one should think also about how one will be using the technology at a later stage in the life cycle.

Activities

1. Interview a student who actively uses technology as a part of life outside of school. What activities does the student do? What benefits does technology offer? What additional ideas do you have for expanding opportunities for the student using technology (e.g., recreation, career/vocational, independence)?
2. Try out a MIDI keyboard and musical composition software. Describe your experience in becoming a composer. What opportunities might technology and music provide for your students?
3. Review the programs of your students and their use of technology. In what areas might technology expand their horizons? List at least five ideas.

References

Burcat, B. (1995). Technology provides independence. *TECH-NJ,* 6(1), 4–5.

Davis, J. (1989). Software solutions for mentally retarded teenagers. *TECH-NJ*, II(1), 8,14.

Holzberg, C. (February, 1995). What works: Technology in special education. *Technology & Learning,* 18–23.

Melly, S. (1986). *Using the Macintosh computer with learning disabled and very young children.* Presentation at the Computer Using Educators Conference, Los Angeles.

Meyers, L. (1990). *The language machine: Using computers to help children construct reality and language.* Presentation at Conoscenze Come Educazione, San Martino de Castrozza, Italy.

Siegel, R., & Freels, D. (1989). Using switches for communication with multiply handicapped, very young children. *Closing the Gap,* 7(5), 20–21.

Sutin, J. (1990). Accessing the muse: Music technology and the handicapped user. *Closing the Gap,* 9(2), 12–15.

Walker, D., and Williamson, R. (1995). Computers and adolescents with emotional/behavioral disorders: Developing social skills and social competency. *Closing the Gap,* 14(3), 24–27.

Wright, C., & Nomura, M. (1989). *From toys to computers: Access for the physically disabled child.* San Jose: Christine Wright.

Chapter 8

Reading, Language Development, and Written Expression with Word Processing and Desktop Publishing

Most of us are accustomed to the benefits in productivity provided by our favorite word processor and cannot imagine writing without this incredible tool. The variety of word processors now available gives us the tools we need to enable all students to express their thoughts in writing and share them with their peers, their teachers, and their families. In this chapter, you will have the opportunity to explore the role of word processing in the larger context of effective literacy development in the classroom and to review your own uses of word processing for increased efficiency, productivity, and effectiveness.

Objectives

By the end of this chapter, you will be able to do the following:

1. Assess your current instructional strategies for reading, writing, and language development
2. Evaluate word processors for features that may be appropriate for you and/or your students
3. Organize your classroom so that word processing is integrated within the reading/writing/language development process
4. Use word processing to enhance your own productivity

Rationale and Research Knowledge

Many teachers who have experienced the power of word processing in their own lives assume that similar breakthroughs will automatically occur for their students. Others use word processing to do traditional drill-and-practice exercises on grammar and writing mechanics and are disappointed that technology is not a magic solution. Still others wonder about how to combine the use of technology with process writing, whole-language approaches, a literature-based curriculum, cooperative learning, metacognitive teaching/ learning strategies, and other important variables.

In spite of the intuitive sense most teachers have that word processing is effective, research results to date are mixed in their support for the role of word processing specifically in enhancing students' written language skills. Students in longitudinal studies of ACOT's technology-rich classrooms, for example, wrote more, more effectively, and with more fluidity (Dwyer, 1994).

Much more is known about what is effective and ineffective in teaching writing. For example, students learn more about writing mechanics by *writing* than by workbook exercises (whether on paper or on the computer screen) on grammar, punctuation, or spelling (Atwell, 1989; Avery, 1993; Calkins, 1994; Graves, 1983; Hillocks, 1984).

Nine instructional recommendations for teaching writing in the exceptional classroom, based on research results, include the following (Graham & Harris, 1988):

- Allocate sufficient time for writing instruction, which includes well-designed and sequenced writing activities.
- Use a broad range of writing tasks, including not only personal narratives/ journal writing but also expository writing with a particular goal (e.g., problem solving, comparison/contrast).
- Create a social climate for writing, with frequent student and teacher sharing and collaborating, as well as highly visible published results (newsletters, bulletin boards, class or team books shared in the school library or other classrooms, etc.).
- Integrate writing activities with other academic subjects, such as having students read or listen to a story and/or have an oral discussion before writing, or complete a related writing activity before reading a story, in addition to such activities occurring in science or social studies.
- Use task-specific metacognitive strategies to aid in the development of processes central to good writing in addition to the consistent use of a conceptual framework of the writing process.
- Provide activities to automatize skills for getting language onto paper—including opportunities to practice keyboarding, sentence combining, paragraph construction, and so on—or use dictation to remove mechanics from the writing process.
- Include activities to develop explicit knowledge about the characteristics of good writing, not just exposure to examples but practice with imitating models accompanied by specific feedback.
- Involve students in setting writing goals, including having specific criteria by which to evaluate their work or the work of peers, and monitor and give feedback on their progress.
- Suggest one or two areas to improve rather than overemphasize errors.

FIGURE 8-1   Inspiration Overview (Reprinted with permission of the publisher.)

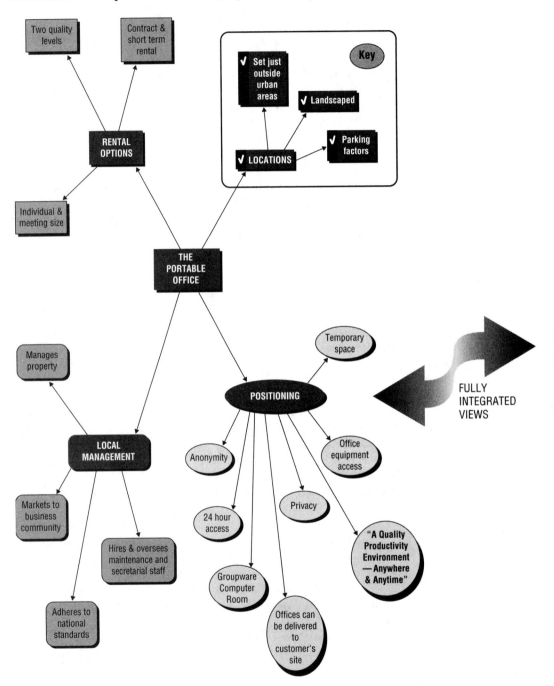

FIGURE 8-1 *Continued*

THE PORTABLE OFFICE

I. LOCATIONS

  A. Set just outside urban areas

    Within the current sales territory, our target market appears to be located in the large suburban areas just outside of Chicago and Detroit. The stability of those locations related to our needs should not undergo any significant changes during the next five years.

  B. Parking factors

    Permits will be negotiated with city governments by our legal department, allowing quick, generalized distribution of units at our discretion.

  C. Landscaped

    Each unit will be placed with a tear-away staircase, plants supplied by our contracted service, and red carpeting which will be installed leading up to the side entrances.

II. RENTAL OPTIONS

  A. Two quality levels

    These standards shall be referred to as The Executive and The Corporate. The Executive model will be the basic unit that can accommodate one to four individuals and includes our basic unit with full amenities. The Corporate model will be a deluxe unit that accommodates four to ten individuals and includes the multi-media presentation computing station.

  B. Contract & short term rental

  C. Individual & Meeting size

III. LOCAL MANAGEMENT

  A. Hires & oversees maintenance and secretarial staff

    Next month, James Conners will present a model of our new process for procuring, training and monitoring support staff for each territory. The program will be executed by Kay Swanson and Fred Berg.

  B. Manages property

    Legal will make a report at our next meeting.

  C. Markets to business community

  D. Adheres to national standards

IV. POSITIONING

  A. Privacy

    We must clearly communicate that a benefit of this product is that it produces on-the-spot privacy for commertial transactions, meetings and general business activities.

  B. Anonymity

  C. Office equipment access

  D. Temporary space

  E. "A Quality Productivity Environment — Anywhere & Anytime"

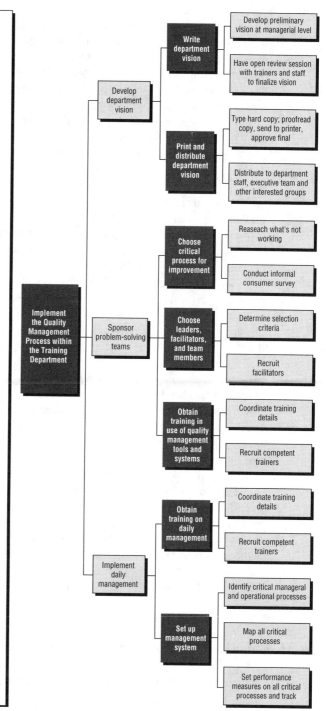

The Process Approach to Writing

The process approach to writing has evolved through analysis of the stages and steps used by successful writers so that novice or developing writers can benefit from the experiences of experts. These stages include planning/prewriting, drafting, revising/editing, and sharing/publication (Florio-Ruane & Dunn, 1987). Rather than a lock-step sequential process, however, writing and reading go together ideally in a cyclical flow, moving backward and forward until results satisfactory to the author/reader are achieved (Rief, 1994).

The *planning stage* is characterized by written outlines, brainstorming, clustering or mind mapping, and lists of ideas, themes, or key words. These activities are ideally suited to a one-computer classroom with a large television monitor or a computer projection device that will allow the teacher to list, group, revise, and expand ideas as students share them. A program such as Inspiration graphically shows ideas in bubbles which can be moved around and when finished can be instantly changed into an outline (See Figure 8-1). Printed copies can then be distributed at the end of the discussion. During this stage, teachers should model the planning process by thinking aloud so that students can see and hear the cognitive processes to be used. It is also important to allocate time for individual student planning and small group sharing.

The *drafting stage* may include individual or small-group collaborative work as students get their ideas on paper. In some classrooms, students may do drafts of their stories at the computer. In others, students may use pencil and paper. In still others, students may dictate their story to a teacher, aide, or peer who writes down the basic thoughts for the student to expand on and revise at a later stage.

Sharing is the first step in the *revising/editing* stage. Students read their stories aloud to a partner, a small group, or the whole class; classmates are instructed to ask questions or give feedback that will help the writer make the story even better than it already is. Activities to learn how to give this precise feedback will help students develop this skill. Students take notes on the suggestions they receive and then return to their stories to make improvements. Once the stories have been completed in terms of content, students turn their attention to mechanics and writing conventions, using peer, teacher, and/or computer feedback (Zellermayer, Solomon, Globerson, & Givon, 1991).

The *sharing/publication* stage allows students to experience being authors responding to an audience. Students are encouraged to share their work by reading it aloud and in printed form, with or without graphics or illustrations. Once students have experienced this cycle several times, their writing is shaped from the outset by wanting to create stories with audience appeal. Desktop publishing programs—which combine features of a word processor with graphic features such as borders, graphics, and formatting capabilities—are frequently used to produce attractive results. A digital camera can be used for illustrations.

The Metacognitive Aspects of the Writing Process

Although the process approach to writing has been implemented widely (Graves, 1983), the metacognitive issues of successful writing are equally important. One recent study found that students working in pairs, using a metacognitive editing strategy, produced higher-quality compositions than did those in a control group where process writing (without the metacognitive editing strategy) was used or those who used a strategy but worked alone (MacArthur, Schwartz, & Graham, 1991). Three features are cited in providing effective strategy instruction for writing (Englert, Raphael, Anderson, Anthony, & Stevens, 1991):

1. Emphasize the role of dialogue in writing development. "Teachers have responsibility to model writing strategies as they 'think aloud' to make visible the normally invisible cognitive processes related to planning, drafting, and revising text. This ensures that students not only see the writing products produced by the more expert and knowledgeable writer, but see the actions and hear the inner dialogue that the skilled writer uses to direct and monitor writing behavior" (Englert et al., 1991).

2. Provide scaffolded instruction in which the teacher bridges the gap between the students' current skill level and the actual developmental level required for independent problem solving. For example, the computer can assist with this scaffolding through written prompts in writing activities that disappear when a product is printed out (e.g., FrEdWriter). Modeling and practicing the use of planning sheets can help organize students' thoughts (See Figures 8-2 and 8-3). By creating templates of these tools, sheets can be tailored quickly to particular assignments or student needs (Sitko, Sitko, & McBride, 1992). Teachers can act as coaches to use dialogue or questions to elicit responses and behaviors.

3. Transform solitary writing into a collaborative activity. "First, as students talk to others about their writing, they practice the inner dialogue of the writer, with opportunities for peers to monitor as well as provide feedback and assistance" (Englert et al., 1991).

Using a Learner-Centered, Literature-Based Curriculum

Many schools are using a learner-centered, literature-based program to integrate reading, writing, and language arts. In this approach, students are introduced to children's literature, develop reading skills with children's literature as content (instead of unrelated workbook drill activities) and engage in writing activities that focus on various aspects of what students have read, as well as other writing activities using a variety of genres. These activities may be summaries, alternative endings, personal responses about similar experiences, or a new story using the same style of writing. A typical schedule for such a classroom is presented in Figure 8-4 (Rief, 1994).

Software such as the Write On! series, with data disks of writing activities related to specific pieces of children's literature for popular word processors make it easier to adopt a learner-centered, literature-based approach. These activities have been designed with the collaborative process writing approach in mind, and they assist the teacher in lesson preparation.

Selecting Word Processing and Desktop Publishing Software

Depending on the students' ages, skills, computer access requirements, and type of computer, teachers, service providers, and parents should look for a word processor that offers students optimum productivity. These features include:

FIGURE 8-2 **Computer-Assisted Writing Project**

Journal and Essay Planner Brainstorm

Steps

1. Decide on a Topic-Thesis. Write it on the Planner.
2. "Brainstorm."
3. Label time-line.
4. Circle the 3 or 4 main points or ideas from your brainstorming. Transfer these main ideas to the Planner. (Boxes under main ideas)
5. Arrange all other good points from the brainstorming under the appropriate main points. Cross out each point on Brainstorm as you place it on Planner.
6. Sequence each main point.
7. Sequence all points under each main idea.
8. Write out a creative introductory and concluding sentence.
9. Write fast draft. Write as fast as you can, don't worry about any mistakes.
10. Proof fast draft. Follow "Proof Reading Sequence."

1 _____	11 _____	21 _____
2 _____	12 _____	22 _____
3 _____	13 _____	23 _____
4 _____	14 _____	24 _____
5 _____	15 _____	25 _____
6 _____	16 _____	26 _____
7 _____	17 _____	27 _____
8 _____	18 _____	28 _____
9 _____	19 _____	29 _____
10 _____	20 _____	30 _____

15 to 20 brainstorming points will give you 3/4 to 1 page of writing.

Time Line

Initial Situation → Building Action → Highest Action → Wrap Up

FIGURE 8-3

Journal and Essay Planner
Topic/Thesis

Name: _____   Date: _____

Main Points/Ideas

Introductory Sentence
(Grab the Reader)

_____

_____

Concluding Sentence

_____

_____

- Size of print (KidWorks, for example, provides large, primary style print, on lines that look like a primary tablet; see Figure 8-5 for a sample).
- Speech synthesis. Auditory feedback is useful in increasing reading fluency as well as assisting in the editing process; for students with visual impairments, it is essential. KidWorks also includes speech synthesis. Other talking word processors include IntelliTalk, Dr. Peet's Talk/Writer, and Write: OutLoud.
- Graphics. Illustrations add motivation to both reader and writer; word processors with built-in graphics libraries are easy to use and fun for writers. KidWorks 2 has graphics

FIGURE 8-4

8th Grade Reading/Writing Workshop

Structure

Monday through Thursday

- Mon through Thurs—5 to 10 min read aloud and/or mini-lesson
- Mon—30 min silent writing
- Tues/Wed/Thurs—individual conferences
- Every other Thurs—response groups
- Mon through Thurs—10 min whole class/mini-lesson/reading

Friday

- Reading aloud—10 min
- Silent reading—35 min
- Whole class share—5 min

Class Expectations

Writing

- Write from 3 to 5 pages of rough draft writing per week (maintenance of working folder)
- Take two pieces of writing to final draft every six weeks (maintenance of portfolio)
- Read writing to at least three peers (response group) and at least once in teacher conference before final draft

Reading

- Read for a 1/2 hr five nights per week (or any combination of days that equal 2 1/2 hrs of reading per week)
- Keep a list of books read

Reader's/Writer's Log

- Collect/respond to/reflect on reading, writing, observations, and discoveries in log with 3 to 5 pages of writing per week

Notes

- Record all notes given in class

Vocabulary

- "Find" at least 5 words per week which are new or unknown (from reading, listening, class shares)
- Write those words in log in sentences found and with definition written in your own words
- Look for and record each new context in which the same word is discovered again (this counts as a new word—same word in context)

Spelling

- Maintain a spelling list in log of words consistently misspelled
- Categorize those words under the four basic rules, exceptions, or usage distinctions

Self-Evaluations

- Set goals every twelve weeks regarding what you want to be able to do better
- Evaluate yourself as a learner every twelve weeks based on goals set and accomplished

FIGURE 8-5   KidWorks Deluxe Sample

which can be used as rebuses (replacing text) or to illustrate stories; Student Writing Center and Storybook Weaver all feature high-quality, engaging graphics.

- Teacher prompts (a question posed to the user that disappears when the composition is printed).
- A match of school and home word processors so that students who need extra time can easily move from classroom to home for completion.
- Formatting. The ability to print a story in columns or insert graphics with flow-around text offers visual appeal in finished products. Student Writing Center and ClarisWorks are popular programs with such features.
- Sound effects. Adding sound effects to a story expands auditory input and engagement for the learner. Storybook Weaver allows the writer to select sound effects for characters and objects in the story.
- Checkers. Spelling, grammar, and style checkers are available to support the emerging writer. Special Writer Coach, for example, provides a powerful, flexible variety of feedback options for struggling writers. It is important to look for programs that offer the features you need but are also easy to use.

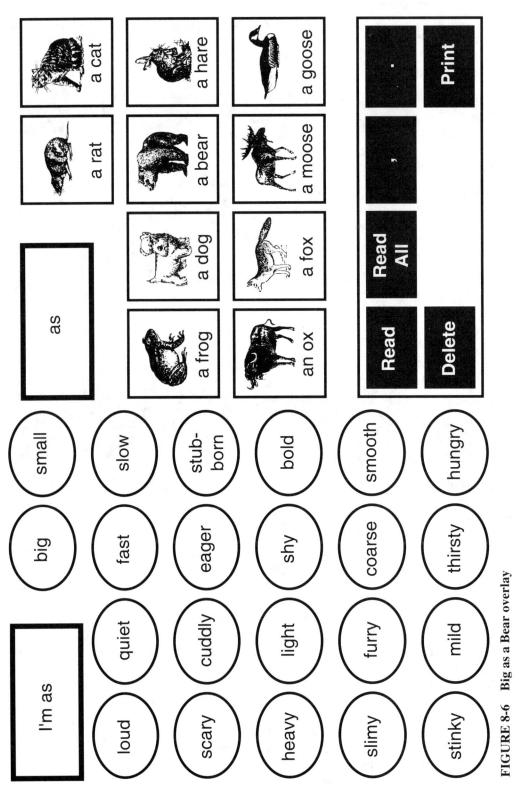

FIGURE 8-6 Big as a Bear overlay

Source: Reprinted with permission of Intellitools.

- Word prediction. Programs that keep track of the writer's word preferences and uses are becoming less expensive and easier to use. Magic Typist, Predict It, and Co:Writer all offer a variety of options that make writing less laborious by allowing the user to select words from a menu of possible choices. This can reduce the typing needed to compose a document.
- Adaptive keyboard/overlays/word processing software. Very young students, students with physical disabilities, or students whose learning disabilities make it difficult for them to use the standard keyboard will benefit from customized overlays for writing using such a tool as IntelliKeys with OverlayMaker and IntelliTalk. In such an approach, the teacher can select a piece of children's literature, design an overlay (see Figure 8-6 for an example), send it to IntelliKeys, load IntelliTalk, and students can use IntelliKeys instead of the regular keyboard, and have the computer read (or read independently) and print out their finished stories (See Figure 8-7). Preliminary research indicates that custom overlays promote increased numbers of student ideas, greater number of sentences, and more positive feelings about writing and peers than using the standard keyboard alone (IntelliTools, 1995).
- Single switch access. For students using a single switch and/or adaptive keyboard with Ke:nx, templates can be made to enable students to make selections to write their stories and get auditory feedback. With the Ke:nx software, the cursor will scan the options on the screen, and the student can make selections by pressing the switch. See Figures 8-8 and 8-9.

Instructional Activities

Some teachers find it helpful to start with a simple writing assignment and build to more complicated activities. Others have a piece of literature in mind and want to jump right in with an integrated approach to reading and writing. One teacher had the class begin by writing a paragraph about a favorite relative. Using Children's Writing and Publishing Center,

FIGURE 8-7   Sample Big as a Bear Story

I'm as cuddly as a rat.
I'm as shy as a cat.
I'm as hungry as a moose.
I'm as fast as a fox.
I'm as stubborn as a bear.
I'm as eager as a dog.

FIGURE 8-8   Scanning Overlay

All About Me!

My name is ____.

My favorite way to travel is by

____.

plane   bus   submarine   train

My favorite holiday is

____.

Christmas   Halloween   Hanukkah   Valentine's Day

Source: Reprinted with permission of the authors, Feit, Hoberman, and James.

FIGURE 8-8 *Continued*

My favorite food is
____.

cake   hamburger   ice cream   pizza

My favorite pet is a
____.

cat   dog   goldfish   horse

FIGURE 8-9   Example of Scanning Overlay

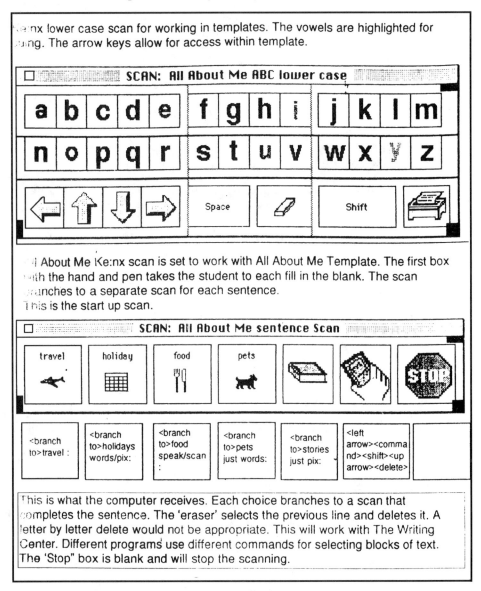

Source: Reprinted with the permission of the authors.

students could add illustrations, printed in color with a color ribbon. Figure 8-10 is an example from that class.

Another teacher wanted to use the children's book *Wilfrid Gordon McDonald Partridge* as a means of introducing the theme of memories to the class. She developed the introductory lesson, and then used the Write On! data disk, Memories, to continue the writ-

FIGURE 8-9 *Continued*

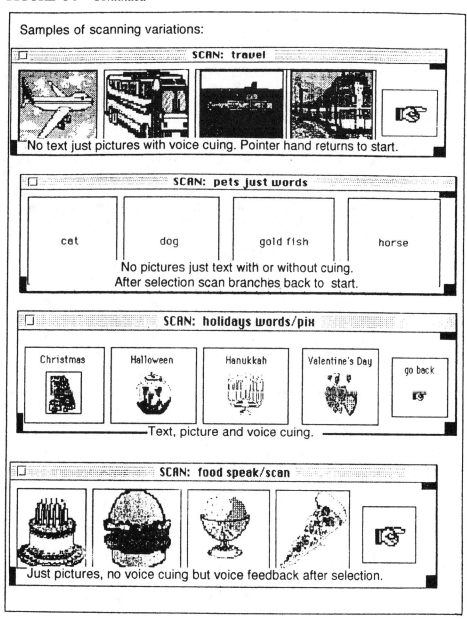

Samples of scanning variations:

SCAN: travel

No text just pictures with voice cuing. Pointer hand returns to start.

SCAN: pets just words

cat   dog   gold fish   horse

No pictures just text with or without cuing.
After selection scan branches back to start.

SCAN: holidays words/pix

Christmas   Halloween   Hanukkah   Valentine's Day   go back

Text, picture and voice cuing.

SCAN: food speak/scan

Just pictures, no voice cuing but voice feedback after selection.

ing activities. Figure 8-11 contains her introductory lesson plan. Figure 8-12 is a set of steps that can be used to develop lesson plans for any piece of literature.

Some teachers begin with a class newsletter. Children's Writing and Publishing Center offers an easy way to format graphics and text in columns, with premade or custom-

FIGURE 8-10   Sample Student Paragraph

MY RELATIVES

My favorite relative is Ryan. He is fun. We like all the same things. We think alike too. He is normal size. He has brown hair. He has a weight of 75 pounds. He can run fast. We like to play army, ride his gocart, ride bikes, fish, and go golfing somtimes too. He likes to let people ahead of him. He helps old ladies across the street. I wish I can see him more then 1 time or 2 times year, but he is my best friend.

by Chris

designed headings. An example of one class newsletter is provided in Figure 8-13. Another teacher had students design and illustrate their own versions of fairy tales (see Figure 8-14).

Teachers report that six general strategies have been helpful in increasing their effectiveness in teaching writing using the word processor. These include the following (Russell, Corwin, Mokros, & Kapisovsky, 1989):

- Read what the student has written and react to it on a personal level. ("After reading that paragraph, I feel like I can almost taste that horrible meal you describe.")
- Help the child clarify or expand his or her writing by asking questions that directly relate to what the child has written. ("What is it about the room that makes it feel cheery?")
- Suggest strategies for expanding or clarifying what the child has written. ("Think back to when you went through the doors into the emergency room. Write about what was going through your mind.")
- Type what the child is saying. The teacher is most likely to type for a student when ideas are flowing and the student is unable to type fast enough to get his or her ideas down or when the student is stuck. Teachers can type short phrases on the computer, based on what the child says aloud, which the student can then expand into complete sentences.

FIGURE 8-11   Literature-Based Lesson Plan: *Wilfrid Gordon McDonald Partridge*

Grade Level: 3–12

Subject: Writing your memoirs

Length: 2–3 class periods

Step 1: Select a Lesson

In this lesson, students discuss memories and the role of sights, smells, and sounds in recreating memories.

Step 2: Make Decisions

Group Size: 4

Group Assignment: random or teacher assigned to assure heterogeneity

Room Assignment: clusters of desks or three chairs at the computer

Materials Needed: one copy of Memories II software (optional); one copy per student of mind map/clustering worksheet; editing checklist; peer review guide

Assigning Roles: no roles used in the lesson

Step 3: Set the Lesson

Task: The teacher reads the book aloud to the class and begins a class discussion. The teacher models the brainstorming/mind mapping/clustering process by recalling a memorable experience and completing a clustering form on the blackboard or on an overhead projector. Students individually think about their own memorable experiences and begin their mind mapping.

In teams, students take turns sharing their mind map of their memorable experience with a partner. After sharing, the partner gives feedback by asking questions about any part of the mind map that was not clear. The partner also makes at least one positive comment about the mind map/memory that was shared.

Students then work individually on their drafts, using their mind maps to help structure the writing and to suggest specific words or images to be used. Each team is assigned to one or two computers and makes decisions about how computer time is divided up equitably. Students may do their drafts at the computer or on paper. Make sure that students double space their work on paper or at the computer for ease of editing.

Each student then reads his or her draft aloud to a new partner on the team. After listening to the draft, the partner gives feedback as follows:

- What did you hear?
- What did you like about the story?
- What are three things that would make this story even better?

When both partners have shared their drafts and given feedback, they make the revisions at the computer or on paper.

The teacher models the *Author's Chair* process by sitting in the designated chair and reading his or her composition and asking the class to respond to the questions above, making notes on needed revisions. The teacher then randomly calls on a student from each team to sit in the Author's Chair and share with the class the edited version of the story, as time permits. All students who sit in the Author's Chair receive special recognition points for their team.

Continued

FIGURE 8-11   *Continued*

> The students complete their final revisions and print out a copy to contribute to a class book of memories, which can be checked out by class members to read, donated to a local nursing home or doctor's office, or used as stories to read to younger children in a nearby school.
>
> *Positive Interdependence:* Each group in which every student turns in mind maps and completed drafts earns points for a team bonus.
>
> *Individual Accountability:* individual compositions; sitting in Author's Chair
>
> *Criteria for Success:* Completed compositions
>
> *Specific Behaviors Expected:* Sharing ideas; complimenting each other on ideas; giving supportive and helpful feedback
>
> **Step 4: Monitor and Process**
>
> *Evidence of Expected Behaviors:* All group members listen and give supportive and helpful feedback.
>
> *Plans for Processing:* The teacher circulates among the groups and notes instances of supportive and helpful feedback. After the stories have been shared, the teacher asks for examples of how well the groups worked together. The teacher then shares examples of good group work from the observations.

FIGURE 8-12   **Cooperative Writing Steps**

> 1. Assign students to teams.
> 2. Read a story or selection of writing aloud, setting the stage for the writing assignment.
> 3. Discuss the story in a large group, culminating in the specific writing assignment.
> 4. Initiate the brainstorming/prewriting stage. (Begin in a large group, then continue in teams.) Mind maps, clustering, and skeleton plans may be used.
> 5. Students write individual mind maps.
> 6. Students share their mind maps in pairs within their teams.
> 7. Students write individual stories at the computer or on paper (emphasis is on content, not mechanics).
> 8. Students read their stories to a new partner on their team. The partner gives feedback: What did you hear? What did you like? Is there anything that is not clear? Where could more details and information be added?
> 9. Students incorporate changes into their next drafts.
> 10. Students read in the Author's Chair (done in teams and/or with the whole class).
> 11. Students edit work with a checklist signed off by a teammate.
> 12. The teacher evaluates/scores/recognizes work.
> 13. The class debriefs the process of writing stories.
> 14. Publish the stories.
>
> *Ground Rule for Teachers:* Never assign a piece of writing that you do not plan to do yourself. Share your mind maps, drafts, and final products with the class. Let the students know that you are all in this together, sink or swim!

FIGURE 8-13   Sample Class Newsletter

THE JONES CONNECTION

DEVONSHIRE SCHOOL
CHARLOTTE, NC
FIRST EDITION
SPRING-1990

THE NEW COMPUTERS

One day Mrs. Jones walked into the classroom and asked us if we wanted to have four computers and a printer in our classroom. We all yelled, "Yes". Then someone said,"What do we have to do to get them?" She said that we would have to use them and be willing to let some outside teachers come in and do lessons with us. She also told us that we would have to work in groups, without fussing too much, and come up with completed work products at the end of allotted times. It sounded like fun to us, so we were willing to give it a try. Now that we know what we are doing , we have others  kids from different classrooms come in and we help them. Sometimes they end up helping us. By now you may be wondering what this program is called. WELCOME TO COMPUCID. There are three of these programs at our school and just a few across the country. The program also has an AppleLink component. We have only been able to link with the Computer Center at Metro and another school in Charlotte. Maybe, next year, some of you will be able to be a part of the program.

A Class Contribution

The Smoking Machine

Our class made a smoking machine. if you would like to see what it looks like, come by Room #118 and see our wall display. We were trying to see what happens to our lungs when we smoke. We smoked one cigarette each day for ten days. Our "lungs" were light brown, that was the tar on them. The one thing that we will all remember is that "SMOKING MAKES YOU SMELL STINK."

By Eric Myers

Rules for Getting Along with the Computer

#1 Always wait until after the red light is off before putting in a program or you might get ZAPPED!

#2 Don't bring food to the computer or it might eat it for you.

#3 Don't leave the diskette out unless YOU want to become a part of the computer.

#4 Don't leave the diskette near the window when it's hot or you will get a sunburn along with the diskette.

#5 If you love the computer very much, don't blow dirt and harful particles on/in it or you might end up being a dirtball.

#6 The mouse won't squeak but it will cause the cursor to run around the screen. Not too fast please.

#7 If you hear a noise and it's not sound effects then you know it's the computer's stomach begging to have a diskette put in.

Alicia Cooper

Wouldn't it be nice to have a bus load of computers?

Source: Reprinted with permission of Carolina Computer Access Center, Charlotte, NC.

FIGURE 8-14   Sample Student Fairy Tale

Cinderella said, I'll do a cartwheel for you if you give me an egg."

Source: Reprinted with permission of Miriam Furst.

- When the child encounters difficulties with the word processor, help him or her focus on the writing itself by assisting with particularly difficult commands or steps.
- Build the child's self-image as a writer by commenting on the strengths he or she has in common with real authors, and by assuring the child that authors share some of his or her same frustrations.

Personal/Professional Productivity

Some popular word processors (e.g., ClarisWorks, FilePro, Microsoft Works) are part of an integrated productivity package that includes data-base and spreadsheet applications. Using these tools together or separately will save time and get the job done more effectively and attractively (Jacoby, 1987). Chapters 9 and 10 will offer specifics on integrating these tools; the ideas that follow concentrate on word processing and desktop publishing.

- Organize the class rosters, name and address lists, and instructional groupings so that when students come in or move away, revisions are easy. (Data bases are even better for this task; see Chapter 9.)
- Write a template or a "stationery file" for any routine correspondence (positive notes to parents, academic or behavior concern letters to parents, notices about upcoming events or conferences), lesson plans, goals and objectives for IEPs, and so forth. Save the template file with a generic title (e.g., parent concerns); save it under a different name when a copy of a specific letter is needed for personal records (e.g., smith.concernltr). (Form letters that use word processors and data bases together are ideal for this task; see Chapter 9.)
- Decorate the classroom. Create banners and headings for showing off student work. Print name tags for students' desks. (After a little training, this task can be delegated to students.)
- Write out classroom rules and policies including homework, absences, field trips, classroom behavior, and so on. A program such as Comic Create or Creative Writer can be used to add graphics and emphasis.
- Design a class calendar using Calendar Maker or KidWorks 2 programs. By designing a monthly calendar template, one will be able to plan ahead and keep students and their families informed of upcoming events. Fill in major holidays, vacation times, as well as tests, trips, and other school and class events that are known in advance. Student birthdays and important deadlines may also be added.
- Set up a homework system. Design a weekly homework assignment sheet template to help students and parents keep track of what is due (see Figure 8-15).

Activities

1. Think carefully about the strategies you use to teach reading, writing, and language arts in comparison to those given in this chapter. Select one aspect of your teaching you would like to expand or concentrate on and describe how word processing could support your success.

FIGURE 8-15

Weekly Homework Assignment Sheet

Big Springs School—Ms. Loew–Room 51

Name _____

Week of _____

Homework Assignments

Classwork

Monday

	Complete	Incomplete	Needs Correction
Math			
Reading			
Language Arts			
Social Studies			
Science			
Spelling			
Tuesday			
Math			
Reading			
Language Arts			
Social Studies			
Science			
Wednesday			
Math			
Reading			
Language Arts			
Social Studies			
Science			

Continued

FIGURE 8-15 *Continued*

Thursday	Complete	Incomplete	Needs Correction
Math			
Reading			
Language Arts			
Social Studies			
Science			

Friday

No Homework, but all uncompleted classwork must be taken home to be completed and signed by parents.

Parent's Signature _____

Source: From *Teaching and Computers,* August/September 1987 issue. Copyright © 1987 by Scholastic, Inc. Reprinted by permission. All rights reserved.

2. Design a literature-based, learner-centered lesson.
3. Videotape yourself teaching the lesson you planned.
4. Visit a classroom where a teacher is using word processing integrated with literacy development. How are the instructional strategies alike or different from the ones presented in this chapter? Summarize your observation.
5. Provide five examples of expanding your own productivity in using word processing.

References

Atwell, N. (1989). *In the middle: Writing, reading, and learning with adolescents.* Portsmouth, NH: Heinemann.

Avery, C. (1993). *With a light touch.* Portsmouth, NH: Heinemann.

Calkins, L. (1994). *The art of teaching writing.* Portsmouth, NH: Heinemann.

Daiute, C. (1986). Physical and cognitive factors in revising: Insights from studies with computers. *Research in the Teaching of English, 20,* 141–159.

Dwyer, D. (1994). Apple classrooms of tomorrow: What we've learned. *Educational Leadership,* 51(7), 4–10.

Englert, C., Raphael, T., Anderson, L., Anthony, H., & Stevens, D. (1991). Making strategies and self-talk visible: Writing instruction in regular and special education classrooms. *American Educational Research Journal,* 28(8), 337–372.

Feit, S., and Hoberman, C. (1995). Magic carpet ride. Presentation at Closing the Gap, Minneapolis, MN.

Florio-Ruane, S., & Dunn, S. (1987). Teaching writing: Some perennial questions and some possible answers. In V. Richardson-Koehler (Ed.), *Educators' handbook: A research perspective* (pp. 50–83). New York: Longman.

Graham, S., & Harris, K. (1988). Instructional recommendations for teaching writing to exceptional students. *Exceptional Children,* 54(6), 506–512.

Graves, D. (1983). *Writing: Teachers and children at work.* Portsmouth, NH: Heinemann.

Hillocks, G. (1984). What works in teaching composition: A metanalysis of experimental treatment studies. *American Journal of Education, 93*, 133–170.

IntelliTools (1995). *An evaluation report for the National Institutes of Health.* Novato: IntelliTools.

Jacoby, S. (1987). Back to school breakthroughs. *Teaching and Computers,* 5(1), 16–20, 29.

Kerchner, L., and Kistinger, B. (1984). Language processing/word processing: Written expression, computers, and learning disabled students. *Learning Disability Quarterly,* 7, 329–335.

MacArthur, C., and Graham, S. (1987). Learning disabled students' composing under three methods of text production: Handwriting, word processing, and dictation. *Journal of Special Education, 21,* 22–42.

MacArthur, C., Schwartz, S., and Graham, S. (1991). Effects of a reciprocal peer revision strategy in special education classrooms. *Learning Disabilities Research & Practice,* 6(4), 201–210.

Rief, L. (1994). A full-time teacher talks about her writer's/reader's workshop. *The Writing Notebook,* 11(3), 24–26.

Rhodes, L., and Dudley-Marling, C. (1988). *Readers and writers with a difference: A holistic approach to teaching learning disabled and remedial students.* Portsmouth, NH: Heinemann.

Russell, S., Corwin, R., Mokros, J., and Kapisovsky, P. (1989). *Beyond drill and practice: Expanding the computer mainstream.* Reston, VA: Council for Exceptional Children.

Sitko, M., and Crealock, C. (1986). A longitudinal study of the efficacy of computer technology of improving the writing skills of mildly handicapped adolescents. Paper presented at the Invitational Research Symposium on Special Education Technology, Washington, DC

Sitko, C., Sitko, M., and McBride, A. (1992). Using technology to help learning disabled students access a process approach to functional writing skills. *Closing the Gap,* 11(3), 12–14, 36.

Zellermayer, M., Solomon, G., Globerson, T., and Givon, H. (1991). Enhancing writing-related metacognitions through a computerized writing partner. *American Educational Research Journal,* 28(8), 373–391.

Chapter *9*

Organizing Information for Social Studies and Science with Data-Base Management

In the Information Age classroom, all students need to know how to find information, organize it, and present it in a variety of ways. Many students (and many adults!) struggle with the increasing information load. Using data-base management tools, students and teachers alike can become more productive and feel more powerful in dealing with an expanding knowledge base!

Anyone who has ever cleaned out a desk in search of a missing file folder or gone through a stack of papers in pursuit of one particular sheet has had experience with data bases—the old fashioned kind! Computerized data bases can be thought of as electronic filing cabinets or electronic index card boxes. Almost everyone has had experience with data-base management through entering data on forms, keeping track of library books checked out, maintaining records of taxes owed, and so forth. In this chapter, you will explore how data bases can help your students learn to organize and retrieve information to answer questions or solve problems. In addition, you will get some ideas on how data bases can enhance your own productivity.

Objectives

By the end of this chapter, you will be able to do the following:

1. Define key data-base terms
2. Identify learning goals for your students that can be met through the use of data bases

3. Design a data base for a specific curriculum unit
4. Plan a series of lessons to teach your students how to use data bases
5. Design and use a data base to enhance your own productivity

What Is a Data Base?

A good place to start with data-base management is by becoming familiar with the terminology used to describe the information to be stored, sorted, and retrieved. A *field* is a category or item of information. In the Our Classroom data base, shown in Figure 9-1, Birthday, Hobbies, and Pets are fields. One set of information is called a *record*. In the Our Classroom data base, all of the information about each student is a record. A *file* is a collection of related records or the category that describes the data base. Our Classroom is the file for the lessons described later. Figure 9-1 shows the relationship of these three terms.

One way of thinking about data bases is to think of a form you have recently filled out and identify the terms. For example, you may have applied for a library card. The library's data-base *file* would be Patrons. Each item on the form you filled out (address, city, state, zip code, phone number) is a *field*. When you completed the application and someone entered that data into the library's data base called Patrons, information about you became a *record*.

Why Learn Data-Base Management Skills?

Many students are hampered by lack of organizational skills. Perhaps they are unable to find their homework when it is time to turn it in, or maybe they do not know how to organize

FIGURE 9-1   Data-Base Management Terminology

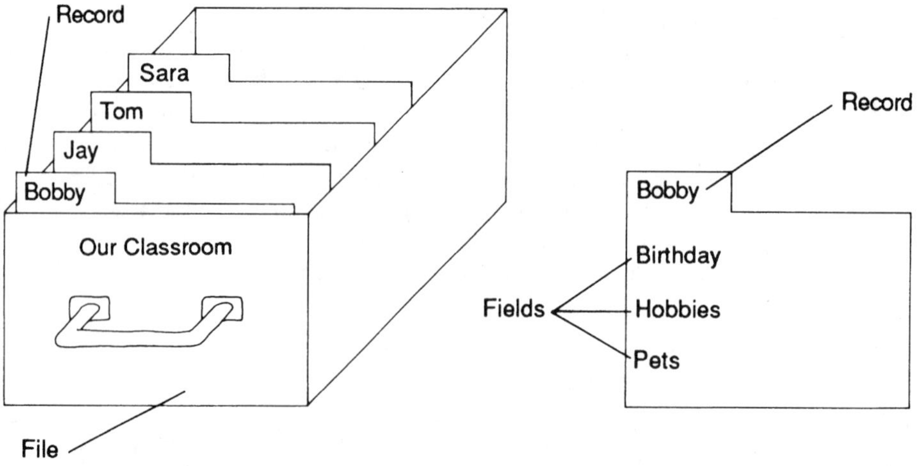

Source: From *Special Magic: Computers, Classroom Strategies, and Exceptional Students* by M. Male, 1988, Mountain View, CA: Mayfield Publishing. Reprinted with permission of the author.

their work on paper, or perhaps they find test questions about comparisons and contrasts baffling. These students may be able to locate information in a textbook, but they are unable to put it in a sequence or framework so that they can remember or express it in a paper, a presentation, a project, or on a quiz.

Data-base management is one of the most empowering solutions to these types of problems. Because it is a general-purpose tool, like word processing, the same program can be used to create, sort, and retrieve files on an unlimited variety of subjects, such as sociology, history, geography, science, or art.

Data-base management is a powerful instructional tool for teachers and students because it helps students perform the following tasks:

- Similarities and differences among groups of events or things can be discovered.
- Relationships can be analyzed. (The types of tools a particular tribe of Indians uses may be related to the type of environment in which they live.)
- Trends can be seen. (How many students in the class were born in the same state in which they now live or have moved more than three times in their lives?)
- Hypotheses can be tested and refined. (Through the sorting and searching capability of a data-base program, students can set a criterion and see how many examples fit.)
- Information can be organized and shared. (If everyone puts information in a common format and saves it in a common file, then the whole class has an organized source of information available to them, which is greater than what students could do individually.)
- Lists can be kept up to date. (Class clubs, book lists, and the like can all be updated and printed out easily.)
- Information can be arranged in more useful ways. (A list of all students with the same hobbies or who live in the same neighborhood may be generated.)

Selecting Data-Base Management Software

Every computer has many different data-base management programs that can be useful instructional tools. Some are designed specifically for student use and may come with sample files. Others come as part of integrated productivity packages that include word processing, data-base management, spreadsheets, and additional applications such as charting and telecommunications (e.g., ClarisWorks and Microsoft Works). Figure 9-2 provides an overview of characteristics of popular data-base management software.

Designing a Data Base

Designing a useful data base requires a good understanding of the data-base terms introduced earlier in this chapter, knowledge of the ways the computer is able to sort information (e.g., by zip code for printing address labels for a bulk mailing or by date to keep track of who has not paid club dues yet), and lots of practice. In the beginning, it helps to organize the data base on paper first. Then ask several people to enter data into the established fields to see if their responses provide useful data. For example, in the Our Classroom database

FIGURE 9-2   Characteristics of Data-Base Software

- Ease of learning
- Ease of use
- Flexibility in formats for data (numbers or text of unlimited length)
- Flexibility in naming fields
- Files of meaningful size
- Ease of manipulation (sorting) and retrieval
- Control over the way information is presented (flexible report formats such as tables, charts, or records)

example presented in Figure 9-1, Pets was a field the students wanted to include. After several students had entered their data, however, they discovered that students had interpreted this in several ways:

- Number of pets (none, 1, 2)
- Type of pets (dog, turtle, cat)
- Pets' names (Muffin, Wiggles, Oscar, Elmo)
- Presence or absence (yes, no)

The students wanted to know which students had what sorts of pets. They need to redesign the data base in order to get the type of information they desire.

In designing a data base, sometimes people confuse the *data* to be entered with the *categories* (fields) of data (e.g., Yurok—Name of Tribe). Others do not spend enough time thinking about how data will be sorted before setting up the fields. (For example, if the city, state, and zip code are put in the same field, the computer will not be able to sort by zip code, which will result in loss of flexibility and productivity.)

Instructional Activities

Hunter (1985) describes three stages of learning with data bases:

1. Using data bases that have been created by someone else
2. Building a data base by completing a form or template created by someone else
3. Designing one's own data base, entering the data, sorting the data into useful categories, and printing out the data to provide solutions to problems

In the first stage, the teacher guides student thinking by providing examples of appropriate fields for an Our Class data base (see Figure 9-3). Then student input can be solicited to generate additional fields (or students can work in pairs to come up with a list, then the teacher can call on pairs to share their ideas, actively involving every person in the class in

FIGURE 9-3 Sample Classroom Data Base

FIRST NAME:

BIRTHDATE:

FAVORITE HOBBIES:

BIRTHPLACE:

FAVORITE TV SHOW:

FAVORITE SCHOOL SUBJECT:

FAVORITE SPORT:

the discussion). Once the final selection of categories (fields) has been made, the teacher can print out a worksheet form for students to complete (or to interview each other). The real power of the lesson begins when the teacher shows the ways the computer can sort the information.

> *For students to be successful at activities that involve searching a data base, they need to know the types of searches available for the data base they are using, and they need to know which search strategy is most effective for a particular type of question. If you don't systematically guide students to analyze the question and consider each strategy, they will find one strategy that works for them and then use it no matter what question comes before them. Allowing this leaves thinking at lower levels and frequently leads to incorrect conclusions. Training students to focus on data base search strategies will help them to learn more about the content they are studying as well as to become better and more critical thinkers. (Hannah, 1987b, p. 16)*

Most data-base programs offer options of arranging, selecting, sorting, or "filtering" (Microsoft Works) records, finding data by entering comparison information, or selecting records using criteria established by the user. Some of the record selection options from data-base management software include the following:

- equals
- is greater than
- is less than
- is not equal to
- is blank
- is not blank
- contains

- begins with
- ends with
- does not contain
- does not begin with
- does not end with

In addition, more than one qualifier can be used, with the use of *and, or,* and *through.* Several practice lessons with worksheets can be conducted in which students learn to sort and print out the data. A worksheet for a Class Favorites data base with fields for Musical Group, Musical Instrument, Food, Song, Ice Cream, Sport, Hobby, Holiday, TV Program, Movie, and so on might initiate the following (Hannah, 1987a):

- One person chose Guns n Roses as the favorite musical group. What is that person's favorite musical instrument?
- He was eating pizza, had a baseball cap on his head, and was humming "Unforgettable." What was his favorite movie?

Another activity appropriate for this first stage of learning about data bases might be U.S. Presidents, with fields for Term of Office, Party, State, Prior Job, and Notes. Students could search for presidents from California who were Republicans after 1900. Venn diagrams help students conceptualize the difference between an *or* selection and an *and* selection (see Figure 9-4). A record selection worksheet (see Figure 9-5) helps students think about how to structure a search before they get to the computer. Students can also be assigned the task of writing questions to challenge each other.

FIGURE 9-4   Venn Diagrams for Selection Criteria

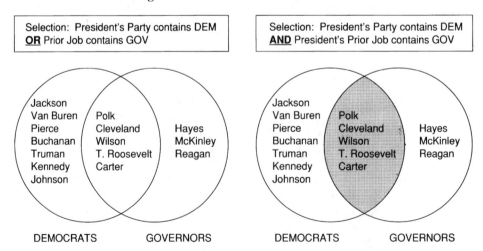

Source: Reprinted with permission of *The Computing Teacher, 14*(9), 1987, International Society for Technology in Education, Eugene, OR. Copyright © ISTE.

FIGURE 9-5   Record Selection Worksheet

RECORD SELECTION
WORKSHEET

1. Question: _____

2. I plan to
select those _____
records that: _____

category	logical operator (comparison)	comparison information	relationship (connector)
☐	☐	☐	and through or
☐	☐	☐	and through or
☐	☐	☐	

3. I found that: _____

4. I double-
checked by: _____

5. Now I plan to: _____

1. equals	5. is blank	9. ends with
2. is greater than	6. is not blank	10. does not contain
3. is less than	7. contains	11. does not begin with
4. is not equal to	8. begins with	12. does not end with

Source: Reprinted with permission of *The Computing Teacher, 14*(9), 1987, International Society for Technology in Education, Eugene, OR. Copyright © ISTE.

In the second stage of learning with data bases, students enter data to complete a data base. As a follow-up to the previous data-base exercise on U.S. Presidents, students might enter the data to complete a similar data base on vice presidents. Each group could be assigned to several vice presidents, with each student in the group responsible for one particular vice president. While the data are entered, students can work in their groups to generate questions to solve by using the search/sort strategies.

In the third stage, students begin designing their own data bases. Figure 9–6 illustrates one lesson that could expand on the Our Classroom theme or link with some aspect of the social studies or science curriculum.

Although presenting data-base management tools in sequential steps may be clearer for some students and teachers, others may find designing a data base for a particular

FIGURE 9-6   Data-Base Lesson Plan

Lesson Title: Lesson 3: Designing Your Own Data Base

Grade Level: 4–12

Content Area: Language, Social Studies, Critical Thinking, Social Skills

Goal: Students will create their own data bases, enter the data, sort the data, and print the information.

Time Required: 3–5 hours

Preparation: Materials needed for each student: paper and pencil; a menu of ideas (can be teacher- or student generated); a sample data base (Our Class); one-page instructions for using the data-base program; one blank disk. Materials needed for the class: one or more computers; one or more printers; one or more copies of the data-base program.

Conducting the Lesson:

1. Introduce the assignment; review the steps in designing a data base.

2. Review the instructions for using the data-base program.

3. Review the menu of data-base ideas.

4. Solicit additional ideas.

5. Ask each student to select a data-base idea and to design the form that represents the fields of data to be collected. Allow time for individual work. Monitor progress and assist as needed.

6. Ask for one student to volunteer to design a form on the computer and to enter his or her data.

7. Assign students to teams of four; have them share their data base and the data (paper copy). Check to make sure each person understands how to enter the data and sort.

8. Assign teams to computers. Bonus points will be given to each team whose members complete the task successfully. Allow time.

9. Ask each team to submit the paper version, a printed version, and the disk on which the data base is saved for credit. Assign bonus points.

Follow-up: Students recruit other students to enter data into their data base.

Source: From *Special Magic: Computers, Classroom Strategies, and Exceptional Students* by M. Male, 1988, Mountain View, CA: Mayfield Publishing. Reprinted with permission of the author.

project a perfectly natural starting place. Taking advantage of the need to organize information about a particularly engaging problem or topic may well be a motivating way of introducing the power of data bases. Mary Anderson at McKinley Elementary School in Arlington, Virginia, uses data bases with students to help them prepare book reports. A simple format with three fields helps students summarize information about each chapter. Figure 9-7 provides an example.

Collaborative Research Tools

In learner-centered classrooms, teachers are helping students learn to do research collaboratively, around real-life problems and authentic situations rather than around traditional topic-focused, teacher-generated subjects (e.g., a report on a particular state). One tool, Researcher, assists students as they define a group research problem. It helps the students assign research tasks, hold each other accountable, share discoveries with those who access their work, and benefit from feedback from classmates. Teachers use Researcher to track group and individual student progress. The program is structured by research phases: Problem, Conjecture, Plans, New Information, and Revision. Each phase is a type of data base which can be sorted by keywords, dates, or researchers. Students can review, comment, or question the work of classmates (see Figures 9-8 and 9-9).

Another research tool to supplement using data-base management tools for collecting information is Note Center. Note Center lets students enter inquiries, hypotheses, conclusions, and reflections into a communal data base. Students use Note Center tools to add images, video movies, and sounds to their data and share them with each other and the teacher.

Personal Productivity

Perhaps the greatest tool for enhancing personal productivity for teachers is the integrated data-base/word-processing function, offered by such programs as ClarisWorks, Microsoft Works, and Filemaker Pro. By designing a data base thoughtfully and with care, and merg-

FIGURE 9-7   A Book Report Data Base

Chapter Title	1. The Battle of the Snow Ball.
Vocabulary	Tussle- To fight or hit.
Question	Why did the boys get in a tussle?
Chapter Title	2. Thinking of Gold.
Vocabulary	bullion- gold
Question	Why were they thinking of gold?

FIGURE 9-8

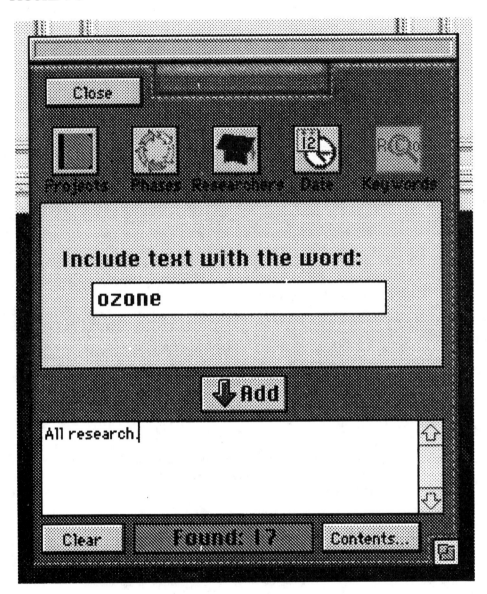

ing it with unlimited forms and form letters created by the word processor, a teacher can perform almost any task related to information about students to communicate with school personnel or parents.

The teacher should consider the information needed about the students and ways in which it is used. He or she should then make a list of all the different types of information

FIGURE 9-9

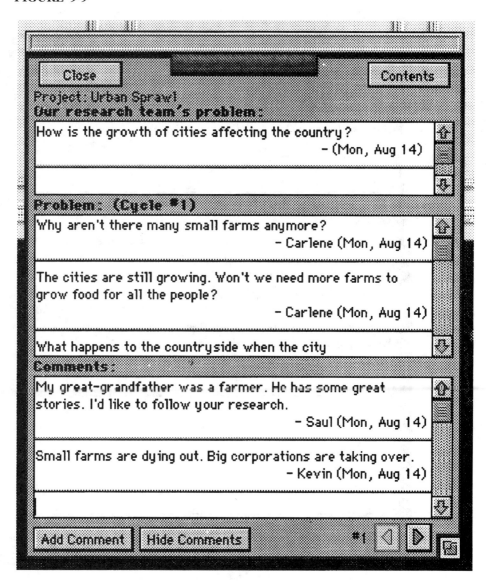

Continued

that are requested (e.g., lists of students who receive free lunches, special education, or Chapter I instruction services; bilingual students; birthdays; IEP review dates; parents' names, etc.). By taking the time to design an effective data base and entering the data, the teacher can produce a report for virtually any purpose with just a few keystrokes and no headaches!

FIGURE 9-9 *Continued*

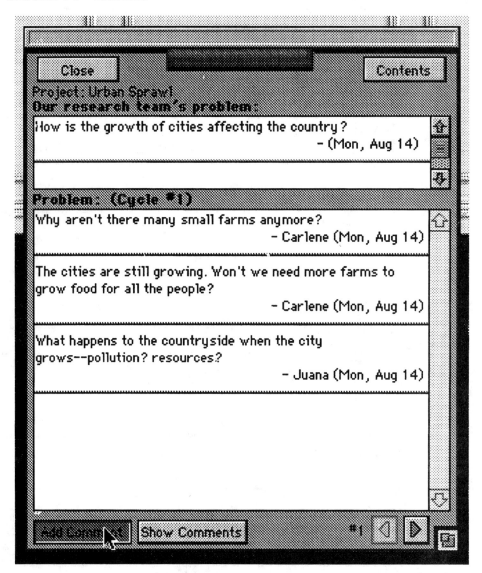

For example, Ms. Jones has 31 students in her fourth-grade class: 6 are bilingual, 4 receive special education services, and 13 receive Chapter I assistance. She thought carefully about the data base that could assist with parent conference notices, class lists (which seemed to change daily), meeting dates to review individual plans, and letters home. Since she planned to use form letters, which could merge data-base information, she chose the following fields:

Student's last name: Student's first name:
Title: Father's Last Name: Father's First Name:
Title: Mother's Last Name: Mother's First Name:
Home Address:
City: State: Zip: Home Phone:
Father's Work Number:
Mother's Work Number:
Student's Date of Birth: Student's SS#:
Special Education (*y* or *n*)
Chapter I (*y* or *n*):
Free Lunch (*y* or *n*):
Areas of Strength:
Areas of Concern:

Once the data for each of her students had been entered, Ms. Jones could print out any lists she needed. She could also send out academic or behavioral progress reports to specific parents, or to all the parents in the class, with personalized information inserted automatically by the computer. New fields could be added as needed without having to redo the data base or reenter data. Reports could be designed with just the appropriate information needed, such as a list of birthdays for each month for the room mother or a list of IEP meetings (also using birthdates) for the students in special education. Name and address labels for letters home to families could be done with the same data base! Even better, Ms. Jone's template for this year's data base can be used again, with next year's students, without redesigning it.

Activities

1. Think carefully about the curriculum you are using. In what areas would data-base management be appropriate for students to learn to organize, retrieve, and report information? Select one aspect of your teaching you would like to expand or concentrate on and describe how data-base management could support your success.
2. Design a data-base management lesson using Figure 9-6 as an example.
3. Videotape yourself doing the lesson you planned.
4. Visit a classroom where a teacher is using data-base management to assist with writing instruction. How are the instructional activities similar to or different from the ones presented in the chapter? Summarize your observation.
5. Provide five examples of expanding your own productivity using data-base management.

References

Hannah, L. (1987a). The data base: Getting to know you. *The Computing Teacher, 15*(l), 17–18.

Hannah, L. (1987b). Teaching data base search strategies. *The Computing Teacher, 14*(9), 16–20.

Hunter, B. (1985). Problem solving with data bases. *The Computing Teacher, 13*(7), 24–28.

Chapter *10*

Spreadsheets

The spreadsheet does for arithmetic and math problems what the word processor does for written language. As with word processing, students can erase, move, insert, and print their work easily. In this chapter, you will explore this powerful way of teaching mathematics and manipulating numbers. You will also have an opportunity to expand your own productivity by using spreadsheets.

Objectives

By the end of this chapter, you will be able to do the following:

1. Define key spreadsheet terms
2. Identify learning goals for your students that can be met through the use of spreadsheets
3. Design a spreadsheet for a specific curriculum unit
4. Plan a series of lessons to teach your students how to use spreadsheets
5. Design and use a spreadsheet to enhance your own productivity

What Is a Spreadsheet?

A *spreadsheet* is a table of information organized into rows and columns (see Figure 10-1 for an illustration). Most people are familiar with paper bookkeeping spreadsheets, such as a budget, where all the numbers across and down must balance and where a change in one row or column affects all the other rows and columns. When an electronic spreadsheet is used and a change is made in one entry, all other entries affected by the change are automatically made. The electronic spreadsheet can also do all the calculations if the appropriate formulas are entered.

As with data-base management, knowing some key terms is a good place to begin becoming familiar with spreadsheets. A *cell* is the intersection of a row and column, identified by coordinates such as A1, B2, and so on. Each cell holds one piece of information, which can be either a *label* (word), a *value* (number), or a *formula* (directions to perform a

FIGURE 10-1   Electronic Spreadsheet

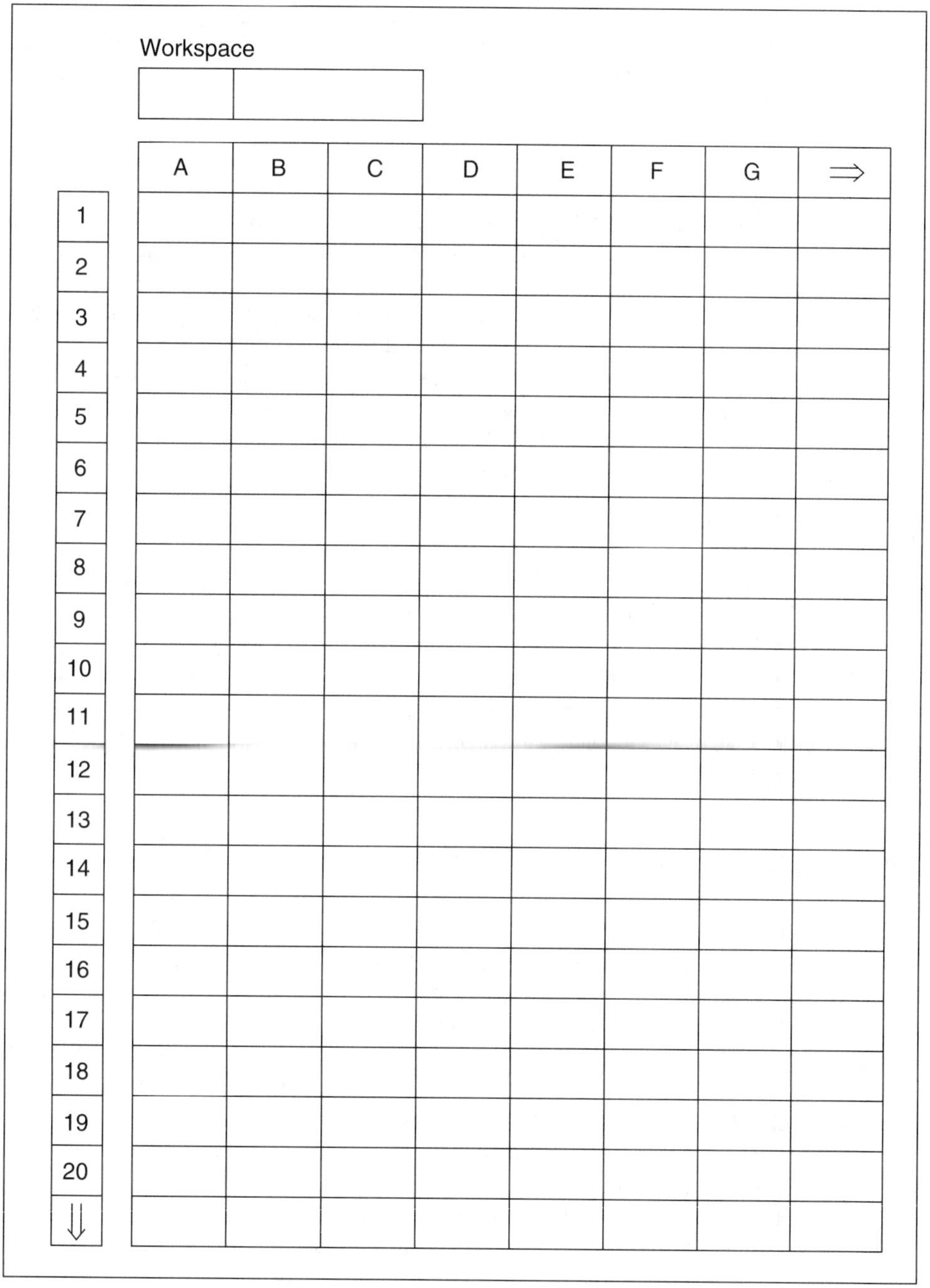

Workspace

	A	B	C	D	E	F	G	⟹
1								
2								
3								
4								
5								
6								
7								
8								
9								
10								
11								
12								
13								
14								
15								
16								
17								
18								
19								
20								
⇓								

Source: Reprinted with permission of *The Computing Teacher,* *14*(9), 1987, International Society for Technology in Education, Eugene, OR. Copyright © ISTE.

calculation such as addition, subtraction, multiplication, or division of values in one or more cells). The *workspace* is the area at the top of the spreadsheet where values, labels, and formulas are entered. The portion of the spreadsheet that can be seen at one time is called a *window.*

Why Learn Spreadsheet Skills?

The use of spreadsheets will enable students to create models of a variety of situations in math, science, social studies, and the like. For instance, students can pose "what-if" questions with numbers and learn about relationships, cause and effect, and actions and consequences. At the very least, an electronic spreadsheet can organize students' math problems and print them out so they can be read. Since the computer can do most of the calculations, students can reach the correct answer only by understanding how to set up the problem, which is a key thinking and problem-solving skill.

Brown (1987a) lists the following reasons for teaching students to use spreadsheets:

- Encourages logical thinking
- Promotes organizational skills
- Encourages problem-solving skills
- Sets the stage for experimentation
- Enables students to view a problem in general as well as in specific terms
- Makes algebraic concepts concrete
- Gives students a new interest in math
- Familiarizes students with a real-life business tool
- Encourages student-adult and student-student interaction
- It's fun!

Selecting Spreadsheet Software

The terms and the basic procedures used to work with spreadsheets are usually the same regardless of the software. The selection of spreadsheet software depends basically on price, power, and whether the user wants software that is integrated with other applications of word processing and data-base management.

Integrated productivity packages such as ClarisWorks or Microsoft Works have spreadsheet programs along with word-processing and data-base management. Using such a package allows for easy transfer among applications, permitting the user to cut and paste a spreadsheet into a memo on the word processor, for example. It also means that the commands to operate one application can be applied to the others, thereby reducing the time it takes to learn how to use the program. Powerful single-purpose spreadsheet programs such as Lotus 1,2,3 and Excel are also available; they are more complicated to learn and somewhat less flexible for classroom use, however.

For most educational and classroom uses, an integrated program is the most flexible choice. It is also the most economical in terms of training time, since the commands used to work with the spreadsheet are the same as, or similar to, those used to work with the word processor or data-base applications.

The Cruncher is a spreadsheet program designed specifically for use in classrooms. It teaches students how to use spreadsheets and graphs in everyday life. It computes, graphs, and talks, and enables students to add animated illustrations and sound effects to their work. The program comes with 10 real-world projects with templates to get started. An example of a sample spreadsheet lesson is included in Figure 10-2. Figure 10-3 is a teacher-design overlay for The Cruncher.

Designing a Spreadsheet

A prerequisite to introducing spreadsheets to students is for the teacher to understand how spreadsheets work. Luehrmann (1986) suggests beginning with a blank spreadsheet to get familiar with moving the cursor from cell to cell, entering information, and editing and

FIGURE 10-2   Cruncher Spreadsheet

	A	B	C	D	E	F
1	Can We Get A Pet?					
2	How Much Will It Cost for One Year?					
3	Purchase Price					
4	One-Time Costs					
5	(fence, tank, house, etc)					
6	Vet care, immunizations					
7	Obedience school					
8	Boarding costs while on vacation					
9	Dog Treats					
10	License and Collars					
11						
12	Grand total is:			$0.00	$0.00	$0.00
13						
14						
15						
16						
17						
18						
19						
20						

Source: Magic Carpet Project. Reprinted with permission of the authors, Feit, Hoberman, and James.

FIGURE 10-3 Cruncher Overlay

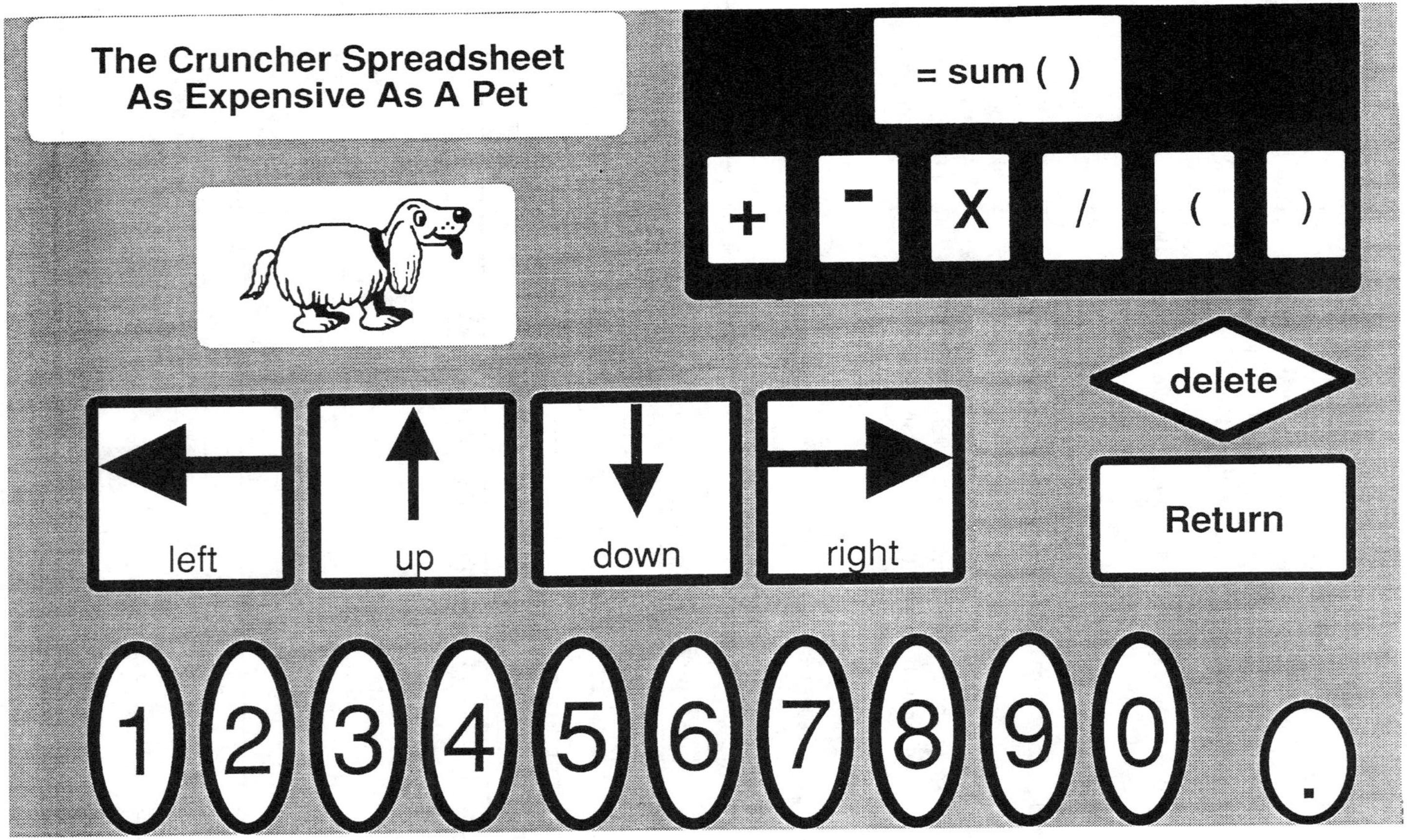

The Cruncher Spreadsheet As Expensive As A Pet

= sum ( )

+   -   ×   /   \   ~

delete

Return

up   left   down   right

1   2   3   4   5   6   7   8   9   0   .

Source: Magic Carpet Project. Reprinted with permission of the authors, Feit, Hoberman, and James.

deleting it. With a blank spreadsheet, whatever is displayed on the screen is the result of the user's own actions, which makes the terms introduced earlier in this chapter more concrete. Brown (1987a), on the other hand, begins with a paper-and-pencil exercise to illustrate the usefulness of spreadsheets (see Figure 10-4). Brown then suggests doing the exercise again with the electronic spreadsheet, entering formulas in the cells. When changes are made, the spreadsheet updates itself automatically.

Whether one begins with a blank spreadsheet or a paper-and-pencil exercise, the potential power of spreadsheet use to solve mathematical problems is quickly revealed. Once the user feels successful in doing examples such as that shown in Figure 10-4, it is then time for the user to design his or her own spreadsheet with real data and to practice making changes. For example, a teacher might think of his or her own classroom materials budget for a three-month period. The top of a column would be labeled Expenses. Then beneath this label, typical expenses such as the following would be listed:

Paper
Pens
Workbooks
Paints
Markers

The first row across the top would be labeled Monthly, and then each column would be labeled with a month (January, February, March, etc.). Now the user is ready to enter "cells" with amounts spent. Once the amounts for each item for each month are entered, a total for each item and a total for each month are needed. The amount in the lower right-hand column should be a Grand Total. Instead of entering the totals, however, a formula should be entered so that the computer can do the calculations. The teacher's next challenge is to think of examples that are appropriate for the students with whom he or she works.

Instructional Activities

The keys to success in introducing students to spreadsheet use are the design and selection of appropriate examples. It is important to sequence the introduction of new concepts, breaking tasks into small chunks so that each concept is understood before moving on to the next.

Depending on the spreadsheet being used, a reference sheet may be designed for students with just the commands they will need for the day's lesson. For a lesson on taking a field trip to the zoo, for example, the students will need to know the following:

- How to move the cursor from cell to cell
- How to record an entry
- How to confirm an entry
- How to edit an entry
- How to enter a formula
- How to read the screen prompts
- How to show dollar values in the cells
- How to show a range of cells in a formula

FIGURE 10-4   Spreadsheet Activity on Grades

Handout: Grades

1. Fill in the CHART handout using the information listed below.

COLUMNS	ROWS
A1 NAME	A3 ARTLEY
C1 TEST	B3 MICHAEL
C2 ONE	A4 BRENNEN
D1 TEST	B4 MARY
D2 TWO	A5 KOSY
E1 TEST	B5 JONI
E2 THREE	A6 LEONARD
F1 FINAL	B6 LORI
G1 AVERAGE	A7 SMITH
	B7 BEN
	A9 CLASS
	B9 AVERAGE

2. Enter the following data into the correct cells.

NAME		TEST ONE	TEST TWO	TEST THREE	FINAL AVERAGE
ARTLEY	MICHAEL	95	100	97	100
BRENNEN	MARY	92	93	90	93
KOSY	JONI	82	85	87	92
LEONARD	LORI	75	82	89	90
SMITH	BEN	100	85	90	94
CLASS	AVERAGE				

3. Figure out the student average for each student and enter the data in the column labeled AVERAGE.
   Write out the formula you used on this line:

   _____

4. Figure out the class average for each test and place this data in the row labeled CLASS AVERAGE.
   Write out the formula you used on this line:

   _____

5. Sorry, but you were given some incorrect information. You need to change a few things.

   BEN received a 78 on TEST THREE.
   LORI received a 100 on TEST ONE.
   JONI received a 68 on TEST TWO.

6. Please enter the new data and then recalculate where needed.

Source: Reprinted with permission of *The Computing Teacher,* 14(4), 1987, International Society for Technology in Education, Eugene, OR. Copyright © ISTE.

Refer to Figure 10-5. Have the students enter the information that is shown in Column A (labels for the various expenses) along with a cell for the Total (A8). In Column B are the values in dollar amounts for the expenses. Cell B8 holds the formula for getting the total; using ClarisWorks, the formula would be expressed @SUM(B3 . . . B7). It may be desirable to have the students try this formula in three learning steps:

1. Entering the total (doing the addition themselves)
2. Doing the formula with numbers instead of cells—@SUM(.75 + 1.00 + 3.50 + .75 + .25)
3. Doing the formula with specified cells

A task sheet might include problems such as:

1. The entrance fee to the zoo has been increased to $1.00. What is the total cost per student now?
2. The bus fare has been reduced to 75¢. What is the total cost per student now?
3. In Column C, put in formulas that will calculate the cost for a class of 30 students.
4. What if another class of 35 students decides to go along on the field trip, too? What is the cost for that class? What is the total cost for the trip for both classes?

It is important for students to note that only by expressing formulas in terms of cells will the computer automatically make changes when values in any related cells are changed. Problems 3 and 4 above will introduce the need to copy or replicate formulas from cell to cell, relative to the information from the row or column being calculated. This is a complex concept and will require practice with lots of examples. Recipes are ideal examples because problems can be constructed around doubling, tripling, and quadrupling the ingredients (Luehrmann, 1986).

Arad (1987) summarizes the following student goals for problem solving:

• Understand the problem.
• Divide the problem into subproblems.
• Identify the appropriate variable(s).
• Set up a table.
• Look for relationships between the different components of the problem.
• Write equations.
• Solve for the correct answer.

In Arad's opinion, spreadsheets offer the ideal medium to solve problems such as the following:

> Mary invested twice as much money at 5% per year as she did at 4% per year. How much was invested at each rate if her annual return is $168?

He teaches students to construct spreadsheet templates to solve such problems. Figure 10-6 shows examples of spreadsheets for solving such problems. In problems such as these, "students can experiment and explore the word problem by entering different values in the variable cell, observing the related changes in the other dependent cells. The change is visible immediately; the problem becomes dynamic. When the student translates the word problem into a dynamic table, the problem becomes real and easier to relate to" (Arad, 1987, p. 15). This approach forces students to break problems into component parts and encourages

FIGURE 10-5   Fieldtrip Lesson Spreadsheet

A Field Trip	B	
		1
		2
Entrance	0.75	3
Bus	1.00	4
Lunch	3.50	5
Snack	0.75	6
Postcard	0.25	7
Total	6.25	8

Source: From *Special Magic: Computers, Classroom Strategies, and Exceptional Students* by M. Male, 1988, Mountain View, CA: Mayfield Publishing. Reprinted with permission of the author.

approximation and estimation by making the change process easier than the tedious paper-and-pencil approach.

Brown (1987b) recommends story problems related to real-life situations of students that require outside research or interviews of experts to gather data. Here are three examples:

Problem 1

You are considering three summer jobs. The first one pays $8.50 an hour, eight hours a day but requires that you purchase three uniforms at $75.00 apiece. The second job pays $5.00 an hour, six hours a day, but offers tips of at least $25.00 per day. The third job pays $10.00 per hour but is only for four hours per day. If you plan to work for thirty days, and money is your only consideration, which is the best job?

Problem 2

You are planning to go to college. Your parents have offered to pay the tuition, but you must cover housing, food, books, and all other expenses. Your three choices are San Jose State University, University of California at Santa Cruz, and De Anza Community College. Which one can you afford? What other variables should you consider?

Problem 3

You are planning to attend the senior prom. You have $200. Design a spreadsheet estimating your expenses and staying within your budget.

Trawick (1995) provides another motivating real-life problem—buying a car (Figure 10-7).

Some concerns have been expressed about the use of spreadsheets to teach math. Teachers will want to consider these concerns in their instructional planning (Johnson, 1987):

- Does the student or teacher construct the spreadsheet template?
- Does using a template really reflect student understanding of the problem? If students construct the template incorrectly, their answers will be incorrect regardless of their understanding of the problem. If they use the teacher's template, may the experimentation process become as rote as the paper-and-pencil equation process?

FIGURE 10-6 Sample Problems and Spreadsheets

Example 2: Mary invested twice as much money at 5% per year as she did at 4% per year. How much was invested at each rate if her annual return is $168?

The student constructs a spreadsheet template based on his/her understanding of the problem:

	A	B	C
		AT 4%	AT 5%
1			
2	AMOUNT	?	2•B2
3	RETURN	.04•B2	.05•C2
4	— — — — — — — — — — — — — —
5	LOOKING FOR RETURN OF $168
6	VARIABLE IS THE AMOUNT INVESTED AT 4%
7	CURRENT RETURN IS: B3+C3

The cells with their formulas.

When the student enters a numerical value (e.g., 800) in cell B2, the other cells adjust accordingly:

	A	B	C
		AT 4%	AT 5%
1			
2	AMOUNT	800.00	1600.00
3	RETURN	32.00	80.00
4	— — — — — — — — — — — — — —
5	LOOKING FOR RETURN OF $168
6	VARIABLE IS THE AMOUNT INVESTED AT 4%
7	CURRENT RETURN IS: 112.00

The resulting values when cell B2 is 800.

Because the student is looking for a total return of $168 and cell C7 currently reflects $112, an investment value larger than 800 must be used in cell B2. Eventually, 1200, the correct value, is obtained. The correct answers of $1200 invested at 4% and $2400 invested at 5% also appear in the table:

	A	B	C
		AT 4%	AT 5%
1			
2	AMOUNT	1200.00	2400.00
3	RETURN	48.00	120.00
4	— — — — — — — — — — — — — —
5	LOOKING FOR RETURN OF $168
6	VARIABLE IS THE AMOUNT INVESTED AT 4%
7	CURRENT RETURN IS: 168.00

The correct answer.

Example 3: One weekend Mike got the blues and decided to visit his brother in Vancouver, 90 km away. On the return trip, he drove 15 km/hr faster than on the trip there. Mike's total travel time was 3½ hours. At what speed did Mike travel on the way back from his brother?

The student constructs a spreadsheet template:

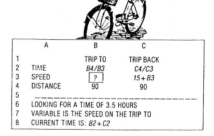

	A	B	C
		TRIP TO	TRIP BACK
1			
2	TIME	B4/B3	C4/C3
3	SPEED	?	15+B3
4	DISTANCE	90	90
5	— — — — — — — — — — — — — —
6	LOOKING FOR A TIME OF 3.5 HOURS
7	VARIABLE IS THE SPEED ON THE TRIP TO
8	CURRENT TIME IS: B2+C2

The cells with their formulas.

The student enters a numerical value in cell B3, and the other cells adjust accordingly;

	A	B	C
		TRIP TO	TRIP BACK
1			
2	TIME	3	2
3	SPEED	30	45
4	DISTANCE	90	90
5	— — — — — — — — — — — — — —
6	LOOKING FOR A TIME OF 3.5 HOURS
7	VARIABLE IS THE SPEED ON THE TRIP TO
8	CURRENT TIME IS: 5

The resulting values when cell B3 is 30.

A faster speed than 30 must be used in cell B3 to reduce the travel time from 5 to 3.5 hours (cell C8). The student experiments with the value, and eventually comes up with 45.

	A	B	C
		TRIP TO	TRIP BACK
1			
2	TIME	2	1.5
3	SPEED	45	60
4	DISTANCE	90	90
5	— — — — — — — — — — — — — —
6	LOOKING FOR A TIME OF 3.5 HOURS
7	VARIABLE IS THE SPEED ON THE TRIP TO
8	CURRENT TIME IS: 3.5

The correct answer.

FIGURE 10-7

Financing A Car Worksheet
Enhanced Spreadsheets   Name _____

Goal   To enter, change, format or print date, and recalculate mathematical
                          relationship using a spreadsheet and to produce charts and graphs.

Specific Directions   Key in the spreadsheet with the information provided; then change
                          the figures as indicated and answer the following questions.

sticker price	$9,000
percentage of sales tax	8.25%
amount of sales tax	*formula*
cost of license plate	$68.80
cost of title	$12.50
loan fee	$100
credit report	$25
total (final) price of car	*formula*
interest rate of loan (percent)	12.25%
term of loan	60 months
percentage of down payment	15%
amount of down payment	*formula*
balance to be financed	*formula*
monthly car payment	*formula*

____ 1. Change the purchase price to $6,500. List the monthly car payment.

____ 2. Change the purchase price to $4,700. List the monthly car payment.

____ 3. Change the down payment percentage to 20 percent on $5,700. List the balance to
be financed.

____ 4. Change the down payment percentage rate to 30 percent on $5,700. List the amount
of the down payment.

____ 5. Change the down payment percentage to 25 percent of $5,700. List the monthly car
payment.

____ 6. Change the sales tax rate to 3 percent on $5,700. List the total cost of the loan
before down payment.

____ 7. Change the interest rate to 9 percent on $5,700 and the sales tax rate to 5 percent.
List the monthly car payment.

____ 8. Change the sales tax rate to 8.5 percent on $5,700 (9 percent interest rate). List the
total cost of the sales tax.

____ 9. Change the interest rate to 11.25 percent on $5,700 and the sales tax rate to 4 per-
cent (25 percent down payment). List the monthly car payment.

____ 10. Change the sales tax rate to 5 percent on $6,000, the loan fee to $120, and the down
payment percentage rate to 20 percent. List the monthly car payment.

Source: Reprinted with permission of *The Computing Teacher,* 22(3), 1995, International Society for Technology
in Education, Eugene, OR. Copyright © ISTE.

- Can we realistically expect math classes to have enough access to computers to make the spreadsheet approach workable? Students need a great deal of practice, hands-on at the computer, for this approach to be meaningful.

Personal Productivity

While spreadsheets are very useful in the curriculum, they also can be used as management tools for teachers. They simplify such tasks as preparing a budget for a field trip, keeping records of classroom lunch money, preparing classroom handouts or visuals, making estimates of expenses and income, balancing budgets, keeping inventories, managing sports or recreational activities, preparing a gradebook, constructing tables or charts, and organizing information for reports. (Turner & Land, 1988, p. 161)

Students are much more likely to respond to spreadsheet activities in the classroom if teachers can model and demonstrate the value of spreadsheets in their own lives. Think carefully about some aspect of your life in which your productivity could be enhanced by using a spreadsheet. Tax time? Use a spreadsheet to keep track of deductions and income. Household budget? Track your expenses, compare actual with projected income, estimate additional needed income, and so on. Fund-raising for a community or school project? Help plan what types of activities yield the greatest result, track expenses, and project how additional investment could yield greater results.

Activities

1. Think carefully about the strategies you use to teach mathematics, social studies, and science. Select one aspect of your teaching you would like to expand or concentrate on and describe how spreadsheets could support your success.
2. Design a spreadsheet activity (Figures 10-2 through 10-7 provide examples).
3. Videotape yourself teaching the lesson you planned. Watch the tape and list what went well and what you will do differently next time.
4. Visit a classroom where a teacher is using spreadsheets to assist with instruction in math, science, or social studies. How are the instructional strategies similar or different from the ones presented in the chapter? Summarize your observation.
5. Provide five examples of expanding your own productivity using spreadsheets.

References

Arad, O. (1987). The spreadsheet: Solving word problems. *The Computing Teacher, 14*(4), 13–15.

Brown, J. (1987a). Spreadsheets in the classroom. *The Computing Teacher, 14*(4), 8–12.

Brown, J. (1987b). Spreadsheets in the classroom, Part II. *The Computing Teacher, 14*(5), 9–12.

Johnson, J. (1987). Editorial reflections. *The Computing Teacher, 14*(4), 15, 45.

Luehrmann, A. (1986). Spreadsheets: More than just finance. *The Computing Teacher, 13*(7), 24–28.

Trawick, L. (1995). Four wheels on the information highway. *The Computing Teacher, 22*(3), 21–23.

Turner, S., & Land, M. (1988). *Tools for schools: Applications software for the classroom.* Belmont, CA: Wadsworth.

$$Chapter \quad 11$$

Telecommunications, the Internet, and the World Wide Web

"When I think about tomorrow and next year and five years from now, what excites me more than anything else is the idea of connectedness, no longer being isolated, making choices to participate in virtually anything" (Brightman, 1995). Telecommunications has ushered in an age of communication, a step beyond the Information Age (Thornburg, 1992).

Classrooms without walls are becoming a reality for many schools where computers are hooked up with modems and phone lines to provide access to peers in other places. Writing activities take on a new importance when one is communicating with people in different cultures and languages about topics in which one is vitally interested and that may contribute to world peace! Current research indicates that properly organized telecommunications activities "enable students to reflect on their own learning, use writing as a tool of both communication and thought, and to create social contexts that are not merely 'passive backgrounds' for learning but arenas for goal-oriented, reflective problem-solving" (Laboratory of Comparative Human Cognition, 1989). In this chapter, you will explore how telecommunications can open up new vistas of learning for your students and expand your own connections with colleagues near and far.

Objectives

By the end of this chapter, you will be able to do the following:

1. Define key telecommunications terms and vocabulary to get started on the Internet and the World Wide Web

2. Identify learning goals for your students that can be met through the use of telecommunications, access to the Internet and the World Wide Web

3. Select an information service, bulletin board, or discussion group to join

What Is Telecommunications?

Telecommunications is the act of communicating from one computer to another over telephone lines. An external or internal modem is used to enable the computer to send and receive signals through the telephone lines. Users can subscribe to commercial electronic networks, such as America On-Line, CompuServe, or Prodigy, and have access to electronic mail, bulletin board services, data bases, and a variety of other services. Universities and educational agencies also provide access to the Internet at little or no cost.

Electronic mail allows the user to send messages to another user's private "mailbox" within the host computer of the electronic network or information utility. Bulletin boards can be used to send and receive information from a wide audience, indexed by subject matter. Data bases allow the user to do research without having to go the library; for example, NEXIS offers full text searches of five major newspaper collections dating from 1977.

A computer with communications software to operate a modem that will link with a selected network or bulletin board enables a teacher to expand the horizons of a classroom and office. The Internet is growing at a rate of 10 percent per month and is expected to have 100,000,000 people on-line by 1998 (Ellsworth, 1994).

The Benefits of Using Telecommunications

Some of the benefits of telecommunications for students described by Tamashiro and Hoagland (1987), who worked with students on a "telecommunicated chain story," include the following:

- *Risk-free self-expression.* Since students are not known by the students with whom they are telecommunicating, they are more willing to take risks in expressing themselves freely.
- *Focus on content rather than personality/physical attributes.* Since communication is done "invisibly," users are free to interact as equals, without the factors that sometimes isolate students (e.g., wheelchairs, canes, sign language, race, appearance, etc.).
- *Cross-cultural respect and curiosity.* Telecommunications projects across national and state boundaries motivate students to learn more about geography, history, culture, and language beyond their own neighborhoods.
- *Self-worth.* Students know that telecommunications is a new field, with implications for new options in work environments, employment, and networking to stay informed. Students feel important when they receive electronic mail and have their work acknowledged by peers around the world. For persons with physical disabilities, the use of telecommunications for shopping, banking, research, and employment offers not just enjoyment but meaningful experiences and economic survival.

The magic of telecommunications is not just taking what students ordinarily do and sharing it with others; telecommunications adds empowerment through access to the entire world, and multisensory, multiple-intelligence activities—combining text, graphics, sound, video, animation. These activities transform students' experience of what schooling and learning are all about. Sauer (1994) describes the benefits of a telecommunications project with her seventh-grade students with learning disabilities, who wrote and videotaped a play in collaboration with a group of students in another town. "The greatest success for me was watching my students create a product of which a student in any class could be proud. Another area that pleased me was the level of interest that was maintained throughout the project. I saw in my students a level of awareness, pride, and interest that I had never seen before. They were willing to work longer, try harder, and share in the give and take necessary to create something with a group. I watched as many of my students worked with other students to develop friendships between their characters" (p. 9).

Students in two elementary schools in Michigan used telecommunications to learn about writing biographies by connecting with senior citizens (Simms & Simms, 1994). "The project was especially meaningful to the students because it gave them an audience for their writing. It gave them a reason for using correct punctuation and spelling. New-found vocabulary and historical information the seniors wrote about often intrigued the students. Academic subject areas were easily integrated into this project. Students spent time on language arts, history, math, geography, and science skills. Equally important were the relationships that developed. Students and their senior 'buddies' had a chance to meet at an end of the year party. This is one of the most valuable projects we have ever done. We have observed an increase in students' self-esteem, leadership, cooperative learning skills, and academic achievement. The integration of ages in a vertical fashion establishes an interaction between the ages that is especially valuable for students from single-parent families and families whose grandparents are living far away. It takes both students and adults beyond their microcosmic world" (p. 26).

Many classrooms are signing up for "on-line expeditions," in which they can "participate" in a bike trip across Africa, a dogsled crossing of the North Pole, or an archeological dig in Central America. One teacher notes, "Each of these trips that I have followed electronically have had certain goals. They teach the students about opportunities in this world. My students don't just live in Missouri, they live on earth, and they're going to share their lives with other cultures" (Smith, 1995).

Teachers cite the value of "authentic" learning experiences, connected to the real world, opportunities to integrate curriculum areas thematically by tackling real world issues, and the motivation of knowing an audience is always available for students to produce more and higher quality work as some of the important outcomes from using telecommunications and becoming knowledgeable about the resources available on the Internet and the World Wide Web.

Crucial to the success of global communication is not just access to telecommunications but rather the structure of activities that require student-to-student collaboration and a teacher-as-facilitator role. For example, in a San Diego classroom where students were jointly producing a newsletter with students in Alaska, writing articles was uninspiring and difficult for students, until the teacher created an "editorial board" of students that had to meet to review articles submitted by their Alaskan counterparts. Students were intrigued to read about seal hunting in Alaska but frustrated by the lack of detail provided in the articles. Likewise, students in Alaska were fascinated by surfing but wanted more than the skimpy reports submitted by the California students. Students on both sides began requesting additional computer time to edit and expand their contributions to the newspaper, and they eagerly suggested improvements for their fellow authors (Levin, Riel, Boruta, & Rowe, 1985).

In another California classroom, students telecommunicated with students in Mexico and discovered a newfound respect for students who could understand Spanish and who had an interest in increasing their skills in both Spanish and English. Students at the Florida School for the Deaf and Blind used writing process and cooperative learning activities on self-selected themes with pen pals in nearby schools, but, for the first time, no stigma of sign language, white canes, or wheelchairs got in the way of making friends (MacDonald, 1989).

The PALS project, which has been in operation for six years and includes over 400 schools in more than 15 countries, features opportunities for students to share questions, answers, research, and creative writing with a sister school across the world. Students work very hard on their writing because of their desire to be understood by their peers on the other end. Every stage of the writing process assumes a new importance. "Students work cooperatively, brainstorming ideas for a first draft, rewriting, and sending a final copy only after much discussion about the cultural connotations of the words chosen" (Erwin, 1989).

One of the advantages of telecommunications activities is that the interactions do not occur in "real time." That is, students receive messages and can work on them off-line, which gives them an opportunity to look up information, consult with a teammate or teacher, and think about and revise responses. Taking the time pressure away from communication allows students to convert their interactions into significant learning experiences.

Aside from students benefiting greatly from structured, cooperative telecommunications activities, teachers also value the electronic contacts, particularly teachers who are isolated. Teachers enjoy having a chance to interact with colleagues and share ideas about teaching strategies. The nature of the technology allows for more thoughtfulness than a conversation while passing in the hall or in a hurried lunch in the teachers' lounge.

What You Need to Get Started

You probably have almost everything you need to get started. Review the following items to make sure:

- *Computer*—recent models are easier to connect than older models, but virtually any computer will enable you to get connected. You will need to consider memory, and audio and video capabilities of your computer to enjoy all the resources available on-line.
- *Modem*—your computer may have a built in modem, or you can get an external (separate) modem, to allow your computer to communicate over the phone lines. Speed is important! Buy the fastest modem you can afford, because it will reduce the amount of time you or your students have to wait as files are downloaded. Modems at a baud rate (speed) of 28,800 are now available.
- *Software*—most productivity software such as ClarisWorks or Microsoft Works comes with a communication software module. Public domain and shareware programs such

as RipTerm for MS-DOS computers and Z-Term or Kermit for Macintosh computers are available from user groups and on-line bulletin boards. Some universities and educational agencies have formatted a software program for easy access to their systems. Commercial on-line service providers will give you the software you need to log on.

- *Telephone line*—these may be very rare in a school situation, although more classrooms are being wired for access every day. You will want to get a "splitter" (available from Radio Shack or other electronic supply houses) so that you can use either the modem or the telephone, without having to hook and unhook wires all the time. You will also want to disable "call waiting" and let others know you are going on-line; if someone picks up the phone, your connection will be interrupted.
- *On-line service*—you may wish to take advantage of a commercial on-line service provider's introductory offer of free time on-line to try out telecommunications before you commit to a particular provider. If you have access through a university or educational agency, you will want to find out procedures for logging on as well as telephone access numbers. Commercial providers (Prodigy, America On-Line, CompuServe) will give you the software you need and the telephone access numbers to log on.

If all this is new to you, use the following steps to orient yourself to telecommunications (Marsh, 1995):

Off-Line

- Open your on-line service software without connecting to the service (using the phone line).
- Explore the menu options and find the disconnect option.
- Compose, save, and address a message to send later when you go on-line (you'll need the e-mail address of a friend, or address one to me; my address is mmale@aol.com).
- Ask a friend to send you a message so that you'll have something to look for in your electronic mailbox).

On-Line

- Send the message you wrote off-line.
- Open any messages you received; save them to answer later (off-line).
- Explore the various areas of the on-line service; note a bulletin board on which you would like to post a message.

The Internet and the World Wide Web

"The Internet is a huge, amazing worldwide system of voluntarily interconnected networks with literally millions of documents, resources, data bases, and a variety of methods for communicating—it has become the best opportunity for improving education since the printing press started putting books in the hands of millions" (Ellsworth, 1994, p. xxii). The World Wide Web (WWW) provides a means of searching for information on the Internet. "The WWW consists of millions of linked files on thousands of computers around the world, accessed with browser software that works with the same kind of point-and-click mouse controls familiar to Windows and Macintosh users" (Hertzberg, 1995, p. 48). Sites on the WWW are called "pages" and are linked together by text that is underlined or in a different color than the regular text. These links are indexed by "Uniform Resource Locator" which provides the Internet address. By clicking on the highlighted text, the user navigates instantaneously from location to location. Some key terms helpful in understanding this process are included in Table 11-1.

The easiest way to connect with the WWW is via a commercial on-line service such as America On-Line, CompuServe, Prodigy, or Genie who offer access to the Internet and web browser software as a part of their service. Commercial Internet Service Providers (ISP) offer direct, high-speed data links to the Internet.

Instructional Activities

The following examples of teacher-initiated telecommunications projects (Dyrli, 1995) just begin to illustrate the potential power of telecommunications in a classroom. With a little bit of practice (and courage!) you and your students can design a web page describing your school or program and link it to web sites that your students like. (See Figure 11-1 for a list of student and teacher favorites and Figure 11-2 for an example of a student-designed Web page).

Online Wagon Train West
Students in schools near the historical Oregon Trail not only use MECC's Oregon Trail software to imagine what the trip might have been like; they also conduct local research and share with other students the supplies they are planning to take and profiles of the travelers

TABLE 11-1   Key Terms

Internet—a worldwide information storehouse accessible to the public

WWW–World Wide Web—a part of the Internet

page—how resources are "published" on the World Wide Web (a "page" on the Web is like a file in a word processor or a record in a data base)

URL–Uniform Record Locator—specifies the location of the WWW resource and what type of Internet application is necessary to access it

browser—software that helps the user navigate around the Internet

chat—real-time conversations among users on-line

gopher—software that helps the user connect to a computer that connects to other computers to gain access to specific resources

listserv—similar to a mailing list or bulletin board; allows the user to participate in world-wide discussions of a large number of topics by e-mail. The topic is usually described in the name of the list.

telnet—enables one computer to dial into another and gain access to its resources

HTML–Hypertext Markup Language—used for formatting WWW pages so that resources can be linked by "buttons"

FIGURE 11-1   Some Web Sites to Visit

Awesome Lists
http://www.clark.net/pub/journalism/awesome.html

Berit's Best Sites for Children
http://www.cochran.com/theosite/ksites.html

Canada's SchoolNet
http://schoolnet.carleton.ca/english/schlnet.html

KidLink
http://gnn.digital.com/gnn/wic/ed.35.html

Newton's Apple
http://ericir.syr.edu/newton/welcome.html

Tenet Web
http://www.tenet.edu.main.html

---

in the wagons. One school near Vancouver, Washington, researched what their town (then known as Columbia City) was like during the western immigration. For more information, contact jmeckel@services.dese.state.mo.us.

Electronic Postcards
Students use the Internet to share HyperCard stacks about themselves. Over 100 schools worldwide have joined this network. Students use word processors, paint programs, scanners, digitizing cameras, video cameras, and sound recorders to design their stack. An example of such a stack done by a class in Arlington, Virginia, is provided in Figure 11-3.

Literature and Science
Students in Catherine Ney's second-grade class in Blacksburg, Virginia, read classics such as The Three Little Pigs and Humpty Dumpty and do science experiments, sharing the results with students in other schools. In The Three Little Pigs, students design, construct, and test three houses for strength. In Humpty Dumpty, students wrap an egg in protective packaging and test its ability to fall from a specified height without breaking. Designs and results are shared with students in other locations. For more information, contact cney@pen.k12.va.us.

Memories of WWII
Ron Adam's seventh-grade students were researching WW II. He posted a message on the Generation to Generation area of SeniorNet on America On-Line inviting volunteers with WWII memories and experience to share to "adopt" his students. By the end of one week, seniors from 18 states had volunteered to participate, with memorabilia arriving by "snail mail" and sharing of photos and notes—electronic and handwritten! The students made

FIGURE 11-2 Student Web Page

transcripts of all the interviews and compiled a book over 500 pages long, bringing history to life for students in a very personal way, and resulting in friendships at both ends of the age spectrum. For more information, contact ronadams2@aol.com.

Victorian Lives and Letters

The Chatback Trust in the United Kingdom has provided computers, modems, and phone hookups for over 100 special education schools; the Trust also sponsors five telecommunications projects for students. In Victorian Lives and Letters, for example, Charles Dickens himself is available to answer questions about his life and work in Victorian London as a young reporter in court and in Parliament and as the writer familiar to so many. Sign up by contacting listserv@sjuvm.stjohns.edu and say subscribe boz your-first-name-your-last-name. Or contact Tom Holloway, tholloway@warwick.ac.uk, for information.

Finding Out about Mammals

Ann Sokoloff, second-grade teacher in Princeton, New Jersey, logs on to the Internet and looks for responses to her search she sent out about mammals on Kidsphere (Ferguson,

FIGURE 11-3   Getting to Know You

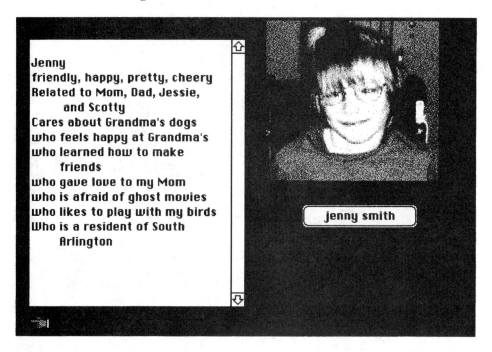

1995). By sending out searches on Kidsphere, Ann lets other teachers know what her students are learning and asks for responses from classes who would like to share information. A third/fourth-grade class has sent a letter describing all the mammals commonly found in Arkansas. As she is reading, two students eagerly search for Arkansas on the map of North America. Ann also has a weather project, in which students share weekly weather information with students from all over the world. In this way, she integrates computers, weather, geography, writing, and math.

Personal Productivity

Teachers, who have not had the benefit of a telephone in their classroom, will find that telecommunications can save hours of time. Sending files electronically not only saves paper but communicates more rapidly. Getting access to information on policies, legislation, litigation, and resources is essential to today's special educator. As the examples above illustrate, no teacher needs to be in a position of trying to teach something without resources. Using a newsgroup or listserv to get advice, suggestions, lesson plans, and so on, means that every teacher has access to a world of ideas and support! For special educators, NCIP-Net (no cost to users) and SpecialNet (subscription fees and monthly charges) offer discussion groups, on-line conferences, and electronic mail to a specialized audience. Learning to use an on-line service provider and getting in the habit of checking electronic mail takes some time; at first, the available information may seem overwhelming. Having access to such an abundance of immediate information is empowering—if you have time to do something with it!

Activities

1. Think carefully about the ways in which telecommunications activities fit in with the curriculum you teach. Select one aspect of your teaching you would like to expand or concentrate on and describe how telecommunications could support your success.
2. Design a telecommunications activity based on some of the activities described in this chapter.
3. Visit a classroom where a teacher is using telecommunications to link students with their counterparts in another part of the country or world. How are the activities similar or different from the ones presented in the chapter? Summarize your observation.
4. Log on to an information network such as America On-Line, CompuServe, or Prodigy. Browse through several bulletin boards and print out three items of interest or concern to you. Summarize the actual or potential benefits to you of subscribing to such a service.

References

Anderson, M. (1995). Personal communication.

Brightman, A. (1995). Imagine the future: It's about concepts, not things! *Exceptional Parent, 25(11),* 41.

Dyrli, O. (1995). Teacher-initiated telecommunications projects. *Technology & Learning, 15(7),* 20–26.

Ellsworth, J. (1994). *Education on the Internet.* Indianapolis, IN: Sams Publishing Co.

Erwin, J. (1989). PALS across the world: Writing for inter-cultural understanding. *The Writing Notebook,* April/May, 3–4.

Ferguson, M. (1995). Second grade students cruise the information superhighway. *TECH-NJ,* 1, 14–15.

Hertzberg, L. (1995). Every educator's WWW. *Electronic Learning, 15(2),* 48–49.

Laboratory of Comparative Human Cognition (1989). Kids and computers: A positive vision of the future. *Harvard Educational Review, 59(1),* 73–86.

Levin, J., Riel, M., Boruta, M., and Rowe, R. (1985). Muktuk meets Jacuzzi: Electronic networks and elementary schools. In S. Freedman (Ed.) *The acquisition of written language* (pp. 160–171). New York: Ablex.

MacDonald, B. (1989). A telecommunications writing project for students who are hearing impaired. *The Writing Notebook,* April/May, 5–6.

Marsh, M. (1995). *Everything you need to know (but were afraid to ask kids) about the information highway.* Palo Alto: Computer Learning Foundation.

Sauer, E. (1994). Creative collaboration online. *The Computing Teacher,* 21(7), 38–40.

Simms, J., and Simms, B. (1994, April) The electronic generation connection. *The Computing Teacher, 21(7),* 9–10.

Smith, M. (1995). The new "trekkie": Students travel from the Arctic to Brazil over wire. *Electronic Learning, 14(5),* 26–30.

Thornburg, D. (1992). Edutrends 2010. San Carlos, CA: Starsong Publications

Tomashiro, R., and Hoagland, C. (1987). Telecomputing a chain story. *The Computing Teacher, 14(7),* 37–39.

Chapter 12

Multiple Intelligences and
Technology: Multimedia
and Hypermedia

Imagine a classroom where technology tools provide the means for reaching every learning style—where students traditionally unsuccessful with linguistically-based paper and pencil activities have a chance to demonstrate their knowledge and understanding through graphics, sound, and video! Howard Gardner's dream of a classroom in which the school's traditional value of linguistic and logical/mathematical intelligences can be expanded to include interpersonal, intrapersonal, visual/spatial, kinesthetic, and musical. Technology can serve as a catalyst to change the roles of teachers and learners so that everyone has an environment to "mess around" with learning, and everyone has a chance to demonstrate their skills. Multimedia and hypermedia options provide a nonlinear means to learn, using sounds, images, and text (Thakkar, 1990). In addition to graphics, text, and sounds, real-life events with narration can be accessed. In this chapter, you will explore the implications of this new and evolving technology for the variety of learners within your classrooms and for your own teaching and learning style.

Objectives

By the end of this chapter, you will be able to do the following:

1. Define multimedia and hypermedia and describe elements of each
2. Identify issues, benefits, and concerns associated with the use of multimedia/hypermedia approaches to instruction
3. Select multimedia/hypermedia equipment and software appropriate for your teaching situation

4. Explore a HyperStudio stack and identify its components
5. Teach a lesson using HyperStudio with your students
6. Describe ways to expand your own productivity using multimedia/hypermedia

What Are Multimedia and Hypermedia?

"Understanding multimedia as a tool for learning requires more than simply knowing about the latest technical developments. Multimedia introduces into a classroom whole new ways of thinking about curriculum, interactions with students, even the nature of learning itself" (Mageau, 1994). Technically, students using a CD-ROM or laserdisks could be considered to be using "multimedia" (p. 28). The power of multimedia and hypermedia comes with the changes in the ways learners have access to and demonstrate their understanding of knowledge—moving from a single dominant presentation and demonstration style (verbal/linguistic, linear/sequential), to an integrated, multisensory learning and demonstration "microworld" (Papert, 1992), where learners have more freedom of choice—in the mode of learning and the order in which learning takes place. For the purpose of this chapter, *multimedia* are the options for expanding beyond text in the presentation of information; *hypermedia* are the software tools for integrating multimedia into a nonlinear, multisensory environment for teaching and learning.

Hypermedia are software applications that operate at two levels: (1) a system that lets the user build applications, similar to authoring but much easier to use; and (2) a system that lets the user employ applications developed by others, but in a much more open-ended way than traditional menu-driven, linear computer-assisted instructional packages to which most people are accustomed. Fortunately, it is much easier to experience HyperCard than to explain it.

The following example provides a glimpse at the possibilities:

Jay taps his foot impatiently while the Macintosh boots up; he's spending his recess time checking the resource library for ideas for his next project. The computer screen comes up and Jay peruses the image of a book shelf whose book titles correspond to the subject matter areas in his school curriculum. Deftly, he slides the "mouse" pointer over the book spine titled "Science" and "clicks" once. The computer screen dissolves to a menu of science topics. Jay's interest is piqued by the "Earthquakes" choice. Ever since the 6.1 temblor during school last October he's been intrigued by the inability of geologists to predict earthquakes. He clicks on the word "earthquakes" and finds himself looking at a world map with fault lines drawn on it and a row of buttons directly underneath. The buttons have names like videodisc, literature, history, local experts. He clicks on the western edge of North America and the screen changes to show a closer view of just that area. He moves to one area where a long line seems to bisect the territory. He clicks on the line; the name San Andreas pops up and the screen displays a closer view of that area, with other minor fault lines now visible. "Great," he thinks, "but are there any images I can use?" He moves the pointer over the small picture of a monitor, labeled "videodisc," at the bottom of the screen. He clicks on the picture

and initiates a video playback of a National Geographic video all about that par-
ticular earthquake zone. "Okay," Jay thinks, "that's good." He interrupts the vid-
eo and clicks on another button, a picture of a book labeled "literature."

    The software brings up a listing of related works of fiction, non-fiction, and
biography. He knows by clicking on a particular title he could view brief previews
and annotations written by students about the various book titles, but recess time
is waning. He's already beginning to formulate the project in his mind. "One last
thing," he thinks. He moves to the "local experts" button and clicks.

    The screen poses a question to him "area of expertise?" and Jay types in cam-
corder. The screen displays a list of several students in the school who have listed
themselves as camcorder experts willing to assist others. "Rad" Jay whispers to
himself, "Dan can be my film editor! I'm outta here." (Polin & Lindon, 1988, p. 40)

Although this classroom vignette may seem ideal, the issue of hypermedia warrants
closer examination. With all of the excitement about multimedia, some people are asking if
simply adding more media will enhance learning (The Cognition and Technology Group at
Vanderbilt (CTGV), 1991).

Rationale for Using Multimedia and Hypermedia in a Classroom

The environments in which multimedia and hypermedia are used are characterized by the
following (Handler, Dana, & Moore, 1995):

- Students learn by doing, as active creators and constructors of knowledge.
- Students learn to analyze and solve problems and communicate clearly through differ-
  ent means and in collaboration with others, rather than in isolation.
- Students transform and use prior knowledge.
- Students learn in a highly supportive environment, with changed roles for teachers and
  peers.

Powerful new technologies offer us the choice of embellishing the existing curriculum
or breaking the mold, or perhaps doing both. Given the demands for teachers to respond to
a variety of different learning needs in the same learning environment, curricular embellish-
ment, as illustrated in the preceding vignette, offers immediate benefits. Imagine a heterogeneous classroom equipped with books that talk, define vocabulary, and illustrate. Discis
books, for example, offer readers the following options (CTGV, 1991):

- The whole book can be read aloud (text is highlighted as the reading progresses).
- Any word or phrase can be pronounced as requested.
- Key vocabulary words can be defined as needed.
- Texts, sentences, or words can be translated into some other language.

Hypermedia can also provide extensive visual support for comprehension. Careful
choice of visual illustrations will help students construct mental models of what they are
reading or hearing (CTGV, 1991).

Another way in which hypermedia can promote effective learning is by promoting organization of knowledge. This book, for example, is organized in a linear, sequential way, with chapter titles, headings, and subheadings. If the book were presented in a hypermedia format, readers could access text, graphics, and video clips of classrooms to fit their computer expertise level, classroom situation, or topical interest.

An area of crucial need for most teachers is to provide the appropriate scaffolding to support students in successfully reaching toward the next learning goal. With hypermedia, this scaffolding is always available and under user control. Although some educators worry that continuously available support could supplant students' development of their own schemas and mental models, others feel that continuous support is far preferable to little or no support at all, which may be the case in most large and vastly diverse classrooms.

In addition to, or perhaps instead of, improving current teaching, hypermedia offer ways for teachers to break out of traditional modes. Students in classrooms with hypermedia have the opportunity to explore environments and generate issues and questions to be researched further; produce knowledge rather than merely receive it passively; and teach others rather than always waiting to be taught by someone else. To attain such goals, however, educators must cease traditional practices of (1) using fact-filled texts and emphasis on drill and rote memory; (2) employing decontextualized basic skill and concept exercises as prerequisites to hands-on relevant activities; (3) presenting technical definitions and formulas in ways that do not connect with intuition, experience, or reality for many students; and (4) treating students as passive recipients of knowledge, rarely getting the opportunity to choose projects, work with others, or contribute to classmates' learning (CTGV, 1991).

Components of Multimedia

CD-ROM: Compact-disc read only memory is a 4¾-inch laserdisc capable of holding 250,000 pages of text, 15,000 high-resolution pictures of 15 hours of high fidelity sound, or any combination of the three. It is an ideal medium for the electronic publication of large data bases and catalogs, and it can reduce search time by hours to those accustomed to leafing through print indexes or periodicals (Mendrinos, 1990). Computer software may be written for and shipped with the CD-ROM product; therefore, it is important to match the specific CD-ROM, computer, and player before making purchases, since all must be compatible to get the desired result. Software on CD-ROM is becoming more prevalent, moving away from the 3½-inch disk format.

Double-sided CD-ROMs are currently in production, which will create the need for players able to read both sides. Speed of players is also a consideration for purchase; quad-speed players are the state of the art at the moment.

CD-ROM storybooks provide scaffolding and support for emerging readers and students from other languages. In addition to superb graphics and lifelike narrative voices, such storybooks also offer a range of language choices and let students record and playback their own readings of a story (Parham, 1995). Table 12-1 contains a sampling of CD-ROM storybooks which teachers may find appropriate for some students.

TABLE 12-1 CD-ROM Storybooks

Program	I Learn Library	Interactive Storybooks	Living Books	Wiggleworks
Publisher	Sanctuary Woods 1825 S. Grant St. #410 San Mateo, CA 94402 (415) 286-6110	Harper/Collins Interactive Order Department 1000 Keystone Industrial Pk. Scranton, PA 18512-4621 (800) 424-6234	Broderbund PO Box 6125 Novato, CA 94948-6125 (800) 521-6253	Scholastic 2931 East McCarty Jefferson City, MO (800) 325-6149
Platform(s) and Unusual System Requirements	• **Macintosh** with CD-ROM drive • **Multimedia PC** (A microphone is recommended)	• **Macintosh** with CD-ROM drive • **Multimedia PC** (Single titles are also available on floppy)	Dual platform CD-ROM for: • **Macintosh** (4 Mb) • **Multimedia PC**	• **Macintosh** with CD-ROM drive (individual titles are available on floppy)
Price	School price: $59.95, including printed copy of book. Lab packs and site licenses are available.	Retail price: $39.95 including printed copy of book.	School price: $79.95 per title, including teacher's guide and printed copy of book. Lab packs and networkable versions available.	School price: $1,750 including 6 CD-ROM (with 4 titles each). 1 cassette version and 6 printed copies of each book, teacher's guide and class-room books. Lab packs and site licenses available.
Grade Level	K–2	Pre-K–2	K–3	K–2
Options	• Read-, sing-, write-, and listen-along modes • Spanish, French, and English language options • Voice recording for singing and reading • Users can hear theme song played by any of eight instruments	• Read-aloud and sing-aloud modes (with songs that can be played separately) • Read-aloud instructions • Playful animated hotspots (including animated subplots) • Page-finding feature	• Read- and play-along modes • English and Spanish language options • Play animated hotspots	• Read- and write-along modes • Authentic-sounding narrations with accents and an array of voices with your-own text composition • Coloring book and your-own text composition • Voice recording feature • Pre-reading story introductions
School-Oriented Special Features	• Vocabulary words are pronounced and animated. • Noun-search feature • Comprehension questions	Several pages of thoughtful suggestions and extension activities for adults in user's guide.	• Whole language and other early skill reinforcement built into hotspots • Well-chosen literature will promote classroom discussion	• Excellent online class management system • Printed activity cards and overview material • Well-chosen literature to promote classroom discussion • Word list feature • Vocabulary pronunciation • Alphabet board

Encyclopedias on CD-ROM are another useful learning tool. Students can search for information systematically and then cut and paste information and graphics into their reports. Table 12-2 provides a sample of CD-ROM reference programs.

Laserdiscs: Laserdisc players equipped with bar-code readers and linked to computers allow lessons to be created that access specific frames from the videodisc to create interactive multimedia lessons with still or motion video. Table 12-3 provides a listing of some laserdisc offerings currently popular with teachers and parents (Shields, 1994; Porter, 1991).

Digital Cameras/Photo CD's: Photo CDs are cameras which store photographs directly on a disk for easy pasting into hypermedia projects. Students on field trips, for example, can use a photo CD camera to take pictures of events, activities, animals, plants, and so on, to incorporate into their projects. Approximately 30 pictures can be stored on each disk. Both Kodak and Canon make these cameras, which currently cost approximately $600.

QuickCam: QuickCam is a small, ball-shaped, inexpensive ($100) video camera which can be used to take movies of students. The field of vision is quite small, but it provides a low-cost option to include movies in student projects easily.

QuickTime (Macintosh) and PhotoMotion (IBM) movies: QuickTime movies, video clips that are transferred to computer disk, can be made by an interface that allows a video camera to be plugged directly into a computer. Students can use videotapes that they prepare themselves, or other videotapes that illustrate the theme or project they are working on.

Scanners: Scanners are similar to photocopiers. They put an image of whatever you are scanning onto your computer screen. You can then edit the image and save it on your computer. Photographs, text, or graphics can be scanned using either a flat-bed scanner or handheld scanner with appropriate software.

TABLE 12-2   Sample of CD-ROM Reference Programs

Title	Category	Publisher
Compton's Multimedia Encyclopeida	Encyclopedia	Encyclopedia Britannica Educational Corporation
Information Finder	Encyclopedia	World Book, Inc.
Library of the Future	Literature	World Library, Inc.
Magazine Article Summaries (MAS)	Periodical Index	EBSCO, Inc.
Mammals, a Multimedia Encyclopedia	Reference	National Geographic Society
New Grolier Electronic Encyclopedia, The	Encyclopedia	Grolier's Electronic Publishing
Newsbank	Newspaper Index	Newsbank, Inc.
Newsbank Index to Periodicals	Periodical Index	Newsbank, Inc.
Reader's Guide Abstracts	Periodical Index	H. W. Wilson Company
Reader's Guide to Periodical Literature	Periodical Index	H. W. Wilson Company
TOM	Periodical Index	Information Access Company
UMI Resource/One	Periodical Index	University Microfilms, Inc.

Source: From "1991 CD-ROM Evaluation Project Completed" (pp. 19–20) by A. Lathrop. Reprinted with permission from *CUE Newsletter,* May/June 1992.

TABLE 12-3   **Sample of Laserdisc Titles**

Title	Producer
Science Sleuths	Videodiscovery
History in Motion	Scholastic
Solar System	National Geographic
Eyes on the Prize	PBS
Jurassic Park	LucasFilms
Animal Pathfinders	Scholastic
Race to Save the Planet	Scholastic

Using Hypermedia to Create a New Type of Learning Environment

Hypermedia, such as HyperCard, HyperStudio, or LinkWay, is made up of five kinds of objects: cards, fields, buttons, backgrounds, and stacks. A *card* is a single-screen display, like an index card. Text or graphics can be displayed on the card, or a card can enable the user to enter text into a text *field. Buttons* connect one card to another; like a button on a machine, HyperCard buttons can make something happen. Buttons can take the user from one card to another, cause certain sections of a videodisc to play, or locate a specific piece of information or visual image from a CD-ROM player. *Background* cards are like clear overlays on which buttons, fields, or graphics are shared by cards in a *stack* (a collection of cards).

HyperCard has five user levels that can be set by the stack user or designer. The levels are browse, type, paint, author, and script. In the *browse* level (used by Jay in the classroom vignette presented earlier in this chapter), the user can flip through cards and stacks, looking for information. In the *type* level, the user can enter or edit text in a field. The *paint* level enables the user to use the painting tools to create graphics to use on the cards. The *author* level lets the user add, move, or delete buttons and fields. The *script* level contains the specific directions to the computer to perform certain functions, such as dialing a phone, turning on a specific frame of a videodisc, producing a sound effect or saying words aloud, and so on. By copying scripts of buttons from stacks created by others, teachers or students can create powerful applications without learning HyperTalk, the programming language that scripts use (Phillipo, 1989; Goodman, 1987).

Figure 12-1 is an example created by Trish, a fifth-grader. The *cards* are a *stack.* On Card 1, there are six *buttons;* clicking in any of those buttons takes Trish to another card in the stack. In Card 2, she copied the place setting from a clip-art file and pasted it on her card. In Card 6, she used the paint tools to draw a picture of herself. In Card 3, at the *type* level of HyperCard, Trish could add to the text in the field; at the *browse* level, she could simply read the information and move on to new choices.

Four potential classroom uses for hypermedia/multimedia include the following (Wilson, 1991):

FIGURE 12-1   Sample Stack

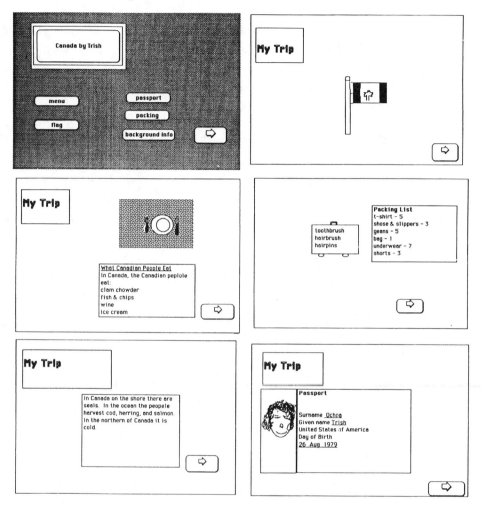

Source: Reprinted with permission of the author, Mary Anderson.

1. Teacher presentations, using a large screen monitor or projection device
2. Student exploration, inquiry, hypothesis testing, and research
3. Student authoring or producing multimedia reports or HyperEssays (Rogers, 1994)
4. Teacher-made materials

Several videodisc producers are publishing stackware with their laserdiscs. A card is created for each frame or movie sequence on the laserdisc. HyperCard searches through the cards for user-defined terms and easily organizes and views the slides and sequences chosen (Phillipo, 1989). Laserdiscs such as the Video Almanac of the 20th Century are wonderful resources (Rogers, 1994) for both teachers and students.

TABLE 12-4 Comparison of Multimedia Programs

Program Titles	List Price	Run Time Version	Import Graphics	Import Text	Spell Check Available	Sound	Create Animation	Color Capability	Access Video Discs	Access VCR Clips	Sample Files Included	Hardware Required
HyperScreen Scholastic, Inc. 2931 E. McCarty St. Jefferson City, MO 65101 1-800-541-5513	$89.95	No	Yes. Additional graphics available from Scholastic Public Domain DOS 3.3 Print Shop Graphics	No	No	Yes. W/ program & additional sound available through the publisher	No	Yes	Yes	No	Yes. Sample files & a short tutorial are included.	Apple IIe Apple IIGS MS-DOS w/ 256 graphics card
HyperStudio (Apple IIGS) Roger Wagner Publishing 1050 Pioneer Way, Suite P El Cajon, CA 92020 1-800-497-3778	$125.00	No	Yes	Yes. Text files from word processors.	Check before import.	Yes. Within program or using a microphone.	Yes	Yes	Yes	No	Yes. Sample files & a tutorial are included.	Apple IIGS At least 1MB RAM. At least 1 3.5-in. drive. Is GS/OS compatible & can be networked.
HyperStudio (Macintosh) Roger Wagner Publishing 1050 Pioneer Way, Suite P El Cajon, CA 92020 1-800-497-3778	$125.00	Yes	Yes. Any PICT, TIFF, EPSN, or MacPaint, clip art from other sources.	Yes. Text files from word processors.	Check before import.	Yes. Within program or using a microphone.	Yes	Yes	Yes	Yes. Can access Quick-time clips.	Yes. Sample files & tutorial included.	Macintosh w/ at least 2MB RAM using System 6.0. At least 4MB RAM using System 7.
HyperCard (Macintosh) Apple Computer Co. 20525 Mariani Ave. Cupertino, CA 95014 1-800-776-2333	$99.00	No	Yes	Yes. Text files from word processors.	Check before import. In HyperCard can check using Hyper-Spell by Heiser.	Yes. Imported or create using a microphone.	Yes	In ver 2.2. In 2.1 thru HyperColor from Heiser.	Use Videodisc Toolkit from Apple or VideoStack from Voyager.	W/Voyager VideoStack.	Intellimation has many stacks available to use as samples or purchase Education Home Card from Intellimation.	Macintosh using System 6.01 or higher.

Program Titles	List Price	Run Time Version	Import Graphics	Import Text	Spell Check Available	Sound	Create Animation	Color Capability	Access Video Discs	Access VCR Clips	Sample Files Included	Hardware Required
Digital Chisel (Macintosh) Pierian Spring Software 5200 SW Macadam Ave. Suite 250 Portland, OR 97201 1-503-222-2044 FAX 1-502-222-0771	Educator Price—$119.00 Site license—$995.00	No	Yes. Libraries on an included CD-ROM & others available from Pierian. Photo-CD access.	Yes	Check before import.	Yes. Import or add your own. Many included.	Yes	Yes	Yes	Yes	A tutorial is included as well as a demo.	Macintosh System 6.01 or higher. 6-8 mgs RAM to use Quick-Time.
Multimedia ScrapBook (Windows on IBM PC or a compatible PC w/Windows) Alchemedia, Inc. P.O. Box 1061 La Conner, WA 98257 1-206-466-5946	$200.00 Site license—$1,600	One time license is $400.00 to make unlimited copies.	Yes. Additional graphics from any source, PCX, or use a scanner.	Yes. Copy & paste.	Check before import.	Yes. W/program, additional sound through the publisher AV Form on Windows machine. CMI machines need sound.	No	Yes	Yes & CD-ROM discs. Photo CD.	Yes	No. Great help files.	Minimum requirements compatible w/ Windows 3.1.
Linkway Live (MS-DOS) IBM. EduQuest 1000 NW 51st St. Boca Ratan, FL 33429-1234 1-408-372-8100	$130.00	Yes	Yes. Any PCX, PCM, PCV, PCI, PCZ graphic can be brought in.	Yes.	Check before import.	Yes	Yes	Yes	Yes	Yes	A tutorial included, no sample files.	Mouse must be properly installed. EGA IBM-486 Windows version available.
SuperLink (Windows) Alchemedia, Inc. P.O. Box 1061 La Conner, WA 98257 1-206-466-5946	$400.00 Site license—$2,000	Yes	Yes. Any PCX, BMP, DIB, GIF, JPEG, FIF, PCM, PCV, PCJ, or PCZ graphic can be brought in as well as photo-CDs.	Yes. Use any font installed on the computer. Cut & paste.	Check before import.	Yes	Yes. Any media w/ Windows CMI driver can be directly controlled.	Yes. Displays up to 24-bit true color mode.	Yes & CD-ROM discs, photo CDs.	Yes	No sample files. LinkWay Live folders can be brought in.	Minimum requirements compatible w/Windows 3.1 minimum 386 & 4MB memory.

Source: Teacher Ideas Press, P.O. Box 6633, Englewood, CO 80155-6633.

Selecting Software

A variety of hypermedia software is available for both Macintosh and IBM-compatible machines. Depending on your budget, your own sophistication with technology, and the needs of your students, an option is available to meet your needs. Table 12-4 presents a comparison of hypermedia programs.

Instructional Activities

Hypermedia learning projects can start when students are very young. In one preschool class, for example, the teacher used HyperStudio to create a talking class picture album. The teacher, Tony LaTess, in Washington Township, New Jersey, took each child's picture with a digital camera. Each child's voice was recorded, giving his or her name and some significant fact. When a child clicked on a button (or touched the picture, using a touch-screen), the child's voice with the introduction was heard (Powell, 1991).

Mary Anderson's class in Arlington, Virginia, also uses a talking class picture book made with HyperStudio. She takes the students' pictures. They must write a summary of significant facts about themselves and record an introduction. When the user clicks the button with the student's name, the introduction is presented. A sample card from this stack is presented in Figure 12-2.

She also used HyperStudio in a project to link the study of Virginia history through music. The music teacher, fourth-grade classroom teachers, resource teacher, and students

FIGURE 12-2   Student Introduction Stack, Arlington, Virginia

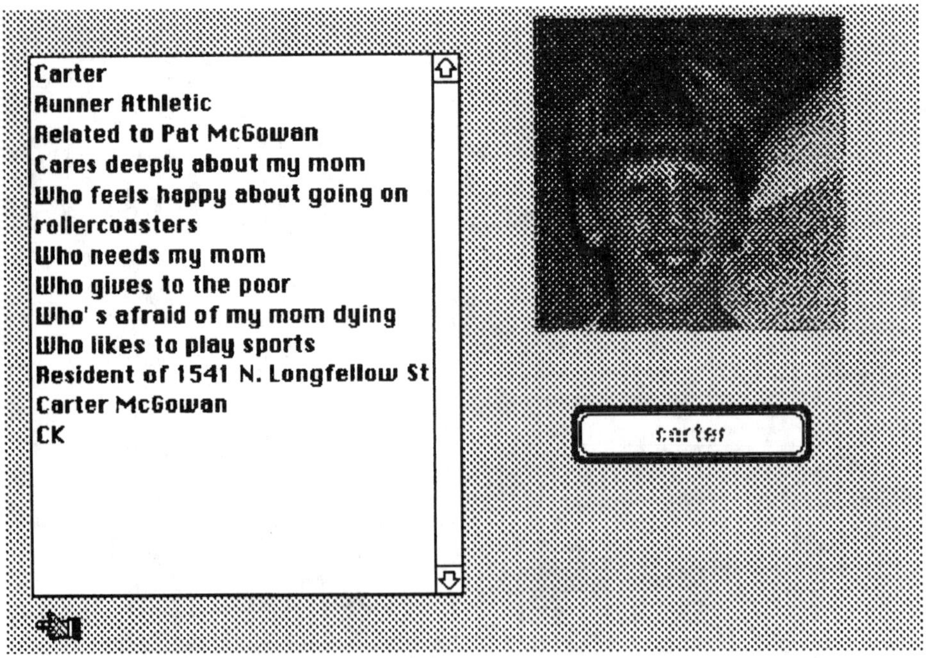

Carter
Runner Athletic
Related to Pat McGowan
Cares deeply about my mom
Who feels happy about going on
rollercoasters
Who needs my mom
Who gives to the poor
Who's afraid of my mom dying
Who likes to play sports
Resident of 1541 N. Longfellow St
Carter McGowan
CK

carter

created a stack that included folk songs, recorded with a Midi keyboard hooked up with the computer, that told about early Virginia inhabitants. Students also created and recorded raps that told about Virginia's life and people. By clicking on a button, the user could select a particular song or learn about some aspect of the project. Figure 12-3 shows the title screen for this stack.

Susan Roscigno and Linda Shearin (1995) used LinkWay with their first graders to study animals. Information was organized into five categories/folders: movement, homes, eating, body coverings, and fantastic facts. Students brainstormed the animals to be researched, coming to a consensus on a variety of animals to illustrate particular characteristics. Using fiction and nonfiction books, art experiences, observations, videos, and laserdiscs, students compared animals. They designed their own animals, describing where the animals lived, what and how they ate, how they moved, and what type of body covering they had. The teachers designed the folders so that they were linked by graphical menus and buttons, making it easy for students to navigate. As they did their research, they used magazines, CD-ROM encyclopedias, digital cameras, and other tools to collect their ideas and information. They used LinkWay Paint skills to create illustrations and clips from a laserdisc and Windows on Science to illustrate examples and characteristics. After their research was complete, parents were invited to view the finished project. The format for this project led into another LinkWay adventure on Weather.

One use of hypermedia is as a scaffold to assist students with reading and writing tasks. Student Assistant for Learning from Text, for example, is a hypermedia template teachers can use to provide support for students who are struggling to compensate for reading difficulties in high-school content area classes (MacArthur & Haynes, 1995). The software added speech synthesis, an on-line glossary, links between questions and text, highlighting of main ideas, and supplementary explanations that summarized important ideas. Students received significantly higher comprehension scores using the software than a software that simply reproduced the elements of the text. Mark Rogers, a resource specialist in Califor-

FIGURE 12-3　Virginia History Title Screen

nia, designed HyperEssays as a template for students to use in producing multimedia research papers. Figure 12-4 illustrates the structure provided for students to use as they did their research (Rogers, 1994).

At Baker Demonstration School, National-Louis University in Evanston, Illinois, seventh graders worked on a Hypermedia Zoo project. Using HyperCard, students and teachers collaborated to establish rubrics for evaluating stacks. Both a teacher- and peer-evaluation process was implemented; two students volunteered to have their stacks reviewed in front of the whole class to provide an example of the collaborative review/evaluation process. Evaluation questions used in the process are included in Figure 12–5 (DiPinto & Turner, 1995).

Students were also asked to do a self-evaluation and reflective summary of what they learned about the subject as well as what they learned about design by constructing a stack. These issues are particularly important as the use of multimedia/hypermedia grows: Is a multimedia report merely more attractive and interesting, or do students really experience enhanced or transformed knowledge in some way (Skillen, 1995)?

FIGURE 12-4   HyperEssay Diagram

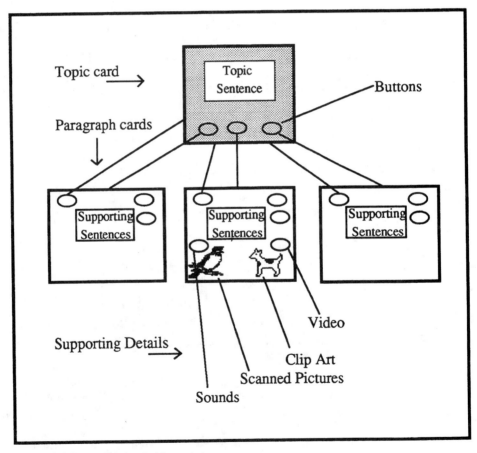

Source: Mark Rogers. Reprinted with permission.

FIGURE 12-5   Review Questions for Stack Evaluation

Content Review

Is the information accurate?

Have you proofread the text for misspellings and grammatical errors?

Have you read it for a general sense of clarity and intended meaning?

Are all the required components included?

Is there additional information beyond the required components?

Are the sources of information cited?

Design Review

Are the links appropriate and do they work?

Are there different paths for navigating through the stack?

How would the user know what to do here?

What is the purpose of this button?

Do the button icons convey meaning?

Do the special effects add interest or distract?

What were you thinking when you created this?

Activities

1. If you have not used hypermedia before, select one of the programs described in this chapter and complete the tutorial. Design a stack that introduces yourself.
2. Select a stack created by someone else and modify it to fit a curriculum, student, or personal need.
3. Select a topic and design a stack. Use the review questions and processes in this chapter to evaluate your stack with a colleague.
4. Design a project for students in your program to make a stack. Include a student stack along with your lesson plans.
5. Visit a classroom where a teacher is using hypermedia. Summarize your observation. How does this environment differ from traditional instructional settings? How do students use hypermedia differently than traditional instruction?

References

The Cognition and Technology Group at Vanderbilt (CGTV) (1991). Integrated media: Toward a theoretical framework for utilizing their potential. Proceedings of the Multimedia Technology Seminar, Washington, DC

DiPinto, V., and Turner, S. (1995). Zapping the hypermedia zoo—Assessing students' hypermedia projects. *The Computing Teacher, 22(7),* 8–11.

Goodman, D. (1987). The two faces of HyperCard. *MacWorld,* October, 104–106.

Handler, M., Dana, A., and Moore, J. (1995). *Hypermedia as a student tool: A guide for teachers.* Englewood, CO: Teacher Ideas Press.

Lathrop, A. (May/June,1992). CD-ROM evaluation project completed. *CUE Newsletter,* 19–20.

MacArthur, C., and Haynes, J. (1995). Student Assistant for Learning from Text (SALT): A hypermedia reading aid. *Journal of Learning Disabilities, 28(3),* 150–159.

Mageau, T. (1994). The (in)sane person's guide to multimedia in education. *Electronic Learning, 14(3),* 28–40.

Mendrinos, R. (1990). CD-ROM: A technology that is steadily entering school libraries and classrooms. *Electronic Learning, 9(4),* 34–36.

Papert, S. (1992). *The learning machine.* New York: Basic Books.

Parham, C. (March, 1995). CD-ROM storybooks revisited. *Technology & Learning,* 14–18.

Phillipo, J. (1989). Videodisc technology and HyperCard. *Electronic Learning, 8(5),* 40–41.

Polin, L., and Lindon, M. (1988). What's hyper about HyperCard? In T. Cannings and S. Brown (Eds.) *Update to the information age classroom: Using the computer as a tool.* Wilsonville, OR: Franklin, Beedle & Associates.

Porter, B. (1991). Are you ready for interactive videodisc? *The Writing Notebook, 8(4),* 38–39.

Powell, R. (1991). Hypermedia creates excitement in a preschool classroom. *TECH-NJ, 4(1)* 1, 12.

Rogers, M. (1994). *HyperEssays: Teacher's guide to creating multimedia compositions with HyperCard.* Santa Cruz: Educational AppleCations.

Roscigno, S., and Shearin, L. (1995). Animals! Animals! Animals! *The Computing Teacher, 22(7),* 27–29.

Shields, J. (1994). Getting the big picture on videodiscs. *Technology & Learning, 15(2),* 48–50.

Skillen, P. (1995). ThinkingLand—Helping students construct knowledge with multimedia. *The Computing Teacher, 22(7),* 12–13.

Thakkar, U. (1990). Using hypermedia in special education. *BMUG Newsletter,* Summer/Fall, 192–197.

Wilson, K. (1991). Bank Street College of Education. Proceedings of the Multimedia Technology Seminar, Washington, DC, 51–57.

Chapter 13

Providing Access

By the time you have reached this chapter, you have an increasingly clear sense of the variety of ways your students can benefit from technology. In this chapter, our focus turns to the issue of making sure that your students have access to the technology: what support is available from legislation to make sure technology is included in IEP's, for example; resources to fund technology the IEP team deems appropriate; and the types of adaptive and assistive devices that may be necessary in order for students to interact with computers.

Objectives

When you complete this chapter, you will be able to do the following:

1. List provisions of federal legislation which support providing access to appropriate technology for your students
2. Identify sources of funding for technology for your students
3. Determine what assistive devices may be appropriate for your students

Legislation

Federal legislation has continued to address the issue of access to technology for students with disabilities. Beginning with PL 94-142, assistive technology can be provided as a related service. PL 99-457 specifies that "technology should relate to any need the child and family have related to learning and/or development, including the need to learn basic self-help skills, to have appropriate adaptive equipment, to develop appropriate social interaction skills, and to receive therapy services" (Armstrong & Jones, 1994).

In 1991, PL 94-142 was amended by PL 101-476, the Individuals with Disabilities Education Act. This legislation defined assistive technology as "any item, piece of equipment, or product system, whether acquired commercially off the shelf, modified, or customized, that is used to increase, maintain, or improve functional capabilities of children with disabilities" [20 USC, Chapter 33, Section 1402(25)]. An assistive technology service is defined as "any service that directly assists an individual with a disability in the selection, acquisition, or use of an assistive technology device." The services include:

A. *The evaluation of the needs of an individual with a disability, including a functional evaluation of the individual in the individual's customary environment*
B. *Purchasing, leasing, or otherwise providing for the acquisition of assistive technology devices by individuals with disabilities*
C. *Selecting, designing, fitting, customizing, adapting, applying, maintaining, repairing, or replacing of assistive technology devices*
D. *Coordinating and using other therapies, interventions, or services with assistive technology devices, such as those associated with existing education and rehabilitation plans and programs*
E. *Training or technical assistance for an individual with disabilities, or where appropriate, the family of an individual with disabilities*
F. *Training or technical assistance for professionals (including individuals providing education and rehabilitation services), employers, or other individuals who provide services to, employ, or are otherwise substantially involved in the major life functions of individuals with disabilities [20 USC, Chapter 33, Section 1401(26)].*

In 1990, policy statements from the federal Office of Special Education Programs (Schrag, 1990) specified that public agencies were not permitted to "presumptively deny assistive technology" before a determination was made as to whether such technology was an element of a free, appropriate public education for that child. Therefore, if an IEP team determined that assistive technology was an appropriate part of a child's program, the technology must be provided by the school district at no cost to the parents.

Section 504 of the Rehabilitation Act of 1973 provides rights and protections for students with disabilities who do not qualify for special education. In 1992, this act was amended so that the philosophy of service delivery was based on a presumption of employability. All state vocational rehabilitation agencies are required to provide a broad range of technology services on a statewide basis, and the technology needs of every client must be addressed in the Individualized Written Rehabilitation Plan (IWRP). The IWRP must contain a "statement of the specific rehabilitation technology services to be provided to assist in the implementation of intermediate rehabilitation objectives and long-term rehabilitation goals" (Alliance for Technology Access, 1994).

The Technology-Related Assistance for Individuals with Disabilities Act (Tech Act—PL 100-407) of 1988 provides funding for states to develop consumer-driven systems of access to assistive technology services, assistive technology, and information. Under the provisions of this act, assistive technology not only includes access to computers, but also to any tool or item that increases, maintains, or improves functional capabilities of individuals with disabilities. Amendments to this act in 1994 provided additional support for system-change activities and to increase outreach and advocacy for under-represented and rural populations.

Funding

While the question of policy and philosophy with regard to assistive device/technology funding seems clear, the reality of funding from the federal government can be daunting and discouraging for both families and professionals alike (Pressman, 1987). For very young children, Part H of PL 99-457, described earlier, is intended to be payer of last resort. However, funding can be obtained through the Early Periodic Screening, Diagnostic, and Treatment services available through Medicaid. Treatments can include the provision of assistive devices and related services for any physical or mental problem identified during the screening and assessment process if such treatment is coverable under federal Medicaid law, even if the treatment is not contained in the state's Medicaid plan (Fox & Yoshpe, 1987; Parette, Hofmann, & VanBiervliet, 1994).

Funding under IDEA and the Tech Act is available for use in supplying technology-related needs, but it is limited, and may require substantial energy expenditure and advocacy to receive it, particularly in school districts unaccustomed to such requests. Parette, Hofmann, and VanBiervliet (1994) suggest five steps for parents and professionals to follow for successful funding of assistive technology. The first step is to obtain a technology evaluation. Some states have established centers where such evaluations are available. The Alliance for Technology Access Center nearest you can provide information on options for assessment.

The second step is to make informed decisions based on the assessment about what are the most feasible sources of funding. The educational planning team should identify a funding advocate familiar with sources of funding and skillful in assisting with parents in justifying the need for the device and fulfilling requirements of the funding agency.

The third step is to document needs and decisions to make it easy for the funding agency to agree to the request. The documentation might include a physician's prescription, the results of the evaluation, and supportive correspondence from professionals involved in the case.

Fourth, different agencies respond to different terminology and wording. Medicaid, for example, funds medical and health-related technology, not educational technology. Using words like "medical necessity" and "restore the patient to his or her best functional level" are important to such funders. A list of suggested do's and don'ts for applications to Medicaid and private insurance are included in Figure 13-1.

Finally, be prepared for an application for funding to be rejected. But don't give up; plan to submit an appeal to one or more levels. Even if the application is not funded, such appeals serve as a means of providing information about new technology to agency personnel, which may ease the way for other applicants to follow.

Identifying Special Needs for Access

The most important thing for a classroom teacher to know about computer adaptations and adaptive devices is that there is a wide variety of solutions for every type of computer and that highly trained specialists in technology as well as in specific needs are available to provide evaluation and suggestions. Many schools and school districts have formed technology teams in which speech/language therapists, occupational therapists, special education

FIGURE 13-1 **Do's and Don'ts in Preparing Documentation**

Do's

When working with young children who have physical disabilities, professionals should demonstrate that these are medical problems and state how the use of the technology would have a therapeutic effect on the child by reducing emotional and psychological frustrations. From this perspective, it can be shown that the acquisition of certain technologies, e.g., a speech prosthesis, involves the issue of medical care.

Remember that many technologies can be motivational factors to increase the child's ability to interact with others. With such increased functional use of the device, there can be a perceptive lessening of the release of anger and emotional frustration.

Remember that cost is **always** a factor. Include in the application a brief description of all the devices for which the child has been evaluated. Include the benefits and drawbacks of each device, price, and why the device was chosen. This will address the possibility of denial due to a cost factor.

Don'ts

Do not assume that because Medicaid or the insurance companies approved a device in your state, that all following applications will be approved. There is no such thing as "precedent setting."

Do not label the device that the young child needs as educational technology, because Medicaid or the insurance companies will not cover the technology for that reason.

If the device is a communication tool or aid, never describe it as such, because they will say that it is not essential to improve the child's **medical condition** as required by law.

Never give the impression that the device is a convenience item. The examining officer will tell you that other alternatives are available at much less cost.

Note. Adapted from Hofmann, A. C. (1989) There is funding out there! In A. VanBiervliet and P. Parette (Eds.), *Proceedings of the First South Central Technology Access Conference* (pp. 7–8). Little Rock: University of Arizona at Little Rock. Reprinted with permission.

Source: Parette, Hofmann, & VanBiervliet, *Teaching Exceptional Children,* 26(3), Sp 94, p. 24.

teachers, computer specialists, and parents work together. The team facilitates the use of technology for inclusion and with maximum cognitive and social development, and it is an essential support system for a classroom teacher in an exceptional classroom.

> *The first time the UAAACT [Utah Augmentative, Alternative, and Assistive Device Communication Technology] Team saw Trisha, she was ten years old. She was multihandicapped and had very poor verbal skills. She was highly unintelligible and spoke with an inappropriately soft voice. She was only able to communicate in situations where she and the listener had a common frame of reference.*
>
> *The UAAACT Team created an overlay for the Unicorn Board in an attempt to facilitate Trisha's ability to communicate information about school to her parents. We used Mayer Johnson Symbols to represent Trisha's daily activities, chores, and feelings. We used Dr. Peet's Talking Word Processor so she could print a letter for her parents every day. She is also visually impaired, so the large print was essential.*

The effects of this simple measure were startling. Trisha began to experience successful communication for the first time in her life. The first sign was her possessiveness toward the computer. The team borrowed her system one day for a UAAACT conference. When we returned it, Trisha ran up and kissed the monitor. She became adamant about writing her letter every day. She also began to speak with appropriate loudness and her intelligibility doubled. It was as if she could finally see the benefit in communication! Now every day, we see added communication skills with Trisha. Her social interaction with staff and peers has increased dramatically. It is gratifying to see the effectiveness of technology. (Pease, 1990)

Success stories like Trisha's provide motivation for even the most timid technology user to identify appropriate resources for access to a computer. Teachers and students in inclusive classrooms have an opportunity to see firsthand the power of technology. Dave Schmitt suggests looking at adaptations from a hierarchical viewpoint. That is, students should use the standard computer to the maximum degree possible and make modifications only to the degree appropriate for a particular situation. For example, a team should try modifying the standard keyboard before using an expanded or alternative keyboard. Morris (1989) calls this approach "least restrictive accommodation."

Schools struggle with questions about when an assistive technology evaluation is required and how to determine what assistive devices and services are really needed for a learner to benefit from a free, appropriate public education. Bowser and Reed (1995) have developed a process and set of questions to guide teams in making appropriate decisions. The questions are presented in Figure 13-2.

In addition, the team should consider the implications of the technology for the family. "Principles of family-driven technology" can be used to guide teams in decision-making and service delivery (Richards, 1995):

- Outcomes of using technology should be clearly understood by the family and should reflect needs and concerns identified by the family.
- Whenever possible, families should be able to borrow and try, or at least view, before a purchase is made (assess for appropriateness; child, space, use, and maintenance issues; comfort level).
- Technology should enhance the existing strengths and resources of the child and family (not be intrusive to the family; be used in natural environments).
- The family should be assisted in disposing of technology when it is no longer in use for their child.
- Appropriate supports should be available to the family to effectively use technology (training, funding).

Modifications to the Standard Keyboard

If a student can use a standard keyboard but it is a slow and difficult process, then modifying the keyboard is the first step. Schmitt (1990) lists 10 ways to modify the standard keyboard:

- Positioning (using a detached keyboard)
- Headstick, mouthstick, utility cuff, or other pointer

FIGURE 13-2   Technology Evaluation Questions

Tech Point #1 • Initial Referral Question

1. Could this student use assistive technology to improve, remediate or compensate for deficits in educational performance.

2. Are there assistive technology options which should be tried before referral?

Tech Point #2 • Evaluation Questions

1. Can the student be accurately evaluated with standard assessment procedures?

2. Does the use of assistive technology as an accommodation during testing enhance the student's performance?

3. What types of assistive technology solutions would enhance the student's educational performance?

4. Are the services of a specialist needed?

5. Is an extended assessment needed?

Tech Point #3 • Extended Assessment Questions

1. Does the type of technology we are assessing actually do what we thought it would do for the child?

2. Which of the technology solutions tried is the most effective?

Tech Point #4 • Plan Development Questions

1. Is the assistive technology that is being considered needed for the child to meet one or more goals on the IEP?

2. Are assistive technology services needed to enable the child to use the device?

3. Was specific assistive technology identified in the IEP?

4. Has periodic review been included in the IEP to identify unanticipated problems with assistive technology and review them?

Tech Point #5 • Implementation Questions

1. What actions need to be taken to assure that the assistive technology identified by the IEP team is used effectively?

2. Who is responsible for each of these actions?

3. Who is responsible for monitoring each aspect of the implementation of assistive technology goals and objectives?

Tech Point #6 • Periodic Review Questions

1. Are the assistive technology devices and/or services that were provided being utilized?

2. Are the assistive technology devices and/or services functioning as expected?

3. Have long range plans (including transitions) for the student's assistive technology use been made?

Source: Bowser & Reed, JSET, XII, 4, Sp 95.

- Moisture guard
- Stickers to mark keys
- Removal of auto-repeat features
- Making the shift, control, and other keys locking
- Keyboard delay
- Rearranged keyboard
- Keyguard
- Speed enhaneement (word prediction, abbreviations)

Adding Alternative Keyboards

If modifying the standard keyboard is not a substantial enough improvement, adding an alternative keyboard is the next step. Alternative keyboards provide options in size, layout, and complexity for individual student needs.

Some examples of alternative keyboards include:

- *Muppet Learning Keys:* a nontransparent keyboard with letters, colors, numbers, and function keys designed to be appealing to young children
- *TouchWindow:* attaches to the computer monitor with Velcro and allows the student to use a finger or pointer to select choices or draw on the screen
- *PowerPad:* a touch-sensitive keyboard with overlays and specific software
- *IntelliKeys:* a transparent, touch-sensitive keyboard that can be customized with a variety of keyboard layouts

IntelliKeys provides a flexible tool for which teachers or parents can easily design communication boards, learning activities, or virtually anything! Overlay Maker software makes the process of programming keys of different sizes, shapes, and colors easy. IntelliPics software provides an environment for authoring learning activities. IntelliPaint is a graphics tool, from which "coloring books" or other graphic design projects can be built. IntelliTalk is a talking word processor, in which students can use their overlays to create and read talking stories. Click-it enables the user to create "hot spots" on the screen using commercially available software, which can then be accessed by scanning routines. Teacher-designed overlays for IntelliKeys are found in Chapters 8 (Figure 8-6) and 10 (Figure 10-3).

Adaptations for Limited Range of Motion

Schmitt (1990) suggests six alternative adaptations for persons with limited range of motion:

- Mouse, trackball, or mousestick
- Joystick
- Joystick coding
- Optical pointing
- EyeTyper or Eyegaze system
- Speech recognition

FIGURE 13-3 Overview of Commonly Used Switches

OVERVIEW OF COMMONLY USED SWITCHES

NAME	EXAMPLE	ACTIVATION	COMMENTS	VENDORS
Flat Switch		Small low force movement of arms, hands, legs, head, etc.	o flat size allows placement under many objects	Don Johnston TASH
Leaf Switch	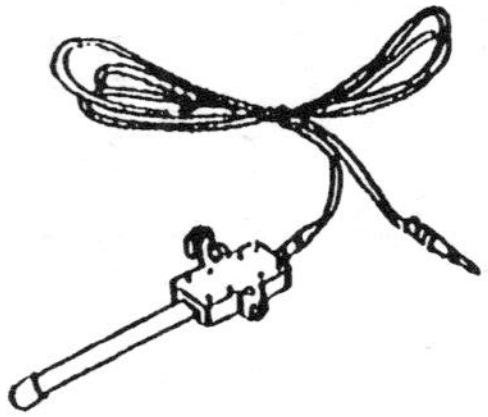	Flexible switch that is activated when bent or pressed gently	o requires mounting o can improve head control, and fine motor skills	Don Johnston Kanor TASH
Mercury (Tilt) Switch	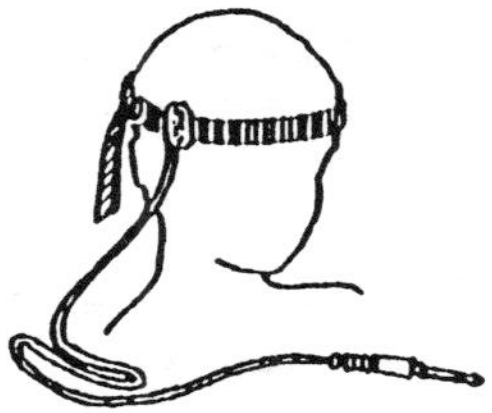	Gravity sensitive switch activates when tilted beyond a certain point	o can improve head or other posture control o attaches easily with velcro strap	HCTS Kanor TASH

OVERVIEW OF COMMONLY USED SWITCHES

NAME	EXAMPLE	ACTIVATION	COMMENTS	VENDORS
Plate Switch		Downward pressure on plate by hand, foot, arm, leg or other reliable movement	o most common o can be covered with different textures o some offer music, light or vibration	Don Johnston Kanor TASH
Sip 'n Puff		Sipping or puffing on tubing	o requires good head and mouth closure o can improve breath control o amount of air pressure adjustable	Kanor TASH
Switch 100 "Big Red"		Light touch anywhere on its top surface	o recommended for young children o click provides auditory feedback o diameter 5"	Ablenet

Continued

FIGURE 13-3 *Continued*

OVERVIEW OF COMMONLY USED SWITCH INTERFACES

NAME	EXAMPLE	ACTION IT MODIFIES	COMMENTS	VENDORS
Battery Device Adaptor		Allows a battery operated device to be activated by switch	o non-permanent o can be used with most on/off toys, radios and tape recorders	Ablenet Don Johnston Kanor
Computer Switch Interface		Allows single switch access to an Apple computer	o accepts 1 or 2 switches o substitutes switches for joysticks	Ablenet Don Johnston TASH
Control Unit		Enables electrical devices to be activated by a switch	o allows children to participate with peers o used with continuous closure or on/off o timer can be set 2 to 90 seconds	Ablenet Don Johnston TASH

OVERVIEW OF COMMONLY USED SWITCHES

NAME	EXAMPLE	ACTIVATION	COMMENTS	VENDORS
Voice Activated		Significant vocalizations (1 to 2 seconds)	o can improve vocalizations o has sound sensitivity control	Kanor

Adapted for use from the Technology/Learning/Collaboration Project
Grant #H024C800228"

Switches

With the appropriate switch and an interface such as Ke:nx, any software program can be accessed. Switches are recommended only when no other modifications have been successful.

Examples of switches include the ABLENET Switch, a 5-inch red circle that makes an audible click when it is pushed; a lever switch, activated by pushing on a lever; a P-Switch, a small button-sized switch activated by even a very small muscle movement; and a tread switch, activated by pushing down on a top plate, which makes it easy to operate with a hand or foot. A list of switch manufacturers is included in Table 13-1. Figure 13-3 illustrates types of switches available.

Speech Output

For students with visual impairments, learning disabilities, language delays, or linguistic differences such that auditory input may make learning tasks more accessible, speech output offers important options. Speech can be either *digitized* human-sounding speech (translation of an actual human voice into data stored on a disk) or *synthesized* robotic-sounding speech.

Meyers illustrates the power of this tool:

When Ryan started working with me, I assumed that he could participate in the normal processes of learning to read and write, if he was given access to writing on a computer with speech output. Since he had minor visual processing problems, the software I used with him "talked" the letters, words, and sentences he was writing in synthesized speech output. He wrote on a standard computer keyboard covered with a clear plastic keyguard. He could put his whole hand on the keyguard and reach his fingers through holes over the keys to type letters. After his first session with me, he took the software program home to use on the computer his parents had bought for him. The next morning, he spontaneously wrote, "Hi mom" and "I love you, Dad." His mother suggested that he write about something unusual that was happening that day, for instance, that he was going to have a

TABLE 13-1   Switches Equipment Manufacturers

Ablenet, Inc. 1081 Tenth Ave. SE Minneapolis, MN 55414–1312	NHATEC PO Box 370 Laconia, NH 03247	TASH 70 Gibson Dr. Unit #12 Markham, Ontario, Canada L3R 4C2
Creative Switch Industries PO Box 5256 Des Moines, IA 50306	Pointer Systems, Inc. 1 Mill St. Burlington, VT 05401	Toys for Special Children 385 Warburton Ave. Hastings-on-Hudson, NY 10706
Don Johnston Developmental Equipment, Inc. PO Box 639 Wauconda, IL 60084	Prentke Romich Co. 1022 Heyl Rd. Wooster, OH 44691	Zygo Industries, Inc. PO Box 1008 Portland, OR 97207

spelling test. Ryan quickly wrote "I HAVE SP" and then completed the sentence "EECH": "I HAVE SPEECH." He was telling his mother that he knew the power that the computer learning tool was giving him. (1990, p. 5)

Enlarged or Braille Text

Students with visual impairments may benefit from either hardware adaptations, such as closed-circuit television, or display processors to enlarge print seen on a screen. Software, such as CloseView, included in the system software, offers large-print capability.

The computer can also print text in braille with the help of a special printer and/or special software. An adaptive device for people who are deaf and blind provides a tactile display of "refreshable" braille, formed by vibrating points that change under the fingertips as the text goes by.

Voice Recognition

Voice recognition, which is still in its early and expensive stages of development, offers a means for people with physical disabilities to operate a computer. Using this device, a student speaks into a microphone a series of words and phrases. Once the process is complete, the computer can execute oral commands. Dragon Dictate is an example of such software.

Alternative/Augmentative Communication

Students whose physical limitations prevent them from using pencil and paper or keyboards, or whose cognitive limitations prevent them from constructing written language, may benefit from alternative/augmentative communication systems. A computer equipped with a speech synthesizer can type text and produce speech heard by everyone. Devices can be programmed with words and phrases for particular situations. Specialists help determine which system is appropriate for a particular student and then train teachers and students alike in the best ways to incorporate the system into classroom life. A list of augmentative communication devices and manufacturers is included in Table 13-2.

Activities

1. Describe your school or school district's policies and procedures related to assistive technology. What policies or procedures could be improved? What policies or procedures are you proud of?
2. What process does your school or school district use to assist parents in getting funding for assistive technology? How could this process be improved to provide greater support for students and their families?
3. Select five assistive technology devices (e.g., switches, keyboards) with which you are not familiar but to which you have access. Try out the device or observe a student using the device. Summarize the benefits of the device and situations in which this device would be appropriate.
4. Make a data base of assistive devices available in your school or district. Include a description of the device, the source of funding, the producer, the location/current user of the device, and situations in which the device might be appropriate. Expand the data base to include assistive devices you feel should be available to students in your school or district.

TABLE 13-2 Augmentative Communication Devices and Manufacturers

Device	Manufacturer
ACS Eval PAC with Real Voice	Adaptive Communication University of Washington Department of Speech and Hearing Science, JG–15 Seattle, WA 98195
Systems ACS Samy	Adaptive Communication
ACS Scan PAC with Real Voice	Adaptive Communication
AIPS Wolf	ADAMLAB 33500 Van Born Rd. Wayne, MI 48184
AudioScan	Detroit Institute for Children 5447 Woodward Ave. Detroit, MI 48202
Dial Scan	Don Johnson Developmental Equipment 1000 N. Rand Bldg. 115 Wauconda, IL 60084
Digital Augmentative Communication Systems	Adaptive Communication
Dyna Vox	Sentient Systems Technology 5001 Baum Blvd. Pittsburgh, PA 15213
Expanded Keyboards for Learning Aids	EKEG Electronics Co. Ltd. PO Box 46199, Station G Vancouver, BC V6R 4G5 Canada
EyeTyper	Sentient Systems Technology
Handy Speech Communication Aid	Consultants for Communication Technology 508 Bellevue Terr. Pittsburgh, PA 15202
Info Touch 20 and 40	Enabling Technologies Co. 3102 SE Jay St. Stuart, FL 34997
Intro Talker	Prentke Romich Co. 1022 Heyl Rd. Wooster, OH 44691
Liberator	Prentke Romich Co.
Light Talker	Prentke Romich Co.
Lightwriter	Zygo Industries, Inc. PO Box 1008 Portland, OR 97207
Mega Wolf	ADAMLAB
Parrot	Zygo Industries, Inc.

Continued

TABLE 13-2 *Continued*

Device	Manufacturer
Peacekeyper	Tiger Communication System 155 E. Broad St. #325 Rochester, NY 14604
Polycom/Polytalk	Zygo Industries, Inc.
Portable Transaction Voice Computer	Voice Connection 17835 Skypark Cir., Suite C Irvine, CA 92714
QED Scribe	Zygo Industries, Inc.
RDS Speech and Learning Center System	Royal Data Systems Route 14, Box 230 Morganton, NC 28655
Real Voice Systems	Adaptive Communication
Real Voice with Small Membrane Keyboard	Adaptive Communication
Say It All Plus	Innocomp 33195 Wagon Wheel Dr. Solon, OH 44139
Say It Simply Plus	Innocomp
Scan Writer	Sygo Industries, Inc.
SmoothTalker Speech Update for Light and Touch Talker	Prentke Romich Co.
Speakqualizer	American Printing House for the Blind PO Box 6085 Louisville, KY 40206
Speller Teller Communicator	Speller Teller Communications 3234 S. Villa Cir. West Allis, WI 53227
Steeper Communication Teaching Aid	Zygo Industries, Inc.
Switchboard	Zygo Industries, Inc.
Talk-O	Innocomp
Touch Talker	Prentke Romich Co.

References

Alliance for Technology Access (1994). *Computer resources for people with disabilities.* Alameda: Hunter House.

Armstrong, J., and Jones, K. (1994). Assistive technology and young children: Getting off to a great start! *Closing the Gap, 13(3),* 1, 31–32.

Bowser, G., and Reed, P. (1995). Education TECH points for assistive technology planning. *Journal of Special Education Technology, XII(4),* 325–338.

Fox, H., and Yoshpe, R. (1987). *Medicaid financing for early intervention services.* Washington, DC: Fox Health Policy Consultants.

Lewis, R. (1993). *Special education technology: Classroom applications.* Belmont: Wadsworth Publishing Company.

Meyers, L. (1990). The language machine: Using computers to help children construct reality and language. A presentation at Conosenze Come Educazione, San Martino di Castrozza, Italy.

Morris, K. (1989). Alternative computer access methods for young handicapped children. *Closing the Gap 7(6),* 1.

Parette, H., Hofmann, A., and VanBiervliet, A. (1994). The professional's role in obtaining funding for assistive technology for infants and toddlers with disabilities. *Teaching Exceptional Children, 26(3),* 22–28.

Pease, S. (1990). Skiing dinosaurs success story. *UAACT Newsletter, II,* 2.

Pressman, H. (1987). Funding technology devices: Ways through the maze. *Exceptional Parent,* 48–53.

Richards, D. (1995). Assistive technology: Birth to Five Years. A Presentation at ConnSense, Cromwell, CT.

Schrag, J. (1990). *OSEP Policy Letter.* Washington, DC, U.S. Office of Education.

Schmitt, D. (1990). *Hierarchy of access.* Lakewood, CO: Colorado Easter Seal Society.

Chapter *14*

Selection of Hardware, Software, and Training Activities

Some readers might wonder why the section on hardware and software selection comes so close to the end of the book rather than at the beginning. The emphasis in this book is on finding useful things that technology can do to change lives rather than on the technology itself. The previous chapters have provided examples and ideas which will make it easier to decide what type of computer in what type of setting will work best for you and your students. In this chapter, some of the basic questions and issues to consider in selecting hardware, software, and training activities are presented.

Objectives

By the end of this chapter, you will be able to do the following:

1. Identify how students and educators will have access to technology in your school
2. Identify the strengths and limitations of different technology configurations (e.g., computer labs versus individual classroom stations)
3. Review considerations in selecting hardware, software, and peripherals

School Access Options

Depending on the philosophy of the school, the degree of interest in implementing technology among its teachers, the leadership of the principal, the perceived needs of the students, and the resources available, school systems have opted for one or more of the following approaches:

1. *Integrated learning systems.* Students use specific computer-assisted instruction software that is usually diagnostic/prescriptive. (The students take a placement test, are placed in a set of activities, and progress through a sequence of activities based on their performance.)

2. *Computer lab.* Typically, a computer lab contains enough computers for a whole class (or half a class) to work individually. The lab may be staffed by a computer resource teacher with or without the classroom teacher of the students who are scheduled to work in the lab. The computers may be networked for printing and/or shared software.

3. *The classroom with one or a few computers.* The computers may be on mobile carts so that teachers can borrow computers from each other for lessons when they would like to have all students at the computer but cannot schedule time in the computer lab.

4. *A few computers.* A learning center or library could house a few computers where students may be sent to do individual projects or assignments.

Each of these models has strengths and limitations, which are reviewed here.

Integrated Learning Systems

An integrated learning system (ILS) is a network of computers that run broad-based curriculum software and a management system that tracks student progress. Some of the reasons school districts purchase such systems include the following:

- Student instruction may be individualized.
- Computer lessons may be integrated with major basal textbooks.
- Test scores of low-achieving students can be improved.

Because of the expense of purchasing such comprehensive systems, their use has been limited primarily to Chapter I schools, which limits access to such programs to specially identified Chapter I students. According to Reilly (cited in Mageau, 1990), features to look for in an integrated learning system include the following:

- Lessons are prescribed based on student performance.
- The management system diagnoses performance while the student is on-line, branching students automatically to more challenging skills or, for students who are not performing adequately, noting the prerequisite skills and moving students to appropriate activities, not just to the next lower level.
- On-line help is given.
- Options for teacher control are available, so that classroom lessons can easily be linked to computer lessons.
- Reports generate customized useful information about specific skills rather than just percentages of correct answers on a particular level.

Unfortunately, none of the systems currently available has all of these features, so school districts have to compare features and judge the tradeoffs. Equally difficult, most of the research on the effectiveness of such systems suffers from one or more of the following problems: the studies were commissioned by the ILS companies themselves; unfavorable results are not typically released; the experimental designs are weak, using no control groups or featuring children in primary grade levels where development could be as responsible for test score increases as the ILS; and important variables such as teacher involvement, time on task, and frequency of exposure are not isolated, thus the source of gains is difficult to pinpoint (Kelman, 1990).

South Bay Union Schools (California), which have demographics common to many schools (68 percent of the students are minority; 25 percent of the students speak little or no English; and 57 percent of the students live below the poverty line, with families with an annual per capita income of $6,500), deal with the limitations of ILSs by adopting an *open architecture* system with the following components:

- An IBM Writing to Read lab is in every school for kindergarten and first-grade students.
- Three IBM PS/2 Model 25 computers are in every second- to sixth-grade classroom on a distributed network, hooked up to a Model 80 file server, with a printer. The file server carries Wasatch Education Systems language arts, as well as math and science courseware, but also runs WordPerfect, Microsoft Works, Children's Writing and Publishing Center, and electronic mail.
- A workstation on every principal's desk is linked to every teacher and student in the school.
- No Chapter I, IBM, or Wasatch funds or model programs were used; all monies came from state or district funds. All decisions are made by a district technology committee, composed of teachers, with a principal as advisor and the assistant superintendent as chair (Mageau, 1990).

In spite of the enthusiasm expressed by South Bay educators for their programs, a number of concerns about the huge growth of ILSs across the country, where expenses now equal the total of all other computer and software purchases, are being expressed.

1. Integrated learning systems tend to diminish interaction between people; in many ILS installations, students work at a remote lab on lessons that may or may not be connected with ongoing classroom instruction.

2. Integrated learning systems promote the use of computers to control students rather than being controlled by them. Most ILSs rely on drill and practice for low-level reading and arithmetic skills.

3. Integrated learning systems tend to promote bureaucratic convenience over educational value.

4. Integrated learning systems tend to flourish in districts where top-down decision making is imposed, with little teacher involvement, even though these efforts are likely to fail in the long run (Kelman, 1990).

The Writing to Read program, and its extensions Writing to Write Form I and Stories and More, is a form of an ILS targeted specifically to primary grades. It incorporates a structured set of reading and writing activities at a cost of $20,000 to $24,000 per lab. In spite of rave reviews seen in the popular press, careful research does not document the powerful effects the program claims (Slavin, 1990). According to Slavin, "The most optimistic reading of the research would suggest that Writing to Read is an expensive means of moderately improving the reading achievement of kindergarten children, with no known long-term effects. A less optimistic reading would question even the kindergarten effects" (p. 216). The students in the studies Slavin reviewed were being compared to students who were receiving no instruction in writing and reading. Riedl states,

> *It is only when we link skilled use of the computer with skilled teaching and good curriculum that we can expect real benefit. When we do put that combination together we will be providing the best learning environment for our students. We can be better teachers with the computer. But, regardless of the claims by hardware and software vendors, the computer cannot do it by itself. It still takes good teachers and good curriculum. (1991, p. 5)*

The Computer Lab

Most schools today have a room equipped with enough computers for a classroom-size group to work. However, many schools dilute whatever positive results might come from contact with the computer in their efforts to provide egalitarian access to all students. Because of teacher reluctance to implement technology, many schools have opted to develop a computer resource specialist to be responsible for computer learning. A different approach is recommended, however—one that takes into account the differing needs of students and their teachers and recognizes the computer as only a tool rather than a solution to the problem of increasing student achievement and motivation.

Three key principles will increase the effective use of computer labs:

1. Labs should be targeted to the teachers who are most interested in and capable of using them, who are dedicated to a specific group of students or subject areas (Pogrow, 1988).
2. The teacher should plan, design, and implement the computer lessons. If a school wishes to have a computer specialist to assist the teacher or to team teach, so much the better.
3. The schedule should accommodate the different needs of students for various activities. Students need intensive, extended time at the computer for some activities (producing a draft of an essay or story) and continuity for others (20 minutes a day for four or a five days a week for math drill and practice to develop fluency and speed on skills introduced and practiced under teacher guidance in the classroom).

The computer lab is the ideal place for students to complete drafts of a composition, edit earlier work, and print final copies. However, most computer labs are not set up for small groups to share their work, or even for teachers to conduct discussions with the whole class about discoveries, challenges, or strategies that are working or not working. It is sometimes difficult to make sure that computers in the lab have exactly the right adaptive equipment a student may need. In some schools, the computer lab is run by a computer specialist, who may or may not be involved in integrating computer activities into classroom curriculum. In other words, the advantages of having one computer for each student may be outweighed by the disadvantages. Do not assume that the computer lab is the ideal place for a computer lesson. If you do need the lab to complete a lesson, think about ways your class can fit into the way the computer lab operates (or work to change the way the lab is set up or has been operated in the past)!

The One-Computer Classroom

By using a large television monitor or a projection plate or overhead projector combination and appropriate software, the one-computer classroom can offer a teacher several possibilities:

1. Present a demonstration or a simulated experiment for the whole class to watch, think about, and respond to in groups or individually.
2. Present a problem for which there are many possible answers or means to the solution, which the students can solve alone or in a group.
3. Provide a means for the whole class to work together on a writing project, including the editing and printing of copies to be distributed to each student.

Some companies, such as Sunburst and Tom Snyder Productions, provide helpful videotapes, at no cost to teachers, with creative ideas for using their problem-solving/higher-order thinking skills software with a whole class. Armed with a presentation device, a teacher can link a computer to the television monitor and bring an effective computer lesson to life. Software such as Safari Search, Puzzle Tanks, and The Factory are examples. Some lesson plans using such software are included later in this chapter.

The Classroom with Several Computers

According to Pogrow (1988), there are three components to effective teaching with the computer:

1. Teaching must be process oriented, with students developing and testing their own ideas rather than being told what to do by the teacher.
2. Teaching must force students to articulate their hypotheses and results, as well as cause and effect relationships. It is the articulation of conscious ideas that produces much of transferable learning, not just operating the software.
3. Teachers must integrate effective noncomputer teaching techniques with computer activities.

Rather than (or in addition to) setting up a computer lab, some schools choose to place five or six computers in several classrooms of teachers who are particularly interested in integrating computer use on a regular basis. Using a computer projection device or a television monitor adapted so that computer images can be projected, a teacher can instruct an entire class by using selected computer software to do a demonstration, list class ideas, and so on. Following the teacher presentation, students then work on application activities in small groups at the computers (or in one-computer classrooms, rotate using the computer and noncomputer activities). After the application activities, students meet again as a large group to compare responses, talk about progress and challenges, and deal with the interpersonal aspects of group work in addition to the content objectives of the lesson.

The strengths of the one- or several-computer classroom model are that it puts the computers where the students are, thereby allowing easy access to technology across subject areas. It also focuses the teacher as the designer of instruction, integrating computer use into curriculum objectives. The primary limitation of the model is the lack of training for teachers in how to combine computer and noncomputer activities, selecting software that is best suited for this type of classroom and the targeted curriculum, and scheduling computer use for students that does not disrupt the lesson.

Without this training, many teachers have used the computer as a reward activity, with students using drill or game software after they have finished their "real" work, or have several students doing drill-and-practice work while the rest of the class works on something else. The software is usually chosen not for its educational value but because it is easy to use with little or no supervision by the teacher. This approach is called *computer accommodation,* in contrast to the recommended approach of *computer integration* (Edyburn, 1991).

School Policies Affecting the Selection and Use of Computers

Ideally, a school should have a committee that makes decisions about the types of equipment and software that are needed and how these resources are placed and scheduled. Teachers, related service providers (speech and occupational therapists), computer resource teachers, parents, and students should all have the opportunity to contribute ideas. Given the scarcity of resources, however, policies may be developed that exclude or reduce access to some students or teachers, which may or may not be related to educational goals. The following are some questions to ask as policies are formulated:

1. How are the decisions made about where to place computers and how the schedule is set up?

2. Do students have access to the computers in a lab, even if there is a computer in the classroom?

3. Is keyboarding taught as a prerequisite skill or as a part of a larger emphasis on writing?

4. Are students encouraged to turn in written work done on a word processor? Are they encouraged to use a spell checker?

5. Who evaluates, selects, and orders software for the school? Where is it kept? Who has access to it?

6. How much training is provided to teachers about maintaining, using, expanding, and adapting the computer? Does the school spend as much on training (consultants, release time, materials) as it does on acquiring new equipment?

7. To what degree are parents involved in the program? Can equipment or software be checked out for home use? Is the lab open in the evenings or on weekends? Are parents actively involved in approaching industry or community groups for computer donations or in raising money for additional equipment? Can parents receive training in how to use the computer with their child?

8. To what degree are students involved in the program? In what ways are their perceptions of computer uses and software addressed in decisions?

Using and Choosing a Computer

The computer has four main components:

- The computer itself is where information is processed.
- The keyboard is where instructions and data are entered and edited.
- The disk drives, which may be internal or external, are classified as *hard disk* (rigid aluminum, with a magnetic coating for the recording of data; can hold a high volume of data and software programs) or *floppy* (3½-inch stiff plastic disks).
- The monitor is where text and graphic information is seen on a screen by the user.

Figure 14-1 illustrates these components on the computer.

Standard considerations in selecting a computer include cost, available software, expandability, ease of use, available peripherals (such as printers or modems), and adaptations that may be appropriate to the various students.

Although most schools or districts may not be able to afford all the needed options at the beginning, it is important to keep an eye to the future. The computers should be useful

FIGURE 14-1   Macintosh Computer

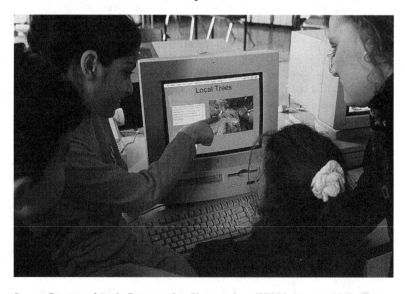

Source: Courtesy of Apple Computer, Inc. Photographers: Will Mosgrove and Julie Chase.

in a number of situations and be adaptable to suit different needs. Many school districts that made decisions based on the purchasing office's considerations (such as cost and frequency of repair) later found that their equipment was not suited for the needs of particular students, could not be expanded, or was not compatible with desired software.

Because of the increasingly modular nature of most computer systems, a simple comparison of different types of computers is almost impossible. Generally, one or two factors may be most important in making a decision to purchase a particular computer, such as specific software compatibility, an adaptive device, or compatibility with other computers in the school or district. The checklist presented in Figure 14-2 will help the classroom teacher ask the right questions and do his or her own comparisons.

Peripherals

Some of the most important peripherals are described here. Each of these items should be considered in light of the different needs of the students.

Printers
Laser quality printers which offer both color and black and white options provide the most flexibility. Cost and speed of printing are primary issues in selecting a printer. Printers can be easily networked in either a lab or classroom situation to maximize resources.

Modem
A modem is a device that permits computers to communicate with each other over a phone line. A computer equipped with a modem allows the user to subscribe to a variety of electronic information services or bulletin boards. (Additional information on the uses of modems and telecommunications is included in Chapter 11.)

---

1. What type of computer do I need? (Consider the compatibility of software at school and home. Is ease of use essential? Is there a particular type of software desired that is specific to one machine?)

2. How much memory do I need? As memory becomes cheaper, software developers continue to produce more memory-hungry programs. Can the computer memory be expanded? (A rule of thumb: Always buy as much memory as possible to lengthen the life span of the computer's usefulness.)

3. How fast a machine do I need? The speed of the computer depends on the chips inside, measured in megahertz. (The higher the speed, the less time will be spent waiting.)

4. What type of printer do I need? For school use, having access to printers networked to all the computers makes sense economically. Printers which offer both color and black and white are most flexible.

5. Should I buy a built-in CD-ROM drive?

6. What type of modem will meet my needs and the needs of my students?

7. What adaptive devices will be needed?

FIGURE 14-2 Checklist for Computer Purchase

Mouse

One way to enter information into the computer without using the keyboard is by using a mouse. A mouse is a small device with a rolling ball in its base that glides over a horizontal surface. The cursor on the screen responds to the movement of the mouse. The student puts the cursor into position on the screen with the mouse, then enters a menu selection by pressing a button on the mouse. A similar input device is the trackball, a rotating sphere built onto the keyboard which can be rotated to the appropriate places on the keyboard for selection, or a trackpad, in which the finger moves across a square to operate the cursor.

Activities

1. Visit a school and survey where the computers are located. During your observation, note how many computers are in use and not in use, and how many students are using them (one student per computer, small group per computer, whole class and one computer, and so on). What changes, if any, would create more opportunities for students to use technology? What strengths do you feel the school's way of organizing access to technology offers?

2. Select three software programs you have not used and try them out with a child. Describe the process the child uses to learn how the software works and what it can do. How is the process similar to and different from your own approach (if you were working by yourself)?

3. Select your three favorite software programs and describe their characteristics and/or why you enjoy them or find them effective. Describe three ways these software programs could be incorporated into classroom learning activities or thematic units.

4. Select a piece of software and integrate it into a classroom learning activity or thematic unit.

References

Edyburn, D. (1991, September). Integrating software into the special education curriculum. Presentation for Lincoln County Schools, West Hamlin, WV.

Kelman, P. (1990). Alternatives to integrated instructional systems. *CUE Newsletter, 13(2)*, 7–9.

Mageau, T. (1990). ILS: Its new role in schools. *Electronic Learning. 10(1)*, 22–24, 31–32.

Mendrinos, R. (1990). CD-ROM: A technology that is steadily entering school libraries and classrooms. *Electronic Learning, 9(4)*, 34–36.

Meyers, L. (1990). The language machine: Using computers to help children construct reality and language. Presentation at Conoscenze Come Educazione, San Martino di Castrozza, Italy.

Pogrow, S. (1988). How to use computers to truly enhance learning. *Electronic Learning, 7(8)*, 6–7.

Riedl, R. (1991). Research notes: Writing to Read in special education. *The Catalyst, 8(3)*, 3–5.

Siegel, R., & Freels, D. (1989). Using switches for communication with multiply handicapped, very young children. *Closing the Gap, 7(5)*, 20–21.

Slavin, R. (1990). IBM's Writing to Read: Is it right for reading? *Phi Delta Kappan, 72(3)*, 214–216.

Wright, C., & Nomura, M. (1985). *From toys to computers: Access for the physically disabled child.* San Jose, CA: Christine Wright.

Chapter *15*

School Policy Issues and Dealing with Change

Recognizing that the traditional models from the past, based on an industrial work force, will not be useful for an information age, schools are currently involved with efforts to restructure their organization. One of the difficulties with restructuring has been agreement on exactly what restructuring is. According to Sheingold,

The central idea underlying restructuring efforts is that the system itself must be reorganized from top to bottom in order to achieve the kinds of learning and thinking outcomes now seen as necessary for students. An organizational structure must be created in which authority and responsibility are aligned—in which those who are charged with getting the job done, namely schools and teachers, have the authority and the support they need to do it. In the long run, this means that schools and districts must be accountable for achieving certain yet-to-be-defined outcomes, rather than for adhering to a set of procedural guidelines and regulations. Educators will have the responsibility for deciding how to reach these goals. (1991, p. 21)

Another difficulty is preparing educators, parents, and students for the changes caused by restructuring as well as evolving technology. In his landmark books, *Mindstorms: Children, Computers, and Powerful Ideas* (1980) and *The Children's Machine: Rethinking School in the Age of the Computer* (1993), Papert states, "We are at a point in the history of education when radical change is possible, and the possibility for that change is directly tied to the impact of the computer." Issues of change and innovation pervade every professional journal, and books warn us of the impact of the evolution from an industrial to an information society (Naisbitt, 1982).

Educators who have preferred to delay the classroom use of computers as long as possible are feeling uncomfortable pressure to move in that direction. At the other end of the spectrum are the early adopters who expound on the benefits of computer use like missionaries seeking converts! Somewhere in between, some teachers in the early stages of computer use are experiencing frustration at the inability to keep up with the latest developments in software.

The implementation of computers in education shares many of the same attributes as the implementation of any other educational innovation. As this book has already discussed, however, the computer is unlike other innovations in two ways: (1) Computer technology changes so quickly that implementation and training efforts are never complete, and (2) Computers in the learning process are developmental tools that can begin at the simplest level and evolve with the learner attaining unlimited skills. Indeed, Papert (1980), who studied with Piaget, believes that computers have the capacity to transform our definition of learning—if schools will stay out of the way. In this chapter, the nature of change is explored as it applies to the implementation of computers in education.

In this chapter, you will have a chance to explore the issues of restructuring and change as they apply to creating inclusive classrooms using technology integrated into the curriculum.

Objectives

By the end of this chapter, you will be able to do the following:

1. Review current policies at your school and school district regarding inclusive classrooms and the integration of technology, and predict what problems may arise as result of (or lack of) those policies.
2. Become actively involved in restructuring efforts to promote inclusive classrooms equipped with appropriate technology integrated into the curriculum.
3. Use a theoretical model to assess your own readiness for the implementation of computers in your classroom and to determine the types of training and assistance that would be most helpful.
4. Develop a plan of action so that your efforts to ensure that all students have access to needed technology are successful.

Gathering Information and Asking the Right Questions

Many of the decisions made in education are based on reactions to problems or crises rather than on systematic planning. Planning, when it occurs, is based primarily on a historical analysis (Cain, 1985). Cain recommends a holistic forecasting approach to planning for computer use, in which individuals responsible for different program elements are brought together to pose questions such as, What is your vision of computer technology in this school district 20 years in the future? Participants are then charged with the task of projecting backwards from that point, in 3- to 5-year segments. In Cain's view, the three major variables that affect planning for the twenty-first century are advancing computer technologies, changes in the work force, and medical developments.

These are some of the developments that affect restructuring, policy making, and planning:

- An information base doubles every 12 months.
- There is a shift from manufacturing to service- and information-oriented occupations.
- Computers can reason, draw conclusions, make judgments, and understand the written and spoken word.
- Robots can perform most household and manufacturing chores.
- Audio and visual technologies will make reading skills decreasingly important.
- Increasing numbers of newborn children have exceptional needs.

Twenty Questions: A Tool for Policy Makers

Just as traditional planners have focused on the past to predict the future, many times people jump to solutions without fully examining the problem. The 20 questions posed below only begin to probe the issues presented in this text; for policy makers, the process for considering the questions is far more important than settling on the so-called right answers. For most school districts, the process of gathering groups of key stakeholders to generate a list of questions may be the best place to start planning and policy making. Categories of questions to consider include political, pedagogical, applications, and institutional.

Political

1. Given that computers can reduce or eliminate the impact of a disability, what is the obligation of our society and our school systems to provide access to these resources?

2. How do we ensure that access to computers is equitable, regardless of socioeconomic status, race, disability, linguistic background, and age?

3. How do we ensure that the applications selected for use in computer-using classrooms are not used to reinforce differences between rich and poor students rather than to reduce disparities (Kozol, 1991)?

Pedagogical

4. At what age do we begin to provide access to computers? How will learning with a computer change what we believe about developmental stages of learning for students?

5. What learning experiences are done best in a computer learning environment?

6. We will soon have access to the entire world of stored information. What are the best ways to use this information? How do we decide what is most important for students to learn? How can this access be a tool for empowerment rather than an instrument of slavery (O'Brien, 1983)?

7. Through the development of talking calculators, speech synthesizers, and software that checks for spelling and grammatical errors, we have already witnessed the possibility that our students may not have as much need for computational, reading, and language mechanics, or handwriting. How will that affect the curriculum?

8. School systems currently operate by sorting students into categories by age, ability/disability, language, socioeconomic status, and so on in order to reduce the variability of the general education classroom. Given research that this approach is ineffective (Oakes, 1985) and a world of work where this model does not apply, how can schools be designed to take advantage of heterogeneity rather than be defeated by it?

9. How can the computer be used as a tool for learning social skills?

10. What is the role of the teacher in using the computer as an instructional tool?

Applications

11. What computer skills should be taught to every student?

12. At what point and in what ways should students be taught keyboarding skills? Will this be outdated in the next five years?

13. In what areas of the curriculum should computer use be concentrated so that students can use computers intensively?

Institutional

14. What considerations influence purchasing decisions? What efforts are appropriate in standardizing software and hardware in order to make computers accessible to students?

15. How should decisions about allocating funds for hardware and software be made? How can schools keep up with new technology acquisitions after their first big acquisition and let go of old technology?

16. How do we ensure that optimal use of computers in classrooms will take place?

17. What do we do when some teachers will use technology and some will not?

18. How do we assess the best uses of computers for each individual student?

19. What are the best ways for educators to evaluate the flood of new software, hardware, and adaptive devices?

20. How can principles of effective training be built in to the implementation of technology in classrooms?

Moving in New Directions

At least eight trends have been identified in classrooms where technology has been implemented extensively (Collins, 1991). These trends also tend to promote the effectiveness of classrooms of students with diverse needs and should be considered in restructuring efforts. These trends focus on shifts from the following:

- Whole-class to small-group instruction
- Lecture and recitation to coaching
- Working with better students to working with weaker students
- Less to more engaged students or passive to more active students
- Assessment based on test performance to assessment based on products, progress, and effort

- Competitive to cooperative goal structures
- A more flexible approach to teaching "the curriculum" for mastery by all students
- Primacy of verbal thinking to the integration of multiple intelligences (logical-mathematical, musical, spatial, linguistic, inter- and intrapersonal)

Building in Change

Apple Classrooms of Tomorrow (ACOT) projects, begun in 1985, have provided a wealth of insights into the course of instructional change and impacts on teachers and students. This program is a consortium of researchers, educators, students, and parents to explore the impact of technology-rich environments in which every student has access to a computer at school and one at home, along with printers, scanners, laserdiscs, videotapes, modems, and CD-ROM players, along with software (Dwyer, Ringstaff, & Sandholtz, 1991).

Conditions essential for success in the restructuring process noted by Dwyer, Ringstaff, and Sandholtz (1991) were (1) change must be recognized as evolutionary and incremental, (2) teachers must be given an opportunity to reflect on their own beliefs about learning and instruction and to develop a sense of the consequences of alternative belief systems, and (3) administrators must be willing to implement structural or programmatic shifts in the environment for teachers who are instructionally evolving.

Three of the discoveries that have been consistent throughout the research conducted in Apple's Classrooms of Tomorrow offer insights (Sandholtz, Ringstaff, & Dwyer, 1991):

1. High access to technology promotes interaction and sharing among staff and students alike
2. High interaction and sharing produce faster implementation of innovations
3. Successful implementation of innovation requires change at multiple levels simultaneously (technology, curriculum, governance, teaching strategies, and ongoing support)

SRI International's case studies of schools deeply involved with restructuring and technology found that

> *Sites that were most successful in infusing technology throughout their entire programs were schools and projects that also devoted a good deal of effort to creating a* schoolwide instructional vision—*a consensus around instructional goals and a shared philosophy concerning the kinds of activities that would support those goals. In some cases preparing technology-savvy students was part of the school's original mission; in others, technology emerged over time as a means to achieve other goals, such as the acquisition of higher-order thinking skills. What appears to be important is not the point at which technology becomes a part of the vision but the coherence of the vision and the extent to which it is a unifying force among teachers. (Means, Olson, & Singh, 1995)*

For those of us who want to be successful "change surfers" in our schools, the following attitudes and behaviors seem critical (Hewlett-Packard Information Systems and Technology Group, 1995):

- Approach change as a process and demonstrate a high tolerance for ambiguity.
- Demonstrate the resolve necessary to sustain major change.
- View the orchestration of roles in the change process as essential to successful implementation.
- Demonstrate a strong commitment by playing an active role in "sponsoring" the change.
- View resistance as a natural and understandable reaction to disruption.
- Understand the strategic importance of school culture and its impact on implementing initiatives.
- Understand that strong "synergistic" teamwork is essential for successful change.

Two tools that are helpful in assessing both individual and schoolwide readiness for restructuring for more student-centered, curriculum-rich experiential learning supported by technology are the Levels of Technology Implementation Survey (Moersch, 1995) and the Levels of Instructional Practices Survey (Moersch, 1994) (Figures 15-1 and 15-2). You might think about the setting and people where you work or live. Where are you now, and where are you going? Where are you in relation to the people you must get along with?

As you think about what technology really means for you and your students, consider the experience of teachers and schools where technology has been a force for change and restructuring. Think about the changes and reforms going on in your school. Do they address the fundamental need of increasing the sense of connection of one person to another and the connection of learner to the excitement and empowerment of learning? To what degree do you and your colleagues have a shared vision of what school and classrooms should be like for students and families?

FIGURE 15-1   Levels of Technology Implementation

0   *Non-Use* Perceived lack of access to technology tools or lack of time to pursue implementation.

1   *Awareness* Use of computers is one step removed from classroom teachers (ILS Labs); computer applications have little or no relevance to teacher's classroom program.

2   *Exploration* Technology tools supplement existing instructional program (games, simulations).

3   *Infusion* Tools such as data bases, spreadsheets, graphing, desktop publishing, telecommunications augment instruction.

4   *Integration* Technology tools provide rich context for understanding concepts, themes, and processes. Multimedia, telecommunications, data bases, spreadsheets, word processing are perceived as tools to solve authentic problems.

5   *Expansion* Technology access is extended beyond classroom. Teachers actively elicit technology applications and networking from businesses, government agencies, and universities to expand student experiences.

6   *Refinement* Technology is perceived as a process, product, and tool to solve authentic problems related to real-world situation or issue. Technology is a seamless medium for information queries, problem solving and product development.

Source: Moersch, 1995. Reprinted with permission.

FIGURE 15-2   Levels of Instructional Practices

	Level 1	Level 2	Level 3
Learning Materials	Organized by the content; heavy reliance on text and sequential instructional materials	Emphasis on kits, hands-on activities (e.g., AIMS, FOSS)	Determined by problem areas under study
Learning Activities	Traditional verbal activities; problem solving activities	Emphasis on student's active role problem solving activities with little or no context; verification labs via science kits	Emphasis on student activism and issues investigations and resolutions
Teaching Strategy	Expository approach	Facilitator; resource	Co-learner
Evaluation	Traditional evaluation practices including multiple choice, short answer, and true-false	Multiple assessment strategies including performance tasks and open-ended and problem-based questions	Multiple assessment strategies integrated authentically
Technology	Drill & practice, ILS little connection between computer and classroom curriculum	Technology integrated into isolated hands-on experiences	Expanded view of technology as a process; tool to find real solutions to real problems

Source: Moersch, 1994. Reprinted with permission.

Increasing the Scope of Restructuring and Participation of Key Stakeholders

One of the difficulties of restructuring efforts is the inclination to focus only on parts of problems and issues. If technology in inclusive classrooms is to become a reality, restructuring must address not only issues of categorical programs and funding, curriculum, grouping practices, decentralized decision making, and so on but also technology and mainstreaming. All participants in the system—superintendents, principals, teachers, other school staff, students, parents, school board members, and community members—must have an opportunity to pose questions and reflect on needed directions for restructuring.

Sheingold (1991) makes these suggestions for broadening the scope of restructuring discussions to include technology:

- Bring technology and learning to the same table when restructuring is discussed.
- Reconsider how technology is organized in the district (decentralize technology budgets and purchasing authority, link technology more closely with curriculum

and instruction, and use teacher committees to make decisions about spending on technology).

- Work toward assembling a critical mass of equipment and expertise. It is far more effective to have fewer students with more intensive access to technology than egalitarian access but no learning outcomes.
- Use the media to convey new images and metaphors of schooling. Traditional images of schooling are very powerful; new images are essential in creating public support for the changes that must be made.

Policy at District and School-Site Levels

Strong leadership, combined with shared planning and decision making at school-site levels, can result in programs with dramatic impact for large numbers of students. What areas of policy should key stakeholders be involved in?

Allocation of Resources

No matter who decides how scarce resources are allocated, not everyone will be satisfied. All policy decisions should result in universal access in an orderly, equitable way, beginning with providing extensive focused computer use in one or two areas and expanding with success. Many districts and schools use a committee to set priorities on resource allocation. The committee—which may be composed of teachers, parents, therapists, and other interested staff—can help with research necessary to assure wise purchasing. Committees can also be useful for evaluating and selecting software.

Effective Training

Districts that have successful programs spend an enormous percentage of their budget on training and staff development. A good rule of thumb is to spend equal amounts for hardware, software, and training.

Traditionally, in-service training for educators has not been very effective in producing change. Even though millions of dollars are spent each year to provide training activities, most of the money is wasted because the training is poorly designed or implemented, and had little or no follow-up. Joyce and Showers (1988) reveal classroom application results from different models of in-service training.

As Table 15-1 shows, the training model that has the greatest impact is one that includes classroom coaching with periodic follow-up. Since the computer is a hands-on tool, much of the available training includes hands-on training. Unfortunately, as Table 15-1 indicates, not even hands-on experience guarantees actual implementation in the classroom. Successful change efforts to implement computers in education will require long-term training with periodic follow-up and coaching.

Coaching means that teachers meet in small groups and observe each other in their classrooms to get support for new ideas and feedback about their teaching procedures and behaviors (Joyce, 1990; Brandt, 1987; MCREL, 1985). Coaching is only successful if it is

TABLE 15-1   Models of In-Service Training and Degrees of Implementation

	Training Stages		
Training Steps	*Knowledge Mastery*	*Skills Acquisition*	*Classroom Application*
Theory (Lecture)* +	Middle/High	Low	Very Low
Demonstration +	High	Low/Middle	Very Low
Practice & Feedback +	High	High	Very Low
Curriculum Adaptation +	High	High	Low/Middle
Coaching +	High	High	High
Periodic Review	High	High	High

Source: From *Special Magic: Computers, Classroom Strategies, and Exceptional Students* by M. Male, 1988, Mountain View, CA: Mayfield Publishing. Reprinted with permission of the author.

Key: Very Low = 5%
 Low = 10%
 Middle = 40%
 High = 80%

Note: The rows are cumulative; the strength of coaching rests on the total effect of theory, demonstration, practice, curriculum, and coaching.

done in an atmosphere of trust and caring—one in which people feel free to help each other improve on current skills. For example, one group of teachers is participating in five day-long training sessions on computers in inclusive classrooms. They are focusing on the following:

- Software planning/integration and curriculum correspondence (reading/language arts)
- Word processing and desktop publishing
- Telecommunications—E-mail and World Wide Web
- Adaptive devices
- Cooperative learning

Between each of the training sessions, coaching teams (two or three teachers) set up opportunities to observe a lesson using the skill being worked on. One teacher is to observe another teaching students using Storybook Weaver to write a story. The coach meets with the teacher to review the lesson plan prior to observing in the class; they agree on the specific focus for the observation (e.g., to see if all of the students are really participating, or if one student is dominating at the keyboard). Most coaches use an observation form along with anecdotal notes so that feedback is precise and meaningful to the teacher being observed.

The coach and the teacher set up a time after the lesson when they can talk about the strengths of the lesson and decide on additional ideas for future lessons. The coaching is a confidential, thoroughly professional process; during the support group meetings, only the teacher who was observed comments on the lesson or calls on the coach for comments.

In addition to the peer coaching sessions, the entire group continues to meet on a regular basis for a one- or two-hour sharing session after the training, where they can pool lesson plans, student worksheets, and solutions to problems they encountered. The support group sets up a mutually agreeable agenda; teachers may decide to bring software to review or an instructional activity to try. Participants review progress they have made since their last support group meeting and identify the skills or activities they will be working on before the next meeting.

These two strategies—peer support groups and peer coaching, added to an ongoing, regularly scheduled, voluntary training program—will assure a more successful implementation of computers in inclusive classrooms.

Funding

Most successful districts aggressively seek funds outside the district, through foundation grants, government grants, and business-school partnerships. Another key to success is the ability to set up a program and put together a combination of needed funding to achieve the desired results. Strong leadership and support are essential at the district level to generate the energy needed to write grants and make contacts with businesses; the efforts result in expanded programs and stronger community support.

Action Planning

Think carefully about the topics and issues presented in this book. Table 15-2 shows a sample action plan that reviews the process of establishing computer technology in an inclusive classroom. List the action you need to take and the date you plan to complete the action. As you finish an action, check it off and evaluate the results. Additional ideas for action items to pursue include:

1. Be clear about whom you are serving: *the students* (not the legislature, the school board, or even the parents). If the students' needs are well served, the rest will usually follow.

2. Get a computer, preferably one that is compatible with the computer you will have in your classroom or in the school's computer lab. Ease of access is essential in the development of skills.

3. From a list of possibilities, select the most empowering, essential thing a computer could do for the students in your class or caseload. Start with that one item and work on it until you and your students get excellent results. Make sure it relates to IEP and curriculum goals.

TABLE 15-2 Sample Action Plan

Action	Completion Date	Results
Interview district, other teachers about plans for getting more computers	5–1	Information on new training available; check out a computer for summer
Go to county office and preview software	5–15	Several ideas for lessons
Observe another teacher using computers in special ed.	5–22	Got sample lessons and a "model" grant
Write a grant to get a computer in my classroom	5–31	Computer arrives Sept. 1

Source: From *Special Magic: Computers, Classroom Strategies, and Exceptional Students* by M. Male, 1988, Mountain View, CA: Mayfield Publishing. Reprinted with permission of the author.

4. Keep instructional materials simple and clear; adapt software manuals and make large charts for the most important instructions.

5. Share your accomplishments with other students, school staff, administrators, school board, and anyone who will listen. Celebrate success!

6. Find a computer users' group that focuses on the diverse learning needs of students and join it. If you can't find one, start one.

7. Find a way of measuring your students' accomplishments with the computer, and get agreement from students, other staff, and parents. Collect the data regularly and let people know what your students are doing.

8. Attend conferences and training and regularly read at least one journal on computers and education.

9. Write a proposal to get needed equipment, software, and training. Develop a form letter to write to software publishers asking to try out software or for software donations. You have nothing to lose!

10. Set up a data base on school and community resources in computers and education, and establish a filing system on state and national resources.

11. Set up a resource room where parents, teachers, and therapists can try out hardware, software, and adaptive devices; review computer publications; receive technical assistance; and meet for training and user groups. If space is at a premium, see if a nearby Alliance for Technology Access (ATA) Center could be visited on an ongoing basis. Another possibility is to locate a room that could be used periodically for such a purpose and bring the necessary equipment to set it up (this approach will wear thin quickly, however).

12. Start a newsletter to share information and ideas about computers and education in your district; encourage teachers, parents, and other staff to share their ideas. Distribute the newsletter widely in the community.

13. Periodically take time out to evaluate the results of your actions and policies in terms of your original vision. Are you still on the right track?

Activities

1. Using the 20 questions in the chapter, interview the principal, a special education teacher, a general education teacher, and a parent. Summarize the results of the interviews in a data base.
2. Select one or more of the recommendations in this chapter to implement. Document the results.
3. Visit an Apple Classroom of Tomorrow or a classroom with a long, successful track record of successful computer use with students of diverse needs. Interview the teacher about school or district policies that supported success or had to be overcome. Ask the teacher for recommendations for new programs just getting started.
4. Using Figure 15-1, review the levels of technology implementation in terms of your own increasing interest in computers for education. Can you identify on what level you are now? How have you changed since you first began implementing technology?
5. Develop an action plan for yourself, similar in format to the one in Table 15-2. Share it with the class.

References

Brandt, R. (1987). On teachers coaching teachers: A conversation with Bruce Joyce. *Education Leadership, 44(5),* 12–17.

Cain, E. (1985). Developing an administrative plan for the implementation of microcomputers. Selected Proceedings of *Closing the Gap's* 1985 National Conference, 14–16.

Collins, A. (1991). The role of computer technology in restructuring schools. *Phi Delta Kappan, 73(1),* 28–40, 75–82.

Dwyer, D., Ringstaff, C., & Sandholtz, J. (1991). Changes in teachers' beliefs and practices in technology rich classrooms. *Educational Leadership, 48(8),* 45–52.

Hewlett-Packard Information Systems and Technology Group (1995). Winners and losers research. Palo Alto: Hewlett-Packard.

Joyce, B. (Ed.) (1990). *Changing school culture through staff development.* Alexandria, VA: Association for Supervision and Curriculum Development.

Joyce, B., and Showers, B. (1988). *Student achievement through staff development.* New York: Longman.

Kozol, J. (1991). Rich child, poor child. *Electronic Learning, 10(5),* 56.

MCREL (Mid-Continent Regional Educational Laboratory) (1985). *What's noteworthy on beginning the school year: Time management, discipline, expectations, motivation, instruction, and coaching.* Washington, DC: National Institute of Education.

Means, B., Olson, K., and Singh, R. (1995). Beyond the classroom: Restructuring the classroom with technology. *Phi Delta Kappan, 77(1),* 69–72.

Moersch, C. (1994). Labs for learning: An experimental-based action model. A paper for the National Business Education Alliance.

Moersch, C. (1995). Levels of technology implementation (LoTi): A framework for measuring classroom technology use. A paper for the National Business Education Alliance.

Naisbitt, J. (1982). *Megatrends.* New York: Warner Books.

Oakes, J. (1985). *Keeping track: How schools structure inequality.* New Haven, CT: Yale University Press.

O'Brien, T. (1983). Wasting new technology on the same old curriculum. *Classroom Computer Learning, 4(4),* 25–27, 30.

Papert, S. (1980). *Mindstorms: Children, computers, and powerful ideas.* New York: Basic Books.

Papert, S. (1993). *The children's machine: Rethinking schools in the age of the computer.* New York: Basic Books.

Sandholtz, J., Ringstaff, C., and Dwyer, D. (1991). Research findings: Technology innovation and collegial interaction: ACOT Report #13. Cupertino, CA: Apple Computer, Inc.

Sheingold, K. (1991). Restructuring for learning with technology: The potential for synergy. *Phi Delta Kappan,* 73(1), 17–27.

Index

Index of Software Titles

Index of Hardware Products